From Cloud Native to AI Native

Catching the Next Wave of Innovation

By Pini Reznik and Michael Müller

From Cloud Native to AI Native

Catching the Next Wave of Innovation

By Pini Reznik and Michael Müller

ISBN: 9798266600997
Imprint: Independently published

This book was produced in collaboration with Write Business Results Limited. For more information on their business book and marketing services, please visit www.writebusinessresults.com or contact the team via info@writebusinessresults.com.

WRITE BUSINESS RESULTS

Acknowledgements

Pini:

Writing a book is never a solitary act, and I am deeply grateful for the community that surrounds me.

To my co-author, Michael: This book was forged in our long collaboration—thank you for making the process so enjoyable. To Kristian, my gratitude for being a trusted partner.

A special thanks to Greg Southey for the long hours in our early collaboration; it was an essential boost to get the book started.

And to the entire team at re:cinq, your ingenuity is a constant inspiration. Thank you for reminding me what's possible when great people work together.

Michael:

To my co-author and friend, Pini. This book is the culmination of countless conversations and shared ideas. Your dedication, energy and insights made this journey not only possible but also rewarding. To Kristian, for being supportive and for your belief in this project.

My gratitude also extends to the entire re:cinq team. Your daily work turning complex technology into practical solutions was a constant source of inspiration and a real-world foundation for the ideas in this book.

And to those who shared their valuable early feedback—Dimitris Thanasopoulos, Arjen de Ruiter, Wil Bruins-Koetsier, Daniel Vaughan, Steve Wall, Edwin Maldonado and many others—our sincere thanks.

This book is a snapshot of a rapidly evolving landscape. My hope is that it sparks conversations and helps us all navigate the exciting path ahead.

Dedication

Pini:

To my wife, Sarit. For a quarter of a century, your love and support have been my foundation. To our children, Shachar and Yonatan, watching you grow has been the greatest adventure.

Michael:

My deepest thanks go to my family. To my wonderful partner, Cathrin, your unwavering support and encouragement were my foundation. To my children, Lukas and Paula, thank you for your patience and for the joy you bring into my life, which always puts everything into perspective.

Contents

Foreword

The pace of technological change is accelerating. Organizations in every industry and region need to reinvent how they work. Pini Reznik and Michael Müller's *From Cloud Native to AI Native: Catching the Next Wave of Innovation* is timely guidance for leaders preparing for what comes next.

Reznik and Müller connect lessons from the Cloud Native journey to the emerging AI Native paradigm. They break down the "waves of innovation" from Waterfall to Cloud Native and set out a clear framework for the next shift. Crucially, they show that Cloud Native is not about tools alone—it requires new team structures, processes and culture. This aligns with the core message of *Team Topologies*: patterns for shaping teams and interactions to improve flow. The authors explicitly reference *Team Topologies* to illustrate the value of clear team boundaries and well-defined interaction modes in organizational change.

A key theme—also strengthened in the second edition of *Team Topologies*—is cognitive load as a design principle for work. The book addresses Cloud Native and AI Native challenges such as distributed-systems complexity and the risk of nanoservices. It also names common pitfalls like "strategic inertia" and "cargo cult adoption", and offers practical pattern-based responses. The message is simple: respect the cognitive limits of individuals and teams to sustain fast, safe flow.

Looking ahead, AI Native signals an "Intelligence Revolution"—systems where AI is not an add-on but part of the core. The authors discuss "model-centric architectures" and "self-evolving systems", and raise important questions about "time reversal": as AI executes faster, humans must focus more on intent, ethics and validation. From a *Team Topologies* perspective, human teams stay central: define the mission, supervise AI operations and ensure technology augments judgment rather than encoding bias. This future also demands strong approaches to ethics, data governance and explainability.

The book is clear that transformation is a journey, not a destination. The six modes of operation—Pioneering, Bootstrapping & Bridge-Building, Scaling, Optimizing, Innovating and Retiring—provide a practical compass for continuous change.

Reznik and Müller have produced an accessible, useful guide for leaders who want organizations that can sustain agility, innovation and wellbeing. By combining Cloud Native lessons with a thoughtful path to AI Native, they equip you to shape the future—not just react to it—so your organization can thrive through the next wave.

Matthew Skelton, co-author, *Team Topologies*

About Matthew Skelton

Matthew Skelton is one of the foremost leaders in modern organizational dynamics for fast flow, drawing on Team Topologies, Adapt Together™ and related practices to support organizations with transformation towards a sustainable fast flow of value and true business agility.

Co-author of the award-winning and groundbreaking book *Team Topologies*, Founder and CEO/CTO at Conflux, and Director of Core Operations at the non-profit Team Topologies, Matthew brings a humane approach to organizational effectiveness.

Preface

Why are so many companies struggling to realize the full potential of Cloud Native, even after years of effort? Despite the promise of Cloud Native, many IT environments remain surprisingly wasteful. This book explores why—and how—AI is poised to disrupt the landscape once again.

Our research revealed a broader story and a different question. Why, even today, are so many companies still struggling to adopt Cloud Native technologies and ways of working? More than a decade has passed since Docker sparked the Cloud Native ecosystem. It's nearly as long since Kubernetes arrived. Yet organizations everywhere continue to face significant challenges.

This widespread struggle with Cloud Native is particularly striking given the increasing emphasis on sustainability. After a year and a half of experimentation, the root of most sustainability-related problems in IT became clear. They stem from poor optimization of public cloud infrastructure. Before focusing on new programming languages or optimized algorithms, teams can therefore achieve dramatic improvements by taking simple steps. These include shutting down unused servers, decommissioning stale test environments, automating scaling down (not just up) and right-sizing virtual machines (VMs). These straightforward measures typically reduce a team's carbon footprint by over 50%. They also lower cloud costs and boost both software quality and development team productivity.

Just as Cloud Native faced initial hurdles, AI is now on a similar path. It's poised to transform everything around us—especially the IT landscape. But many businesses are still unsure how to integrate AI into their products and processes. They often struggle to distinguish between traditional machine learning (ML) and newer generative models. They lack clarity about practical use cases. In the Cloud Native world, discussions center on AIOps and development tools like GitHub Copilot. However, AI tooling itself remains immature, much like the Cloud Native ecosystem back in 2020.

This raises several important questions. Why do so many in IT fixate on advanced ideas like sustainability and AI when so many companies can't even build efficient internal development platforms (IDPs)? Why do cloud costs remain so high when, in almost every case, we can reduce them by 50% to 70% through simple infrastructure management best practices? And why are so many enterprises still stuck in slow, bureaucratic processes that keep them from delivering value to customers at the pace they want?

When we told people we were writing this book, many suggested we focus on newer, more eye-catching ideas for a broader audience. Instead, we chose to write this book for those who haven't yet fully wrapped their heads around Cloud Native and the transformational shift it represents. We made that choice because we know how many organizations are still struggling to get the full benefit of a Cloud Native environment and because we can see another technological evolution is just around the corner.

Over the past decade, we built and grew a Cloud Native consulting firm to 120 people. Then we founded a new consulting company focused on sustainability, AI and Cloud Native. During that time, we read hundreds of books and worked with dozens of companies to see how organizational transformations really happen. Cloud Native is a fundamental change. Yet if you don't take a holistic approach, it rarely yields its promised benefits. More often, it complicates daily work.

It has been six years since Pini published his first book, *Cloud Native Transformation: Practical Patterns for Innovation.*[1] In that time, we've gained a more nuanced understanding of Cloud Native and the processes that make or break a transformation. We've drawn on a range of books and resources—each providing valuable insights—to refine our models and reinforce our points with expert perspectives. Today's Cloud

---

1 Reznik, P., Dobson, J. and Gienow, M. (2019) *Cloud Native Transformation: Practical Patterns for Innovation*. O'Reilly Media.

Native ecosystem features a wealth of stable, reliable tools. Development practices and team structures (like those described in the book *Team Topologies*) are well-documented. This maturity allows us to outline a clear vision of what a successful Cloud Native setup looks like. This is a vision based on proven patterns and real-world experiences.

In this book, we'll show you how Cloud Native transformations should work—and why they often fail. We'll explore both organizational and leadership aspects, as well as specific technical patterns that successful teams commonly adopt. We'll also offer a step-by-step process to help you assess your current state, define clear goals and chart a path to achieve them.

This book is primarily for technical managers and decision-makers—CTOs, CIOs, engineering directors, operations leaders and other IT professionals. However, it will also resonate with developers and operators who wonder why their companies lag behind the "fancy startups" showcased at KubeCon and other Cloud Native conferences. If you're already immersed in a productive, efficient Cloud Native environment, you may find ideas here to explain—or replicate—your success in a more systematic way.

We understand the temptation to skip the chapters about Cloud Native transformation if you have already been through this process, but we encourage you to give them your attention. See this as an opportunity to identify any mistakes you made and to check that you didn't overlook any important steps.

Later chapters delve into the practices of mature Cloud Native companies and prepare you for the next wave of transformation. Remember, these shifts are ongoing. This means the ability to execute a transformation is a crucial managerial skill. The next wave is coming, likely driven by AI, but its exact form remains unclear. This is why it's essential to carry out research and explore opportunities now, before this new wave breaks.

A language for navigating the waves

How do we talk about complex technological and organizational shifts? Often, we lack the vocabulary to discuss possibilities beyond our immediate experience. Architect Christopher Alexander encountered this when designing buildings. Clients understood rooms and doors, but not deeper architectural principles. His solution was not just to gather requirements, but to teach his clients a "pattern language". [2] In other words, a shared vocabulary describing recurring problems and proven solutions. This enabled richer collaboration and better design choices by making the "unknown unknowns" discussable (bring this language to your team with a hands-on pattern cards workshop: https://re-cinq.com/patterns).

Similarly, this book employs a pattern language for navigating the waves of technological innovation, from Waterfall to Cloud Native, and towards the emerging AI

2 Alexander, C., Fraser, M., Ishikawa, S. and Silverstein, M. (1977). *A Pattern Language: Towns, Buildings, Construction*. Oxford University Press.

Native paradigm. Patterns, in this context, are distilled insights drawn from both academic knowledge and practitioner experience. They represent reusable solutions to common problems encountered during transformation or within specific technological eras. They serve as general best practices, clearly explained in accessible language. They are not rigid, one-size-fits-all blueprints.

By learning this language, we can have deeper conversations about the challenges and opportunities ahead. It helps us identify successful approaches (patterns) and recognize common traps (pitfalls—known risks) and flawed strategies (anti-patterns—initially appealing but ultimately harmful solutions).

This library builds upon earlier work, including patterns developed for Cloud Native transformation, refined through continued experience. It covers both patterns related to the *process* of transformation itself (often applicable across waves of innovation) and patterns characteristic of specific *paradigms* (Waterfall, Cloud Native, AI Native). As you read through the stages of transformation and the discussions of different technological waves, we will refer to these named patterns and pitfalls. A complete reference library is also available in the Appendix. Our goal is to equip you with this language to help you open up discussions and make more informed choices on your own transformation journey (full pattern language can be found online at https://re-cinq.com/patterns).

Part I

Breaking Ground—The Shift from Waterfall to Cloud Native

This first part of the book will take you on a journey through the significant shifts in the IT landscape. We begin by navigating the evolution of IT, tracing the path from traditional Waterfall methodologies to the rise of Agile, and the foundational concepts that paved the way for Cloud Native.

We will then delve into what Cloud Native truly represents. It is a transformative shift that goes beyond mere tooling to encompass architectural principles, operational practices and crucial cultural changes. Finally, we'll explore the broader "Waves of Innovation" theory. Here we'll examine models like the Three Horizons and the Product Lifecycle to understand how technological shifts emerge, mature and eventually give way to new paradigms, setting the stage for the AI Native future (take our AI Native Assessment to see how prepared you are: https://re-cinq.com/ai-native-assessment).

Chapter 1

Navigating the Evolution of IT

Both of us started out in different IT environments, but had similar experiences in our early years. We found Waterfall methodologies weren't fit for purpose while the rise of Agile felt like a breath of fresh air.

Pini's perspective: first experience with Agile

I've been in the IT industry since 1997, working with everything from mainframes to modern cloud platforms. My first role was at Intel, writing Perl scripts on Digital Equipment Corporation (DEC) VAX machines to analyze production data. The goal was to help engineers improve chip production process quality. From there, I've worn many hats—from hands-on developer to technical leader—across a range of companies. On my journey I've witnessed first-hand how the IT landscape has continually evolved.

One of the earliest major shifts I observed happened around 2000. I was working at Check Point, the company that pioneered the first firewall and VPN. I joined in 1999, at the height of the internet bubble. At the time, Check Point followed a traditional Waterfall approach. We spent months in planning, about seven or eight in development, then performed a massive "big bang merge". At this point we tested the result and released everything on CDs. It was a predictable but slow-moving cycle—one big annual release plus occasional minor updates.

All seemed fine until the big merge for version 5.0, which was supposed to wrap up about six weeks before launch. Suddenly, after all major development branches were integrated, nightly builds broke and fixes didn't take. Because each full build took five hours, we could only attempt one or two a day. This led to a very slow feedback loop. After weeks of chaos, leadership created a war room of 20 key people. The focus was solely on stabilizing the product. It took four more months of around-the-clock work to get 5.0 out. This delay cost the company significant revenue and damaged its reputation for reliability.

That painful experience sparked a deeper appreciation for iterative development and continuous integration (CI). Martin Fowler's seminal article on CI, *Continuous*

Integration,[3] appeared that same year, but at Check Point, we were already feeling the problems it addressed. We built our own CI server—before CruiseControl existed—and gradually moved towards more Agile practices. This looked like smaller iterations, frequent merges and cross-team collaboration. Around 2001, the Agile Manifesto crystallized these ideas, emphasizing shorter cycles, teamwork and automation. Conway's Law (which states that organizations design systems that mirror their communication structures) also became more apparent. Technical improvements like CI thrive only when matched by organizational changes, such as adopting Agile.

Michael's perspective: a gradual evolution towards agility and CI

My own journey into the shifts transforming IT began not in software, but in the structured worlds of electronics and telco/networking. Like Pini's early experience at Check Point, project management was dominated by traditional Waterfall planning. Detailed Gantt charts dictated timelines months out, offering a comforting illusion of predictability.

Unlike Pini's trigger—a dramatic merge failure—my move away from Waterfall was more gradual. We started by aligning teams around broader goals, empowering them to break down tasks, and implementing regular updates

3 Fowler, M. "Continuous integration". Available at: https://martinfowler.com/articles/continuousIntegration.html.

on progress and obstacles. It was an initial step away from rigid upfront planning. My first real encounter with formal Agile methodologies, however, came later when I transitioned into software and system engineering. Even then, agility often remained isolated within specific teams, rarely coordinated across organizational silos. The communication friction and integration headaches between these Agile pockets and the rest of the Waterfall-oriented organization were palpable, highlighting the limitations even without a single catastrophic event.

My introduction to CI concepts coincided with the move away from laborious, manual server and software configuration towards automation. While Pini was building custom CI tools early on, my initial steps involved leveraging automation scripts, later adopting standard tools as they matured.

When the Agile Manifesto emerged in 2001, I remember reading it and finding the principles resonated deeply. It articulated the gut feelings many of us had about better ways to work. Yet, seeing it genuinely implemented "in the wild" took time. Even in a software project management course around 2008, Waterfall was presented as the standard, with metrics like kilo lines of code (KLOC) emphasized. It wasn't until after university that I saw Agile truly applied in practice.

Conway's Law, however, was something I observed impacting outcomes much earlier, even before knowing the formal term. I saw first-hand how the rigid, siloed structure of a telco negatively affected its ability to deliver changes swiftly, despite having capable engineers.

Later, during my time in the German Air Force, we achieved high-quality service delivery within a siloed environment. Crucially, we were aligned on goals and had near end-to-end responsibility—something counterintuitive perhaps.

Still later, I experienced how a more aligned structure at an e-commerce platform positively influenced delivery, enabling faster feedback and innovation. Understanding how to consciously shape or navigate organizational structures became a key learning. It mirrors Pini's observations on the link between technical improvements and organizational change.

Pini's perspective: embracing Docker and the rise of Cloud Native

By 2013, a decade after I'd first used CI and Agile, I saw another seismic shift. It started when I saw the recording from PyCon US 2013, where Solomon Hykes presented Docker. Everything clicked in five minutes. Docker[4] made packaging and distributing software simple and consistent, solving problems that had bothered us for more than ten years.

I'd used Solaris Zones (a form of operating-system-level virtualization) and chroot (a way to isolate processes) to isolate or share environments, but they never worked

---

4 Hykes, S. (2013). *The Future of Linux Containers.* PyCon 2013. Available at: https://www.youtube.com/watch?v=wW9CAH9nSLs.

seamlessly across different architectures, and distribution remained clunky. Docker changed that. It also arrived just as we were shifting to huge, always-online systems, which demanded a new kind of infrastructure management. Docker containers opened the door to a more dynamic, distributed approach. They allowed horizontal scaling across many machines instead of buying ever-bigger servers. In 2014, I co-founded a consulting firm centered on containers—an ecosystem that would soon be called Cloud Native. Michael joined the new company soon after.

Michael's perspective: the Docker "aha!" moment

Like Pini, the Docker "aha!" moment I experienced around 2013 was immediate for me, although driven by slightly different pains. We were pushing hard on CI/continuous development (CD) for Infrastructure as Code (IaC) but battling constant environment drift with our VM-based testing setups. This led to the classic "works on my machine" syndrome, surfacing issues painfully only in production. Spinning up fresh VMs for each CI/CD run was too slow and the hypervisor APIs were clunky for automation.

Docker instantly solved these issues. It was lightweight, offering consistent packaging, immutable artifacts and speed. As we adopted it, its potential beyond just testing infra code became clear. At HolidayCheck, where I led operations, we became early adopters. We moved towards Docker and, initially, Mesos for orchestration, migrating software workloads too. This is where my path first crossed with Pini's, through our engagement with Container Solutions.

Before Docker, VMs were my primary isolation tool. While I'd experimented with Solaris Zones and chroot out of interest, they weren't daily deployment tools like VMs.

Later, at SwissCom, I joined an innovation department focused on new technologies. When Google released Kubernetes, I dove in immediately. Having felt the operational complexities of Mesos, Kubernetes' design philosophy resonated. Mass adoption within SwissCom took time, but the exploration solidified my conviction in its industry-changing potential. This led me to join Container Solutions shortly after, establishing the Swiss office with a former HolidayCheck colleague.

While our initial paths into the industry diverged, our experiences converged significantly as Cloud Native technologies matured. We both witnessed the profound impact of these shifts not just on technology itself, but on team structures, operational mindsets and the very definition of efficiency. Our collective journey through consulting and hands-on leadership led us to several shared conclusions about navigating this evolving landscape.

Why Cloud Native matters: scalability, speed and resilience

At its core, we learned that Cloud Native is about building and running software that takes full advantage of the cloud's on-demand resources. In these environments, physical hardware is abstracted away by providers like Amazon, Google, Microsoft or internal teams managing private clouds. The defining feature is that developers can programmatically request resources—servers, networks, storage—within seconds. This on-demand, limitless feel is what makes IaC truly possible and fluid: describe the desired state in a file, and the cloud (public or private) spins it up.

This shift was driven by software systems getting ever larger, fuelled by the explosion of mobile devices, the rise of big data and the increasing demand for always-on services. Traditional monolithic designs struggled, pushing the industry towards distributed architectures relying on horizontal scaling. This is where Cloud Native's core ingredients proved essential: immutable infrastructure, containers, microservices, declarative APIs and orchestration.

We saw immutable infrastructure—treating resources as disposable and replacing rather than modifying them live—become practical, largely thanks to containers (like Docker) packaging applications and dependencies into lightweight, repeatable units. The power of this immutable automation for both applications and infrastructure felt transformative. It enabled robust, fully automated CI/CD pipelines for everything.

Crucially, this fuelled the "pets v cattle" transition, a journey many of us remember well. Early in our careers, treating servers like unique pets—perhaps affectionately named after Simpsons characters like Marge and Homer—was common practice. If Marge's /var partition filled up, we'd manually log in, prune logs, restart services, maybe apply a quick patch and diligently update a shared text-file runbook. Configuration "management" might have been a shared folder ambiguously named "latest-configs-FINAL-v2". These machines had unique histories requiring careful tending.

Incidents, like a critical kernel panic late on a Friday when the only person remembering the quirky LVM setup was unreachable, highlighted the fragility. The chaos and wasted time often led to a clear resolution: "We must reach a point where losing any single server at any moment is a non-event." That marked the conscious start of adopting the "cattle" mindset—designing for disposability and automation. When Docker came around, this became significantly easier to achieve, triggering a transformation across the industry.

Complementing this operational shift, microservices break down large applications into smaller, independently deployable chunks. Declarative APIs allow teams to define the system's desired state—how many replicas, which settings—while the underlying platform ensures reality matches the blueprint. Orchestration, typically via Kubernetes, automatically coordinates these containers, handling scaling, healing and deployment. Finally, continuous delivery pipelines ensure every code change remains release-ready, allowing reliable deployment at high speed.

When done right, Cloud Native operates like a factory assembly line: each station (service) is focused and an orchestrator keeps things flowing smoothly. This contrasts sharply with the monolithic approach, akin to a handcrafted watch—intricate but difficult to modify or repair without halting everything. In Cloud Native, component failure or upgrade doesn't stop the entire system. This fundamental shift enables teams to move fast while staying resilient. It provides the foundation for how technical capabilities can enable and necessitate new organizational structures.

The importance of organizational alignment

However, we consistently observed that Cloud Native isn't just about tools. According to Conway's Law, organizational structure and communication patterns directly influence software design. So, if you want the benefits of microservices and containers, you also need the right team structures.

Through our work, including extensive consulting engagements helping organizations navigate the shift towards a Cloud Native operating model, we've encountered a vast array of team structures and witnessed first-hand how critical organizational alignment is. While not dogmatic about any single framework, we've found *Team Topologies*[5] particularly effective. Its concepts are relatively simple and easy for diverse stakeholders to grasp. This makes it a valuable tool for illustrating the benefits of clear team boundaries and interaction

5 Skelton, M. and Pais, M. (2019) *Team Topologies: Organizing Business and Technology Teams for Fast Flow*. IT Revolution Press.

modes when starting an organizational change initiative. It outlines types of teams—stream-aligned (owning end-to-end delivery for a service), platform (building shared tools), enabling (providing temporary expertise) and complicated-subsystem (focusing on niche areas)—and how they should interact.

With the right team topology, you avoid the coordination nightmares that occur when responsibilities overlap haphazardly. The contrast between aligned and misaligned organizations is stark. We saw classic cases of negative Conway's Law in action too. For instance, in one telco, even as parts of the organization tried adopting newer tech, deploying a seemingly simple update involved multiple siloed teams (development, core network ops, IT systems ops, security), a lengthy change process and a change advisory board (CAB) at the end. It took at least six months to get something out, completely negating the potential benefits of microservices due to the rigid structure.

Conversely, we experienced success at an e-commerce company that tackled organizational structure alongside technology. They formed stream-aligned teams with end-to-end ownership, supported by a dedicated platform team. This clear structure, akin to Team Topologies, enabled rapid, independent deployments and faster feedback loops. This alignment is what makes continuous delivery, microservices and fast feedback loops truly possible.

The power of a hybrid approach: centralized control and distributed execution

A key reason for the Cloud Native model is the ability to scale horizontally through microservices and dynamic infrastructure. In principle, that suggests a more decentralized approach, with multiple services running independently across many nodes. However, while pure decentralization sounds appealing initially, our practical experience confirmed that managing coordination and policy across truly distributed systems at scale becomes incredibly complex. Time spent with systems like Mesos highlighted some of these challenges. Coordinating tasks and state across different frameworks involved significant operational overheads.

This aligns strongly with insights from Google, highlighted by engineers like Amin Vahdat and Google's VP of Infrastructure Eric Brewer based on their experience with precursors to Kubernetes like GFS and Borg. They found that a "logically centralized, hierarchical control plane with a peer-to-peer data plane" often outperforms attempts at full decentralization. It might seem counterintuitive if you assume "everything should be peer-to-peer", but at hyperscale, centralizing certain intelligence and orchestration tasks keeps the system simpler to manage. Meanwhile the data plane (where the actual work happens) remains decentralized and distributed for scalability and resilience. Conversations around this time emphasizing "centralize control, distribute execution", profoundly shaped our understanding of building and managing large-scale systems. Google, operating at billion-user scale, needed this robust, partially centralized model.

Through practice, we independently arrived at a similar conclusion: this hybrid approach offers the best pragmatic balance. It simplifies state management, policy enforcement and provides a unified point of interaction. Therefore, Kubernetes' architecture—with its central control plane (API server, etcd, controllers) handling the desired state and the distributed data plane (kubelets on worker nodes) executing tasks—immediately resonated. It felt like a natural evolution addressing the complexities we'd seen in earlier systems, serving as a validation and refinement of this hybrid principle.

The declarative nature exposed via the API was particularly powerful. It shifted the paradigm from imperative orchestration ("do this, then that") to defining a target state ("make reality match this description"). This perfectly aligned with the push towards GitOps and robust automation. For us, it didn't challenge our understanding of distributed systems as much as it provided a more effective and manageable pattern for the crucial control plane aspect, balancing the need for global coordination with the flexibility of distributed services.

The efficiency imperative

When Docker, Kubernetes and continuous deployment became popular, many teams focused on shipping features faster. At first, it felt like we'd solved everything. Resources appeared at the click of a button, updates could go live daily and velocity soared. But speed without efficiency quickly inflated monthly bills and complicated daily operations.

The hidden problem is technical debt. If a performance issue cropped up, teams might simply scale up to a bigger VM rather than fix the root cause. Sure, an extra $100 a month for more capacity doesn't seem terrible, but it can hide a deeper flaw. Eventually, you pay for these shortcuts when usage spikes—think Black Friday—forcing more desperate fixes and piling on more debt. This vicious cycle erodes both productivity and stability over time.

We've watched organizations become so captivated by new technology that they ignored inefficiencies. That is until costs ballooned, or the complexity became unmanageable. True Cloud Native maturity, then, isn't merely about embracing containers or microservices. It's about balancing speed and scale with mindful resource use. That keeps the system resilient, the bills manageable and teams free to innovate without technical debt dragging them down.

The Cloud Native maturity gap

Plenty of companies attempt to "go Cloud Native" by taking their monolithic applications and "lifting and shifting" them into containers or VMs. This often makes the environment more complex rather than yielding the expected agility. Other frequent pitfalls we observed include the chaos resulting from unclear service ownership, where scattered workflows and wasted effort abound due to a lack of accountability.

Then there's the rapid, ever-changing ecosystem of tools. Here it's easy to get swamped by new solutions or adopt multiple conflicting approaches, leading to debilitating tool sprawl. Without a coherent strategy covering architecture, teams and processes, Cloud Native migrations stall, leaving the real benefits just out of reach.

Often, the initial rush for speed in Cloud Native adoption leads to efficiency being overlooked. We recall many instances, early on or with clients, where teams deployed services to Kubernetes without proper resource requests and limits. Things seemed fine under low load, but instability or random Out Of Memory Kills (OOMKills) would emerge as usage increased because the scheduler was flying blind. Costs would also creep up as teams scaled up infrastructure rather than optimizing code or tackling performance bottlenecks at their source.

Another pattern we frequently encountered was the "distributed monolith". These are hastily created microservices with excessive dependencies, increasing latency and complexity. Addressing these typically required implementing robust observability, educating teams on resource management (sometimes introducing cost allocation/showback via FinOps) and embedding performance tuning into the development cycle.

Our consulting work confirms these common maturity pitfalls like "lift-and-shift" disappointments, unclear ownership and tool sprawl. Beyond those, we frequently see the following issues:

- A lack of genuine platform thinking (treating Kubernetes as just VMs++).

- Cargo-culting practices being adopted without understanding the underlying context (e.g. implementing microservices everywhere regardless of need).
- Neglecting the developer experience on the new platform.
- Critically, underestimating the required cultural shift.

Ultimately, we concluded that true Cloud Native maturity transcends specific tools. It hinges on key cultural and process changes:

- Treating the internal platform as a product focused on developer experience.
- Fostering a deep DevOps culture of collaboration and shared responsibility.
- Implementing mature automation, including DevSecOps and GitOps.
- Ensuring ubiquitous observability is built in.
- Establishing clear ownership aligned with architecture (invoking Conway's Law again).
- Always maintaining a focus on delivering tangible business value by effectively balancing speed with stability, security and cost-efficiency.

From maturity to maturity: contrasting Waterfall and Cloud Native setups

The Cloud Native maturity gap highlights the struggles many organizations face in reaping the full benefits of modern approaches. But what does a truly mature, highly functional setup look like within different paradigms? Understanding the characteristics of both well-executed Waterfall and advanced Cloud Native environments provides crucial context. Each, when operating optimally according to its own principles, presents a distinct picture of software development and delivery, shaped by specific patterns.

> A full list of patterns can be found in Appendix 2 at the end of the book. Each pattern is mentioned by its name and its identifier in round brackets (). For example: *Batch Processing (WF12)*.

The mature Waterfall powerhouse

Imagine a large financial institution that has perfected the Waterfall model over decades. This organization excels at predictable, large-scale project delivery where requirements are stable and compliance is paramount. Its maturity isn't defined by speed, but by rigorous control and reliability within its operational constraints.

- **Predictability through planning:** Every major initiative begins with *Comprehensive Upfront Design (WF01)*. Months are dedicated to gathering requirements and creating detailed specifications, ensuring every aspect is documented before implementation begins. This meticulous planning minimizes ambiguity later in the process.
- **Structured execution:** Work proceeds through *Sequential Phase Execution (WF02)*. Dedicated

teams handle distinct phases—analysis, design, coding, testing, deployment. Formal *Phase-Gate Quality Control (WF03)* ensures each stage meets predefined standards before handoff. A *Centralized Planning & Coordination (WF04)* body, likely a project management office (PMO), oversees the master schedule, resource allocation and risk management using tools like Gantt charts.

- **Controlled integration and release:** Components are developed in relative isolation and undergo *Late-Stage Integration & Testing (WF06)*. While this can lead to "integration hell" if poorly managed, in a mature setup, it's a carefully orchestrated process. The culmination is often a *Big Bang Release (WF07)*, deploying the entire system update in a single, coordinated event, perhaps annually or semi-annually. Architecture often follows a *Layered Architecture (WF09)* pattern within a monolith, and capacity is increased through *Vertical Scaling (WF08)*—adding more power to existing servers.

This mature Waterfall setup delivers reliability and predictability for large, slow-moving projects. Its strength lies in control and thoroughness, and it is suited for environments where requirements rarely change mid-project. However, its inherent weakness is its lack of speed and adaptability in dynamic markets.

Waterfall/Monolithic patterns

If you recognize these patterns from your daily work, then your organization is likely operating within a Waterfall/

monolithic paradigm (the full set is in the online patterns library: https://re-cinq.com/patterns).

WF01 – Comprehensive Upfront Design: Invest heavily in initial design for detailed implementation specifications.

WF02 – Sequential Phase Execution: Divide projects into discrete, ordered phases with formal sign-offs.

WF03 – Phase-Gate Quality Control: Implement formal reviews as quality gates after major phases.

WF04 – Centralized Planning & Coordination: Use central PMO for planning, resources and progress tracking.

WF05 – Comprehensive Documentation: Mandate thorough, formal documentation as primary phase output/input.

WF06 – Late-Stage Integration & Testing: Integrate separately developed components late, then system test.

WF07 – Big Bang Release: Release entire integrated system in one large deployment event.

WF08 – Vertical Scaling: Increase capacity by enhancing resources (CPU, RAM) of existing hardware.

WF09 – Layered Architecture: Organize monolithic code into distinct horizontal layers (UI, Logic, Data).

WF10 – Centralized Version Control: Use a central SCM repository for code version management.

WF11 – Shared Database Integration: Multiple modules directly access a single, shared database schema.

WF12 – Batch Processing: Execute large-scale data updates periodically during off-peak hours.

WF13 – Manual Build & Deployment: Rely on documented manual procedures for application deployment.

WF14 – Config-as-Data Services: Store application configuration as structured data separate from binary.

The Agile Cloud Native factory

Contrast this with a thriving e-commerce company that has fully embraced Cloud Native maturity. Their environment is optimized for speed, resilience and continuous adaptation to market demands. It operates like a well-oiled factory, capable of delivering value rapidly and reliably.

- **Continuous value flow:** Instead of large, infrequent releases, this organization practices *Iterative Value Delivery (CN01)*. This means shipping small, valuable increments frequently, often multiple times a day. This is powered by a highly *Automated Validation Pipeline—CI/CD (CN02)*, ensuring every code change is built, tested and ready for deployment automatically.
- **Decoupled and dynamic architecture:** The system is built using *Microservices Architecture (CN03)*, breaking functionality into small, autonomous

services. Each service is packaged using a *Containerization (CN04)* pattern, often managed by *Dynamic Scheduling (CN05) (Kubernetes)*. This allows teams to deploy and scale their services independently. Changes are deployed using *Immutable Infrastructure (CN06)*, where new instances replace old ones, enhancing reliability.

- **Developer empowerment and insight:** The organization is structured to *Optimize for Flow (CN07)*, often using cross-functional teams aligned with services (like *Team Topologies* structures). An IDP built using *Platform Engineering/IDP (CN08)* practices, abstracting infrastructure complexity. Systems are designed for *Observability (CN09)*, providing deep visibility into performance and behavior. The entire architecture is built with *Design for Failure (CN10)* in mind, anticipating and handling failures gracefully using patterns like circuit breakers.

This mature Cloud Native setup achieves high velocity and adaptability. It allows teams to innovate quickly, scale effortlessly and maintain high availability, making it ideal for competitive, fast-paced digital environments. Its success relies on automation, decoupled architecture, empowered teams and a culture of continuous improvement.

By understanding the characteristics and underlying patterns of these mature paradigms, organizations can better assess their own state, define clearer goals and appreciate the fundamental shifts required when moving from one wave of innovation to the next (use our online assessment to get started: https://re-cinq.com/ai-native-assessment).

Paradigm fitness: context matters most

It's crucial to emphasize that neither of these mature paradigms—Waterfall or Cloud Native—is inherently superior or flawed. Each emerged as a product of its time and technological context, shaped by a form of natural selection based on the prevailing challenges and opportunities. Waterfall represented the optimal solution for managing complexity in the era of mainframes and limited computing resources several decades ago. Indeed, it continues to serve many large organizations effectively for massive, stable software systems today.

However, in the current landscape defined by horizontally scalable cloud compute and rapidly shifting market demands, Cloud Native has emerged as the winning paradigm for many. It provides the agility and speed necessary to outmaneuver competition and scale innovations quickly.

The fundamental mistake, therefore, isn't necessarily choosing the "wrong" paradigm for your context—although that can certainly hinder progress. The far more common and damaging failure is selecting the *right* paradigm for the current era (like Cloud Native) but implementing it poorly. Treating a disruptive shift like Cloud Native as merely an incremental tool adoption *(Incremental Facade (AP04))* or mimicking practices without understanding the principles *(Cargo Cult Adoption*

(AP05)) prevents organizations from ever achieving the high performance and true benefits the paradigm offers. True maturity comes from mastering the chosen paradigm, not just adopting its labels (contact the authors for an in-depth assessment of your organization's paradigm fitness: https://re-cinq.com/ai-native-assessment).

By understanding the characteristics and underlying patterns of these mature paradigms, organizations can better assess their own state, define clearer goals and appreciate the fundamental shifts required when moving from one wave of innovation to the next.

Key takeaways

Over the past 50 years, the software world has evolved from artisanal craftsmanship, through the monolithic and Waterfall-dominated control era, into today's Agile and Cloud Native ecosystems. Each stage has enabled us to build ever-larger systems.

The journey through these eras of software development teaches us several key lessons:

1. **Scalability with Cloud Native:** Properly built Cloud Native environments let you reach scales older methods never could.

2. **New complexities:** Distributed systems can become unwieldy and expensive if not managed with care.

3. **Conway's Law matters:** To truly reap the benefits of Cloud Native, teams must be structured to support microservices, CI/CD pipelines and fast iteration.

4. **Balancing scale and efficiency:** Speed is great, but unrestrained resource consumption leads to ballooning costs and hidden technical debt. Efficiency ensures you don't need to slow down your own progress.

5. **Centralized control, distributed execution:** A hierarchical control plane with a peer-to-peer data plane—like Kubernetes—offers a proven model for managing large-scale systems.

Done thoughtfully, Cloud Native is the "well-oiled factory" for software development. With the right architecture, organizational alignment, and awareness of cost and complexity, it delivers both speed and stability. This allows organizations to innovate continuously without losing momentum. It's the latest chapter in our industry's ever-evolving story, picking up where old methods faltered and setting the stage for whatever comes next. In the following chapters, we'll delve deeper into the principles and practices of Cloud Native and explore how organizations can successfully navigate this transformation.

Scan the QR code to access our comprehensive patterns library. Use the interactive tools and pattern cards to identify which paradigm your organization currently operates in and map your own transformation journey.

Chapter 2

Cloud Native–
A Transformative Shift

What is Cloud Native, really? It's more than just a buzzword or a collection of tools. It's a fundamentally different way of building and running applications, one that fully leverages the power of the cloud. At its core, Cloud Native is about achieving speed and agility without sacrificing stability and resilience. It's about empowering teams to deliver value to customers faster, adapt to changing market demands quickly and scale systems effortlessly.

Think of Cloud Native as an approach, not a destination. It's a set of architectural principles, operational practices and cultural norms. It involves building and deploying applications as microservices. In other words, breaking down large applications into smaller, independent services. Cloud Native uses containers, like Docker, to package those services into lightweight, portable units. This also means using platforms like Kubernetes to dynamically manage and orchestrate those containers, automating deployment, scaling and management. And it requires embracing automation and continuous delivery. This automates the software delivery pipeline for frequent, reliable releases.

Crucially, Cloud Native demands a DevOps culture, breaking down silos and fostering collaboration between development and operations. These core tenets reflect key Cloud Native paradigm patterns such as *Microservices Architecture (CN03)*, *Containerization (CN04)*, *Dynamic Scheduling (CN05)* and the *Automated Validation Pipeline (CN02)*, enabling the speed and resilience characteristic of this approach.

But simply adopting these technologies doesn't automatically make you Cloud Native. Many organizations fall into the trap of "doing Cloud Native" without truly *being* Cloud Native. They might use containers and Kubernetes, but if they haven't also transformed their organizational structure, processes and culture, they're likely missing out on the full benefits. This is where we turn our attention to transformational change.

What is transformational change?

Not every "change" is a full-fledged transformation. Swapping out a database or adopting a new testing tool can make a team's life easier, but it won't fundamentally alter how the entire organization operates. Transformational shifts, on the other hand, affect team structures, culture and business models all at once. When a company leaps from Waterfall to Agile or from a monolith to microservices, it's not just a matter of introducing new tools. It represents a shift away from traditional monolithic patterns like a *Layered Architecture (WF09)* often coupled with *Shared Database Integration (WF11)*, towards the fundamentally different approach of *Microservices Architecture (CN03)*. It requires a radical overhaul of how work gets done.

We define transformational change as a deep shift in how a company operates, driven by major technology leaps that require new team structures, processes and culture. These shifts happen for two main reasons. First, when a new technology (internet, containers, cloud, AI) is so advantageous that the old ways become less viable. Second, when customer needs or market forces change so drastically that delivering value requires a totally different approach. Examples of such a shift include subscriptions instead of licenses, daily updates instead of annual releases, or using mobile or a web browser instead of a mostly disconnected PC. These factors make old structures obsolete, forcing companies to rethink everything.

Why Cloud Native *IS* transformational

Impact on teams

Agile represented a transformational shift because it fundamentally altered how teams worked. Instead of the traditional Waterfall approach, with its characteristic Waterfall patterns like *Sequential Phase Execution*

(WF02) and reliance on handoffs (often leading to the *Siloed Handoffs (AP19)* anti-pattern), Agile demanded cross-functional teams collaborating continuously. This aligns more closely with the Cloud Native pattern *Optimize for Flow (CN07)*. Daily stand-ups, short feedback loops and iterative development became the norm. This wasn't just about faster releases; it was about shifting ownership and decision-making power to the teams themselves. This fostered a more collaborative and adaptive culture.

Cloud Native is similarly transformational, but on a larger scale. It's not just about adopting Docker, Kubernetes and microservices. It's about restructuring your entire organization to leverage the cloud. Microservices reshape teams, leading to smaller, cross-functional groups that own services end to end. This structure is necessary to fully leverage microservices and achieve the goals by setting up *Team Topologies*. Container orchestration and continuous delivery pipelines demand new operational practices and a DevOps mindset. The on-demand nature of cloud resources forces a shift in how you plan capacity and manage costs. Cloud Native requires us to fundamentally rethink how software is built, deployed and operated.

Impact on culture

These technological and team structure changes force a cultural shift. Decision-making power often moves from managers to teams. The result is greater collaboration and reduced hierarchy. Leaders must trust their teams to make decisions and adapt quickly. The old, predictive, milestone-based planning approach gives way to "inspect and adapt", which is driven by customer feedback and continuous learning. Organizations must also embrace a higher degree of risk tolerance. That means understanding that experimentation and occasional failures are part of the learning process. And, because Cloud Native enables rapid iteration, continuous learning becomes a core part of the organizational culture.

Impact on business models

Cloud Native doesn't just change how you build software. It changes what you can build and how you deliver it. The speed to market increases dramatically. This allows you to respond faster to customer needs and competitive pressures. The scalability of cloud infrastructure also enables you to handle massive growth (or sudden spikes in demand) without major disruptions. In addition, the cost structures shift from large, upfront capital expenditures to more predictable, pay-as-you-go operating expenses. This can enable new business models, like subscription services, that were previously impractical.

The *Innovator's Dilemma*

Clayton Christensen's *Innovator's Dilemma* explains why even thriving companies stumble when disruption hits.[6] Leaders must decide: keep polishing what works, or jump into the unknown, risking short-term disruption for long-term survival. Getting the timing right is critical. Move too early, you might burn resources on immature technology. Wait too long, you can lose your market lead.

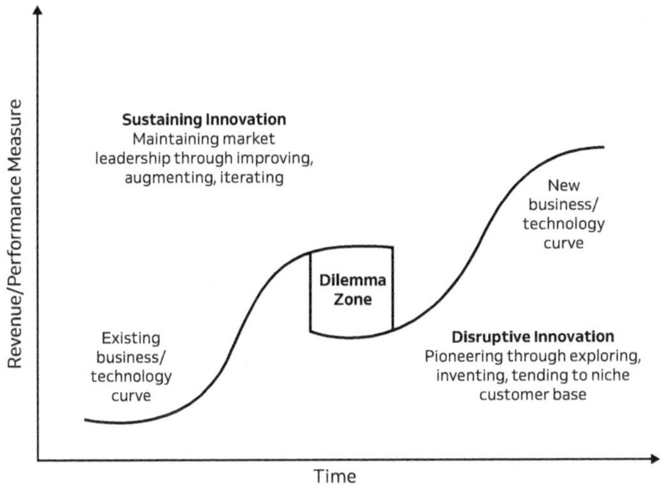

Figure 1: *The Innovator's Dilemma*

The history of business is littered with companies that failed to adapt to transformational shifts. Kodak, for instance, invented the digital camera in 1975, yet

6 Christensen, C.M. (2003) *The Innovator's Dilemma: The Revolutionary Book that Will Change the Way You Do Business.* Harper Paperbacks.

clung to its legacy film business. This proved to be a strategic misstep that ultimately led to its downfall. This underscores a critical point: even industry pioneers can fail if they ignore disruptive innovation.

Similarly, Blockbuster dominated the video rental market but underestimated the power of streaming. This mistake allowed Netflix to completely redefine the industry. The lesson for incumbents is clear: be willing to disrupt your own business model before someone else does.

Nokia, once the undisputed king of mobile phones, provides another cautionary tale. While the company continued to improve its traditional phones incrementally, it failed to grasp the transformative potential of iOS and Android. Internal attempts to catch up, like Symbian and Maemo, didn't solve problems fast enough. Market dominance can evaporate surprisingly quickly if you underestimate the impact of a true platform shift. In many ways this is another example of what happens when you don't keep up with disruptive innovation in your sector.

Finally, Yahoo's story serves as a potent illustration of how even dominant players can falter when they fail to navigate transformational waves, highlighting the critical cost of missed opportunities and a lack of strategic focus. The company's inability to capitalize on the nascent search market by acquiring Google, or recognize the disruptive potential of social media epitomized by its failed bid for Facebook, represent pivotal strategic missteps. Coupled with failures to adapt to mobile, integrate key acquisitions like Flickr and Tumblr effectively, or maximize returns from investments like Alibaba, Yahoo found itself adrift. Rejecting Microsoft's substantial takeover offer further underscored an inability to realistically assess its position as the competitive landscape shifted dramatically around it.

Consequently, the vacuum left by Yahoo's strategic inertia was rapidly filled by more agile and focused competitors. Google, famously spurned in its infancy by Yahoo, cemented its dominance in search and advertising, becoming the default gateway to the internet. Facebook surged, capturing the social dimension of the web that Yahoo overlooked. While other players like Microsoft also interacted with Yahoo strategically, it was the ascendance of Google and Facebook that most starkly demonstrated the consequences of Yahoo's failure to adapt. Ultimately, the once-mighty internet giant became a cautionary tale, its core assets passed between larger entities like Verizon and Apollo Global Management. Yahoo serves as a stark reminder that navigating the waves of innovation requires foresight, agility and the decisiveness Yahoo lacked.

But, as we know, new technology doesn't always lead to business failure. Some companies have successfully navigated major transformations, demonstrating the power of embracing change. Microsoft, under CEO Satya Nadella, provides a prime example. By pivoting to a "cloud-first" strategy, Microsoft revitalized its business and became a leader in cloud services. This demonstrated that even established giants can execute bold strategic pivots.

Adobe offers another compelling case. By shifting from one-time software sales to a subscription model with Creative Cloud, they unlocked new growth and increased customer loyalty. This example demonstrates the power of adapting the revenue model. IBM, although a slower transformation, reinvented itself from a hardware-focused company to a provider of cloud and AI services. In doing so, it showed that even legacy businesses can remain relevant with a long-term commitment to adaptation.

However, Netflix's evolution is perhaps the most dramatic. Starting with DVD-by-mail, its leadership anticipated the shift to streaming and built an infrastructure to dominate that market. From this strong foundation, the company expanded into original content creation. Now Netflix is a global media powerhouse. This demonstrates how you can create an entire new market for your business by anticipating future trends.

Finally, Amazon's transformation of its internal server capacity into AWS, a leading cloud provider, offers a different perspective on transformation. The AWS example highlights how internal capabilities, when properly leveraged, can be turned into significant external products and revenue streams.

In each case, the leaders at the organization in question committed to a major transformation. They understood that incremental changes were not enough.

Focus on one transformation at a time

Geoffrey Moore's *Zone to Win* emphasizes the need to focus on one major transformation at a time.[7] While incremental improvements and small-scale experiments are always valuable, there's only enough organizational energy for one all-consuming shift in the "Transformation Zone". Splitting focus leads to half-finished projects and frustrated teams.

The *Zone to Win* framework provides a vital strategic lens for established enterprises facing the inherent tension between optimizing their current operations and positioning themselves to capture the next wave of disruptive innovation. Moore posits that successfully managing both requires recognizing that different types of initiatives demand fundamentally different management approaches, resources and executive oversight. At its heart, the model contends that an organization cannot effectively pursue multiple large-scale transformations simultaneously. Attempting to do so inevitably fragments focus and energy, hindering the successful adoption of truly disruptive change. To manage this, *Zone to Win* delineates four distinct operational zones:

---

7 Moore, G.A. (2015) *Zone to Win: Organizing to Compete in an Age of Disruption*. Diversion Books.

The Performance Zone (Horizon 1): This constitutes the core business operations delivering the products and services that generate the vast majority of current revenue and profit. The mandate here is sustained performance, predictability and efficiency. Management focuses on hitting near-term targets, defending market share through incremental improvements (sustaining innovation) and optimizing established processes. Success is measured through conventional business metrics. This zone typically commands the largest share of resources.

The Productivity Zone (Horizon 1): Operating in support of the Performance Zone, this encompasses shared services and functions like IT infrastructure, finance, HR and legal. Its focus is on enabling the efficiency and effectiveness of the core business through cost savings, process improvements, standardization and compliance. While indispensable, it is fundamentally a cost center aimed at optimizing the current operational model, not generating new revenue streams directly.

The Incubation Zone (Horizon 3): This zone functions as the enterprise's internal R&D or venture arm, tasked with exploring and nurturing nascent, high-potential disruptive innovations. These are not mere incremental improvements but potential next-generation franchises capable of creating entirely new lines of business (often targeted at eventually generating >10% of total revenue). Management here mirrors venture capital, providing staged funding based on milestones within small, entrepreneurial teams. The goal is learning, validation and identifying candidates with genuine potential for massive scale. The key is understanding that most incubated ideas will ultimately fail or be exited rather than becoming the next core business.

The Transformation Zone (Horizon 2): This critical, yet temporary, zone is arguably the most challenging. It exists solely to take one highly promising, validated initiative (typically emerging from the Incubation Zone) and scale it into the enterprise's next major Performance Zone. This is an inherently disruptive, high-risk, resource-intensive undertaking that directly challenges the status quo and existing power structures. Moore emphasizes that success demands singular focus—only one initiative can occupy this zone at a time. It also requires direct, unwavering CEO sponsorship, significant cross-organizational resource reallocation and a dedicated, often command-and-control, leadership style to overcome internal resistance and navigate the inevitable disruption to near-term performance.

By segmenting initiatives and resources across these zones, the *Zone to Win* framework provides leadership with a disciplined model to manage the inherent conflicts between running the existing business efficiently and investing effectively in the disruptive innovations required for long-term relevance and growth. It forces difficult choices about resource allocation and strategic focus, ensuring that efforts to catch the next wave are given the distinct conditions and executive backing necessary to succeed without crippling the core operations that fund the journey.

	Disruptive Innovation	**Sustaining Innovation**
Revenue Performance	**Transformation Zone** Horizon 2	**Performance Zone** Horizon 2
Enabling Investments	**Incubation Zone** Horizon 3	**Productivity Zone** Horizon 3

Figure 2: *The Zone to Win* framework

Leadership, culture and the human side of change

It's important to remember that technology alone doesn't drive transformation; people do. Leaders must create a culture that embraces change, encourages experimentation and provides psychological safety for teams to learn from failures. They must also set clear priorities and ensure accountability, using metrics to identify bottlenecks and address underlying issues.

As a leader, you need to recognize that endless "transformation" is exhausting. A true transformation has a beginning, a middle and an *end*. But declaring it "done" doesn't mean you stop improving. A finished transformation means the new structures, processes and culture are stable enough to be your new baseline.

Companies that never finalize a transformation get stuck in half-baked implementations, wasting resources and losing out on the benefits. This is not a club you want to join. Therefore, it's important to know what "the end" of your transformation will look like so that you can build on the culture, ways of working and technology you have successfully implemented. We'll share how to tell when it's time to move from one stage to another throughout your transformation in Part II.

Visualizing Cloud Native transformation: the importance of holistic maturity

Embracing Cloud Native is far more than a simple technological upgrade. It is a profound transformational change. It reshapes not only how applications are built and run but also fundamentally alters team structures, operational practices and organizational culture.

Many attempts to "go Cloud Native" falter not because the technology is flawed, but because the organization fails to adapt its culture, processes and structures in concert. We've seen companies attempt to layer Cloud Native tools on to unchanged Waterfall processes, resulting in "the same old organization—just running Kubernetes". This highlights a critical lesson: success hinges on holistic development.

To help organizations visualize this journey and assess their progress, we can use a maturity matrix. This tool serves as a mirror, allowing a company to compare its current state against the characteristics of both mature

Waterfall and mature Cloud Native paradigms across several critical dimensions (take our free, interactive AI Native Assessment to see where you stand: https://re-cinq.com/ai-native-assessment).

The power of this matrix lies in its ability to highlight the interconnectedness of these areas. It illustrates the fundamental shifts required to move from a legacy state to a high-functioning Cloud Native environment:

- **Culture and leadership:** The move is from command-and-control structures and functional silos to cross-functional teams empowered by a DevOps culture.
- **Product and experience:** The focus shifts from being purely feature-focused with a generic UX to developing a data-informed strategy with API-driven services.
- **Development and delivery:** Manual processes, periodic and risky releases are replaced by automated CI/CD pipelines enabling rapid, iterative delivery.
- **Architecture and design:** The architecture evolves from monolithic applications and technology sprawl to microservices and containers specifically designed for scale.
- **Platform and operations:** The operational model transitions from reactive monitoring and manual interventions to proactive self-service enabled by IaC.
- **Data and intelligence:** Data management transforms from siloed data used for historical

reports into centralized data lakes supporting foundational analytics.

- **Trust and security:** The security posture matures from perimeter security and late-stage manual testing to integrated DevSecOps practices and Zero Trust models.
- **Governance and compliance:** Governance shifts from manual checks and reactive compliance to policy-as-code and continuous compliance.
- **Sustainability:** The approach to efficiency evolves from basic carbon accounting and manual efforts to cloud-optimized resource usage and green IT policies.

A common pitfall is the "unbalanced approach", where an organization might surge ahead in one area—say, adopting microservices (architecture and design)—while its team structures remain siloed and its delivery processes are still manual and periodic. Such imbalances create significant friction and prevent the organization from realizing the full benefits of speed and agility. Conway's Law often reasserts itself, leading to a "distributed monolith" where new technology is constrained by old organizational design.

True Cloud Native maturity requires concurrent advancement across all these dimensions. A spike in one area without corresponding growth in others often indicates a superficial or stalled transformation. By understanding that progress must be made on all fronts, organizations can avoid the common trap of treating Cloud Native as a purely technological fix and instead foster genuine, sustainable transformation.

Maturity category	Legacy: Waterfall	Current: Cloud Native
Culture and leadership	Functional silos; command-and-control	Cross-functional teams; DevOps culture
Product and experience	Feature-focused; generic UX	Data-informed strategy; API-driven services
Development and delivery	Manual processes; periodic, risky releases	Automated CI/CD; rapid, iterative delivery
Architecture and design	Monolithic applications; technology sprawl	Microservices and containers; designed for scale
Platform and operations	Reactive monitoring; manual interventions	IaC; proactive self-service
Data and intelligence	Siloed data; used for historical reports	Centralized data lakes; foundational analytics
Trust and security	Perimeter security; late-stage manual testing	DevSecOps practices; Zero Trust models
Governance and compliance	Manual governance; reactive compliance checks	Policy-as-code; continuous compliance
Sustainability	Basic carbon accounting; manual efficiency	Cloud-optimized resource usage; green IT policies

Figure 3: *Cloud Native Maturity Matrix*

Key takeaways

- **Beyond tools:** Transformational change goes beyond picking a new platform or library. It reconfigures team structures, company culture and often the very way business is done.
- **Two big shifts:** Moving from Waterfall to Agile and from monoliths to Cloud Native each redefined how software is built, who builds it and how organizations compete. We can learn valuable lessons from these shifts and apply them to the new wave that is already building.
- **Timing is everything:** The *Innovator's Dilemma* shows that clinging too long to what worked yesterday can leave you behind when a big disruption hits.
- **One transformation at a time:** Trying to juggle multiple massive changes simultaneously often leads to stalled, incomplete efforts. Focus on the one that matters most.
- **Finish what you start:** Set a clear endpoint to avoid transformation fatigue. Once the new approach stabilizes, you can reap its benefits and look ahead.

By understanding these ideas—and recognizing the difference between an improvement and a true transformation—your organization is far more likely to navigate the Cloud Native shift successfully. After all, in a world where entire industries can change overnight, the ability to transform effectively isn't just helpful. It's crucial to long-term survival.

Wondering where you are on your transformation journey? Scan the QR code to take our free AI Native Assessment. It will help you benchmark your current maturity and plan your next steps effectively.

Chapter 3

Waves of Innovation

The history of software development unfolds in waves—major technological and cultural shifts that transform how we build, deliver and manage products. Each wave disrupts the status quo and eventually becomes the norm, until the next arrives. We've seen this with Waterfall (the legacy wave) and Cloud Native (the current wave). Now, AI Native looms, promising to fundamentally alter everything from application design to team structures.

Before diving deep into these waves, it helps to have a quick framework for spotting where a new idea fits and how it matures over time. Two popular models—Three Horizons and a six-stage Product Lifecycle—offer that perspective.

Three Horizons

- **Horizon 3:** Early research, "blue sky" thinking—this is where radical or long-term ideas germinate.
- **Horizon 2:** Disruptive innovation—turning experimental concepts into viable solutions that challenge the status quo.
- **Horizon 1:** Sustaining and optimizing—where proven products or processes are refined and leveraged for ongoing returns.

Product Lifecycle (six stages)

- Research → Development → Introduction → Growth → Maturity → Decline

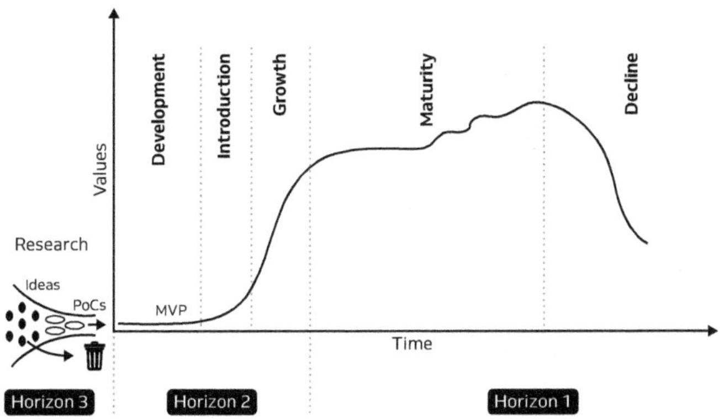

Figure 4: *Product Lifecycle*

Using these quick references, you can categorize a product or initiative according to how radical it is (Horizon 3, 2 or 1) and which phase of development it's in (from Research to Decline). But our focus here is on the modes of operation—the day-to-day mindsets and processes that make each wave of technology adoption possible.

Six modes of operation

Through years of observing technology adoption across organizations of all sizes, we've identified six distinct modes of operation. Each mode represents a particular way of operating and none is strictly tied to any single horizon or lifecycle stage. Instead, these modes can appear at different times, sometimes overlapping, within the same organization. Think of them like tools in a toolbox, where each is designed for specific tasks and conditions (use the patterns as real tools in our collaborative cards workshop: https://re-cinq.com/patterns).

These six modes are:

1. Pioneering

2. Bootstrapping & Bridge-Building

3. Scaling

4. Optimizing

5. Innovating

6. Retiring

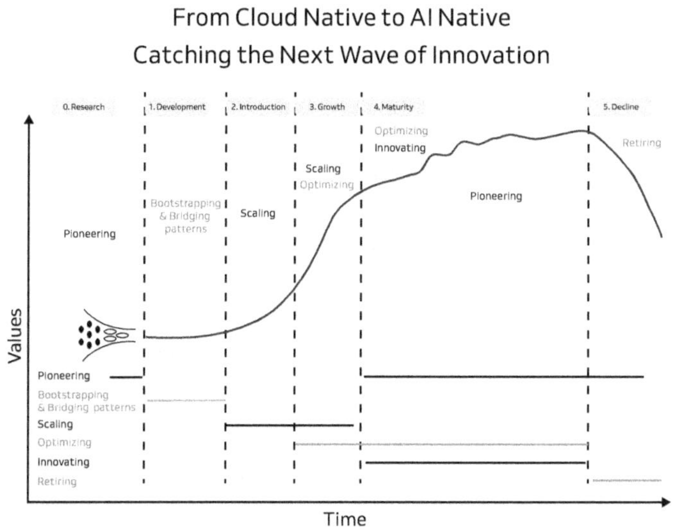

Figure 5: *The six modes of operation*

1. Pioneering

Pioneering is exactly what it sounds like—exploring unknown territory with minimal constraints. Teams in this mode:

- **Experiment fearlessly:** They work on raw ideas, unburdened by extensive bureaucracy or rigid guidelines.
- **Move fast and fail safely:** Quick prototypes and proof-of-concept experiments let them learn without incurring huge risks.
- **Generate inspiration and curiosity:** Their findings often feed the rest of the organization, igniting interest in new tools, languages or architectures.

Historically, Waterfall itself was once a "pioneering" model for large-scale software development. Decades ago, the notion of a structured, step-by-step approach to coding and testing was a breakthrough. It brought order to an otherwise chaotic process. Over time, Waterfall went from pioneering to mainstream and then, eventually, to legacy.

In today's environment, Cloud Native was also once "pioneering". Docker containers and orchestration with Kubernetes were radical ideas before they became widely accepted. Now we see AI Native in a similarly pioneering light. From large language models (LLMs) to advanced automation, these technologies are new frontiers, waiting to be tamed as we write this in 2025.

Patterns for Pioneering:

TF01 – Learn and Explore: Research emerging tech; assess relevance with minimal initial investment.

TF02 – Skunk Works Team: Small, autonomous team experiments rapidly, insulated from standard processes.

TF03 – Reduce Cost of Experimentation: Lower barriers to trying new things safely and cheaply.

TF04 – Sandbox Environment: Provide safe, isolated spaces for exploration and prototyping.

TF05 – Test Hard Things First: Prioritize early PoCs on most critical, uncertain technical aspects.

TF06 – Proof of Concept—PoC: Execute focused PoCs to validate or refute new concepts.

TF07 – Demo Your Ideas: Communicate progress engagingly to build understanding and support.

TF08 – Ideas Shelf: Maintain backlog of deferred ideas for future options.

TF09 – Business Case: Articulate rationale, benefits, costs and risks for initiatives.

TF10 – Finance Topologies: Adopt differentiated funding models for operations, transformation and innovation.

2. Bootstrapping & Bridge-Building

Once a pioneering idea shows real promise, teams shift into Bootstrapping & Bridge-Building mode. This is where they turn nebulous experiments into something tangible and viable in two distinct stages:

- *Bootstrapping:* Creating the minimal foundations—like a small set of microservices, a functional AI demo or the first iteration of an internal DevOps pipeline.
- *Bridge-Building:* Connecting new capabilities to existing systems or workflows. For instance, hooking a containerized service into a legacy monolith or integrating an AI model with older business processes.

During the initial Waterfall to Agile transition, organizations used bridging to keep the lights on in their Waterfall-based infrastructure while piloting short sprints in smaller teams. Likewise, in a Cloud Native push, you might maintain your monolithic core while slowly introducing containerized microservices around its edges. As for AI Native, you may start by connecting AI-based analytics to existing data pipelines or letting an ML model process logs before you trust it with user-facing tasks.

This mode is crucial because it reduces organizational fear. Instead of demanding a "big bang" overhaul, it offers a measured, incremental approach. That's how pioneering concepts survive contact with "the real world" of budgets, existing customers and established business goals.

Patterns for Bootstrapping & Bridge-Building:

TF11 – Executive Commitment: Secure active, visible executive backing for transformation priority.

TF12 – Appoint Transformation Champion: Designate an empowered leader to steer transformation execution.

TF13 – Form the Core Team: Establish dedicated, cross-functional team for Minimum Viable Product (MVP) and core practices.

TF14 – Vision First: Clearly define and communicate strategic vision to guide choices.

TF15 – Cultivate Psychological Safety: Foster a safe environment for experimentation, mistakes and learning.

TF16 – Research Through Action: Build MVP and bridges to uncover real-world challenges.

TF17 – Adaptability over Efficiency: Prioritize adaptable designs during bootstrapping, deferring heavy optimization.

TF18 – Deliver the MVP: Build the smallest valuable product version for crucial early feedback.

TF19 – Thinnest Viable Platform: Strictly prioritize MVP scope, deferring non-essential features.

TF20 – Delayed Automation: Introduce automation iteratively, starting with stable, proven tasks.

TF21 – Best Tool for the Task: Allow core team flexibility in selecting bootstrapping tools.

TF22 – Bridge the Old World: Design explicit integration layers between new and legacy systems.

TF23 – Staged Funding: Release funding in tranches tied to achieving specific milestones.

3. Scaling

Eventually, as the new approach proves itself, you need to scale. This is where an idea transitions from a niche initiative into something widely adopted and mission-critical. This presents as:

- *Focus on automation:* Repeated tasks get automated. CI/CD pipelines become fully fleshed out, enabling daily or even hourly deployments.

- *From cross-functional teams to more specialized teams:* Larger, more diverse groups collaborate—Dev, Ops, QA, security, data science. The aim is to handle bigger user volumes, more data and stricter uptime requirements.
- *Governance and standardization:* At scale, you can't have every team inventing the wheel. Common platforms, coding standards and governance practices ensure consistency across the organization.

In the legacy Waterfall era, scaling meant you had large PMOs, detailed Gantt charts and big committees. By contrast, Cloud Native scaling uses container orchestration (like Kubernetes) to distribute workloads. It encourages microservices architecture and relies on platform teams for shared tooling. For the AI Native wave, scaling might involve massive compute clusters to train large models, specialized hardware for inference or orchestrating ML pipelines across data lakes. The goal in all cases is consistent, repeatable delivery at high volume.

Patterns for Scaling

TF24 – Platform as a Product: Manage internal platform (IDP) with a product mindset.

TF25 – Establish Platform Team: Formalize dedicated team for IDP roadmap, operations, evolution.

TF26 – Dev Starter Pack: Develop comprehensive resources to accelerate new team productivity.

TF27 – Reference Architecture: Define documented, proven architectural patterns for consistency.

TF28 – Internal Service Catalog: Create catalog of platform capabilities for discoverability and reuse.

TF29 – Build the Right Thing: Use tight feedback loops to ensure the platform meets needs.

TF30 – Prepare for Scale: Proactively enhance platform scalability, reliability and tooling.

TF31 – Reverse Conway Maneuver: Design team structures to promote desired target architecture.

TF32 – Gradual Onboarding: Roll out platform to teams in manageable, supported cohorts.

TF33 – Strangle Legacy: Systematically decommission legacy components, redirecting to new equivalents.

TF34 – Protect the Core: Maintain essential stability for critical legacy systems until retired.

TF35 – Holistic Transformation: Address changes in teams, processes and culture alongside technology.

4. Optimizing

Once scaling is in place and your new wave of technology or product is stable, it's time to optimize. This mode focuses less on radical change and more on refining what you've already built. It embodies:

- *Lean principles:* Removing waste, improving efficiency and maximizing flow.
- *Predictable, mature operations:* Detailed documentation, refined CI/CD pipelines, stable architecture.
- *Measuring and monitoring:* Using key performance indicators (KPIs) and operational metrics to identify bottlenecks or performance issues, then systematically eliminating them.

Optimizing can apply to different waves over time. Companies that operate using Waterfall processes, often reach a mature and stable state that is somehow predictable but slow to adapt to any shift or change. For a Cloud Native organization, you might optimize how container images are built, how frequently you can deploy or how effectively you're using cloud resources. For AI Native solutions, optimization could revolve around model efficiency, cost-effective GPU usage or refining user experiences.

This mode is vital for extracting the full potential from a new technology wave. It prevents the chaos of indefinite "beta" states and helps an organization benefit from its investment.

Patterns for Optimizing:

TF36 – Measure What Matters: Track key metrics for platform adoption and performance outcomes.

TF37 – Data-Driven Decision Making: Foster culture of decisions informed by data and analysis.

TF38 – Establish Team Communication APIs: Define clear interaction modes between teams for better flow.

TF39 – Automation Everywhere: Relentlessly pursue automation for repetitive tasks across software development lifecycle (SDLC).

TF40 – Lift and Shift at the End: Migrate stable legacy apps late if rewrite offers little benefit.

TF41 – Finish the Transformation: Define completion criteria; pivot focus to continuous improvement.

TF42 – Continuous Optimization: Embed a culture of regularly reviewing, measuring and enhancing operations.

TF43 – Efficiency over Adaptability: Prioritize performance and cost optimization for mature systems.

5. Innovating

At first glance, you might expect "Innovating" to be the same as "Pioneering". However, there's a nuance. Pioneering mode is about exploring the brand-new, whereas Innovating mode is about continuous improvement and staying open to fresh ideas even when you're already operating at scale. This means:

- *Continuous discovery:* Teams regularly gather feedback from users, stakeholders and data analytics.
- *Rapid testing of incremental improvements:* Building small features or enhancements, releasing them fast to see if they boost engagement or efficiency.
- *Culture of curiosity:* Encouraging staff to suggest improvements or new directions. Leadership fosters a safe space for "outside-the-box" thinking.

In the Cloud Native wave, for example, an innovating team might experiment with service meshes, advanced observability or serverless components. Meanwhile, the bulk of the organization remains in Scaling or Optimizing modes. Similarly, an AI Native team might incorporate new research breakthroughs or refine existing models with more advanced algorithms—without discarding the entire production pipeline.

Crucially, Innovating mode ensures a business doesn't stagnate once it's "done". Even a stable product can keep evolving in small but impactful ways. This means you can keep riding the current wave effectively while also scanning the horizon for the next wave.

Patterns for Innovating:

TF44 – Maximize ROI: Focus on leveraging the platform to drive business value.

TF45 – Minimize Cognitive Load: Enhance IDP to abstract complexity with clear paved paths.

TF46 – Avoid Reinventing the Wheel: Encourage reuse of existing capabilities and shared services.

TF47 – Enable Self-Service: Build robust self-service capabilities into the IDP.

TF48 – Cultivate Observability: Implement comprehensive observability (logs, metrics, traces) for insight.

TF49 – Nurture Incremental Innovation: Leverage platform agility for rapid, frequent, small, valuable changes.

TF50 – Specialized Teams: Utilize appropriate team structures and increase specialization where needed.

TF51 – Minimize Surface of Innovation: Encourage teams to innovate on top of stable IDP.

TF52 – Reflective Breaks: Institute regular, structured opportunities for teams to reflect.

TF53 – Foster Learning Organization: Implement mechanisms for knowledge sharing and systemic adaptation.

TF54 – Dynamic Strategy: Adopt dynamic strategy with short-term objectives and regular sensing.

TF55 – Periodic Checkups: Implement structured health checkups for key systems and processes.

6. Retiring

Retiring focuses on the graceful decommissioning of outdated technologies or processes. This ensures minimal disruption and resource waste. Teams in this mode focus on:

- *Systematic decommissioning:* They create and execute plans to phase out legacy systems, applications or infrastructure.
- *Data migration and archiving:* They ensure data is properly migrated, archived or destroyed according to compliance and business needs.
- *Knowledge transfer and documentation:* They capture and transfer institutional knowledge from retiring systems to prevent data loss and maintain operational continuity.

Historically, the transition away from mainframes or outdated programming languages would necessitate a "retiring" phase. In the Cloud Native context, this might involve retiring older VM-based applications as containerized replacements are fully deployed. For AI Native, Retiring mode could mean decommissioning older, less accurate models in favor of newer, more efficient ones. It can also mean decommissioning older integrations through business process automation with a newer and easier to manage integration such as model context protocol (MCP).

This mode is essential for managing technical debt and ensuring that resources are focused on current and future technologies. It prevents the accumulation of outdated systems that can become security risks or hinder innovation.

Patterns for Retiring:

TF56 – Minimal Legacy Change: Freeze non-essential development on retiring legacy systems.

TF57 – Free Up Resources: Proactively redeploy personnel, infrastructure and budget from retired systems.

TF58 – Sunset Gracefully: Execute planned shutdown of obsolete systems, managing data.

TF59 – Team Reduction/Reallocation: Manage human resources by reallocating or reducing associated teams.

(You can find all the transformations patterns online: https://re-cinq.com/patterns.)

Waves of Innovation: legacy, current and next

Waterfall: the legacy wave

Waterfall once revolutionized software delivery, making large projects feasible in an era of mainframes and early desktop computing. It aligned perfectly with the constraints of the time—big releases, physical media distribution, monolithic architectures, heavy documentation and a clear chain of command. But as markets sped up, Waterfall's long planning cycles and vertical scaling limits became liabilities. Today, it's primarily a legacy wave. It is still present, but losing ground to more iterative and flexible approaches.

Cloud Native: the current wave

Cloud Native has transformed how teams build and run software. Containerization, microservices, DevOps and orchestration platforms allow quick scaling, frequent releases and global resilience. This wave has made it standard practice to deploy multiple times a day, auto-scale services in response to demand and continuously gather feedback from real-world usage. Large enterprises and startups alike have embraced Cloud Native's agility. Many are still mid-journey. They are perhaps in Bootstrapping & Bridge-Building mode as they link legacy monoliths to modern microservices. Or they could be in Scaling mode with mature container orchestration.

AI Native: the next wave

On the horizon, AI Native promises an even more radical shift. While AI isn't new, its practical application at scale is becoming more visible. This is thanks to massive compute availability, improved algorithms and the business demand for data-driven decisions. Embracing AI Native means automating tasks and decision-making in ways not possible before. It involves personalizing user experiences through real-time behavioral insights and redefining product design to incorporate learning and adaptation as core features.

Just as Waterfall gave way to Cloud Native, Cloud Native is already preparing to integrate AI workflows. This includes training and serving ML models, using advanced data pipelines or adopting "MLOps" practices. We're seeing Pioneering AI labs, Bootstrapping pilot projects and some early adopters already hitting Scaling mode with global AI-driven features. Over time, those will shift into Optimizing and Innovating modes as the technology matures.

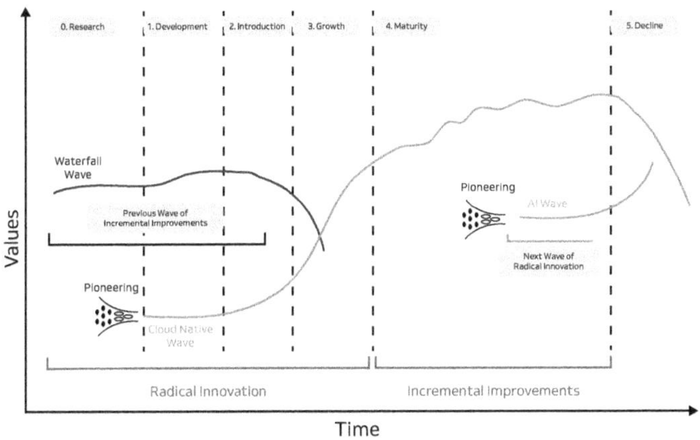

Figure 6: *The Waves of Innovation*

Putting it all together

Each new wave of technology doesn't necessarily replace the old wave overnight. This gradual transition allows organizations to leverage existing investments, minimize disruption and learn from early adopters before committing fully to a new approach. Instead, organizations often run multiple waves in parallel. Legacy systems in a Waterfall framework may remain in Optimizing or Retiring modes. Cloud Native projects might be in full Scaling or Optimizing and Innovating modes. AI Native initiatives may just be Pioneering, with a few key people in a dedicated lab or small pilot team.

The real challenge is orchestrating these waves so that they don't crash into each other. That orchestration comes from a solid grasp of the six modes and their roles, as well as a broad perspective on which horizon or lifecycle stage each initiative occupies. By knowing how to pioneer, bootstrap & bridge-build, scale, optimize, innovate and retire effectively, you can exploit each wave of technology without sacrificing organizational stability (discuss your strategic challenges directly with the authors: wavesofinnovation@re-cinq.com).

Key takeaways

- **Waves of technology:** Waterfall was once revolutionary, but it became legacy. Cloud Native is now dominant. AI looms as the next major shift.
- **Six modes of operation:**
    - **Pioneering:** Exploring uncharted ideas with minimal constraints.
    - **Bootstrapping & Bridge-Building:** Creating minimal foundations and linking new tech to existing systems.
    - **Scaling:** Automating, standardizing and ensuring reliability for large-scale adoption.
    - **Optimizing:** Refining stable systems for greater efficiency and performance.
    - **Innovating:** Sustaining creativity even in mature environments.
    - **Retiring:** Decommissioning outdated tools and technologies.

- **Horizons and lifecycle:** Three Horizons map how radical or mature an idea is. The six-stage Product Lifecycle goes from research to decline. These models allow you to understand where an idea will fit into your broader organizational plan.
- **Parallel existence:** Multiple waves and modes can coexist within a single organization; leadership must coordinate them to avoid friction. But we must remember that only one transformation can continue at any given time.
- **Future forward:** AI Native promises to disrupt the current Cloud Native wave, just as Cloud Native overshadowed Waterfall. Organizations that learn

these six modes now can ride each wave effectively, rather than being swamped by change.

By integrating these concepts, you can better manage the chaotic process of technology adoption. Whether you're still struggling with a Waterfall past, scaling Cloud Native solutions or experimenting in AI prototypes, understanding how to shift among these six modes of operation is the key to continual evolution—and staying ahead of the next wave.

To explore these concepts further and stay ahead of the curve, scan the QR code. You'll find the Waves of Innovation hub, featuring our podcast, upcoming events and a newsletter dedicated to the evolving AI Native ecosystem.

Part II

Riding the Wave–Scaling and Mastering Cloud Native

Having understood the historical context and the nature of Cloud Native transformation, Part II focuses on the practical steps involved in successfully navigating this wave. We will break down the transformation journey into distinct phases, starting with "Step 0: Pioneering mode", where research labs explore future technologies, and "Step 1: Making the decision for Cloud Native transformation", which emphasizes the crucial leadership commitment required.

The subsequent chapters will guide you through "Step 2: Bootstrapping & Bridge-Building" to establish an MVP. Then "Step 3: Scaling and Retiring" to onboard more teams while decommissioning legacy components, followed by

"Step 4: Scaling and Optimizing" to expand across the enterprise and fine-tune systems. We will then look at "Step 5: Optimizing and Innovating" for continuous improvement. Finally, we come back to "Step 6: Pioneering mode"—this time looking ahead to the next disruption, potentially AI. This part of the book will also provide context on transformation timelines and the interplay of operational modes (map your own timeline with the Waves of Innovation pattern cards workshop: https://re-cinq.com/patterns).

Chapter 4

Old Maturity and Deciding to Transform

Is your organization ready for a Cloud Native transformation? For many companies still rooted in Waterfall methodologies, this question is more complex than it seems. Most software companies have already adopted Cloud Native technologies. Only a few laggards have yet to begin the transition. This chapter is mainly for those with very traditional enterprises that are starting the Cloud Native journey. In other words, you are still almost entirely on the Waterfall wave and planning to jump to the Cloud Native wave. In later chapters, we will discuss those already deep into Cloud Native and their preparations for the upcoming waves of innovation (our online assessment can help you answer the readiness question: https://re-cinq.com/ai-native-assessment).

That said, even if you have made considerable progress on your Cloud Native journey, you will still find value in revisiting the early stages. This is your opportunity to look at your Cloud Native transformation through the lens of the next wave of innovation, and work out how you can apply the lessons you learned from that process to the AI Native era.

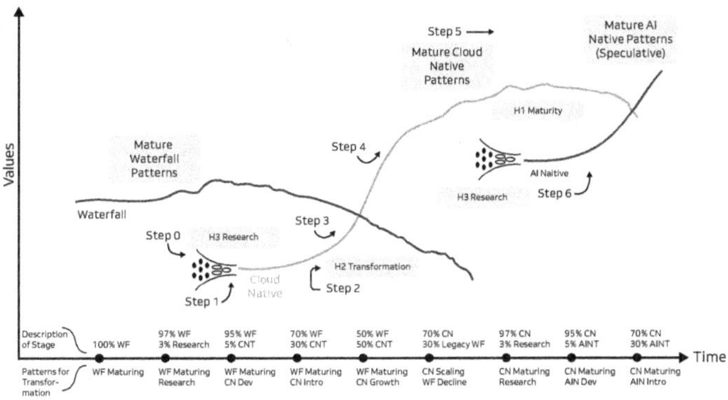

Figure 7: *Waves of the innovation journey: Waterfall, Cloud Native and AI Native*

Step 0: Pioneering mode—Creating a research lab for future technologies

Every major transformation in business begins with a spark of curiosity. Someone needs to ask, "What if...?" and then chase the answer. They often do so without a clear roadmap or a guarantee of success. In traditional, legacy-bound organizations, that spark can easily be suffocated by bureaucracy or risk-aversion. That's why the first phase of any large-scale modernization—be it Cloud Native adoption, a new AI initiative or any other cutting-edge venture—requires a Pioneering mode.

Start by forming a research lab capable of exploring technology frontiers, testing wild ideas and ultimately mapping out the path forward. This initial phase often necessitates establishing a dedicated *Skunk Works Team (TF02),* insulated from standard organizational processes to allow for rapid experimentation.

While every major transformation *begins* with Pioneering, *thriving* organizations maintain ongoing Pioneering efforts as part of their regular operations. However, most organizations operate in stable environments and confuse incremental innovation (business as usual) with radical innovation (requiring transformational change). Therefore, Step 0 is introducing the Pioneering mode. This is a prerequisite for successful transformation.

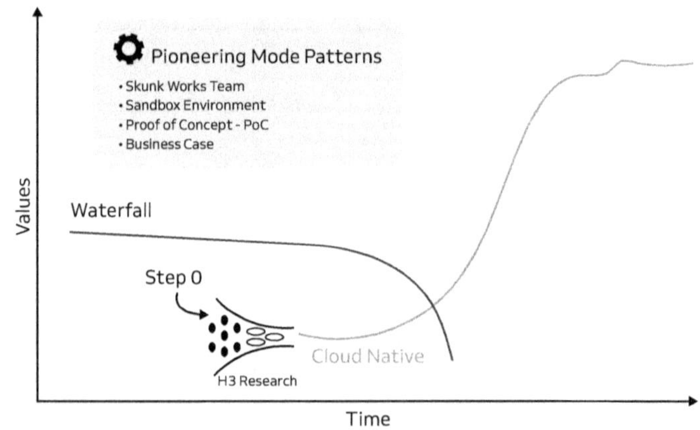

Figure 8: *Pioneering mode on top of the old maturity*

Why Pioneering mode matters

In many organizations entrenched in Waterfall practices, teams have spent years or even decades optimizing existing systems. They have well-worn procedures, specialized committees and entire divisions committed to perfecting (and preserving) the status quo. These structures, while effective for stability, can be hostile to rapid innovation. Teams familiar with older technologies often don't have the exposure or bandwidth to experiment with new paradigms. In essence, a business that has thrived under Waterfall is likely to be less adaptable once markets begin moving faster or when new technologies threaten to disrupt established ways of working.

Pioneering mode is the antidote to that inertia. It does not force the entire organization to "go Cloud Native" overnight—an approach almost certain to fail. Instead it isolates a small, empowered group whose sole mission is to explore emerging tech and demonstrate its potential. This specialized team effectively serves as the tip of the spear. If they discover something valuable, it can eventually spread through the rest of the business. If they fail to find value, the risk and costs remain contained. This approach actively seeks to *Reduce Cost of Experimentation (TF03)*, often by leveraging a dedicated *Sandbox Environment (TF04)*, ensuring that exploration doesn't destabilize core operations.

Goals and mindset

Succeeding in Pioneering mode requires a specific mindset at a team and organizational level. This mindset needs to start in the research lab with a focus on discovery. The goals for a research lab are:

- *Explore and experiment:* The research lab's immediate responsibility is to scout various Cloud Native technologies, frameworks, tools or methods. This typically includes container orchestration platforms like Kubernetes, serverless models, microservices patterns and any up-and-coming solutions that might soon become industry standards. This aligns directly with the *Learn and Explore (TF01)* pattern, requires *Skunk Works (TF02)* and heavily relies on ability to *Reduce Cost of Experimentation (TF03).*
- *Build a strong knowledge base:* As the lab experiments, it also accumulates an in-depth understanding of these technologies—documenting best practices, identifying pitfalls and measuring readiness for broader organizational use. To get new insights we use the pattern *Proof of Concept – PoC (TF06)*, share ideas to get feedback and educate the team—*Demo Your Ideas (TF07)*—and collect useful ideas on the *Ideas Shelf (TF08).*
- *Gain stakeholder buy-in:* Through PoCs and early demonstrations, the lab wins trust from leaders and business units. These short-term wins are essential for moving beyond "science project" status. We must always justify the leap to the new wave by creating a *Business Case (TF09)* and later make sure

that budgets are allocated correctly by applying *Finance Topologies (TF10)* for effective budget allocation.
- *Fail fast, learn fast:* By running quick, low-stakes experiments, the lab reduces the chance of large-scale, expensive failures down the line. This approach aligns with the core Cloud Native mantra of iterating rapidly and learning continuously. We start with the difficult questions to de-risk the core ideas by using the pattern *Test Hard Things First (TF05)* and reduce the risk of damaging current products and business reputation by experimenting in a *Sandbox Environment (TF04)*.

The backdrop of a Waterfall organization

To fully appreciate the Pioneering mode, imagine a legacy enterprise operating under Waterfall processes. They release updates on a strict yearly or quarterly cadence. Many employees have spent their entire careers there, rarely encountering new frameworks or development methods beyond the company's well-established approach. Some might attend conferences or read industry news in their spare time, but they struggle to put these discoveries into practice because the organizational machine resists change.

In such an environment, it's not unusual to see attempts at modernization fizzle out. For example, a small group might set up a mini Kubernetes cluster or do a brief DevOps "workshop", only to find that existing management frameworks—purchasing committees, risk assessments, deployment approvals—instantly stifle broader adoption. Alternatively, the company might buy a platform like OpenShift hoping it will solve all their problems overnight. But because they apply the same old Waterfall processes on top of it, they render the new platform underused or ineffectual. This story repeats across industries. Champions of modern approaches eventually leave out of frustration, or their pilot projects remain sidelined as "special cases".

Around 2018–2019, we worked with a Nordic financial institution on their Cloud Native journey. A manager and their team had researched and adopted Cloud Native technologies, creating a small but successful setup. Despite being a personal initiative, it proved Cloud Native's potential. However, higher management reverted to bureaucracy. They initiated a vendor selection process and handed over the task to those with little knowledge. They failed to treat it as a transformation, neglecting the necessary adjustments to architecture, structure and culture. Disappointed by leadership's response, most of the initial research team left soon after.

Despite significant investment in tooling, adoption rates for new technologies remained extremely low 12 months later. The original small Kubernetes setup was abandoned after the team members responsible left the company.

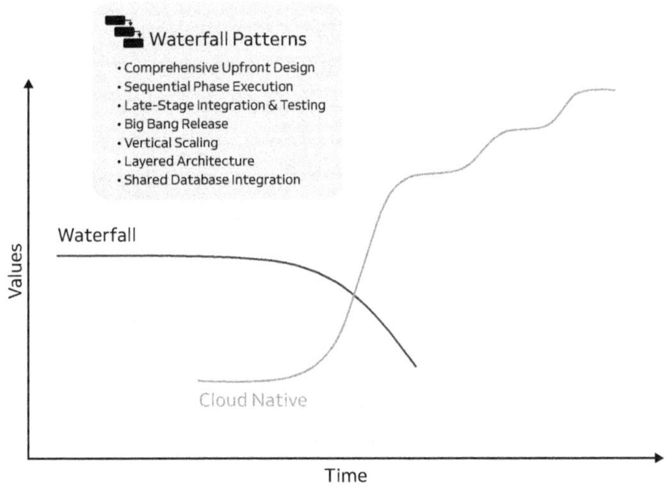

Figure 9: *Waterfall maturity*

Creating the research lab

The simplest solution to break this cycle is to carve out a research lab with the following key features:

- *Autonomy and freedom:* The lab should function outside normal organizational hierarchies. It needs the ability to select its own tools, set up its own environment and make quick decisions without waiting for multiple approvals, as demonstrated in the *Skunk Works Team (TF02)* pattern.
- *Dedicated (but limited) budget:* While the lab's funds don't have to be huge, it's critical they be earmarked and protected. Nothing kills innovation faster than having to request a new line item for every software license or cloud experiment—and then waiting months for sign-off. See the F*inance Topologies (TF10)* pattern.

- *Sandbox environment:* This team should not operate in a critical production environment. Instead, it works in a separate sandbox or dev/test environment. This ensures they can experiment freely and push boundaries without risking real customer data or revenue-generating systems. See the *Sandbox Environment (TF04)* pattern.
- *PoC-driven approach:* The lab's success is measured in short, tangible PoCs. For instance: "Let's containerize one small internal service and see if we can reduce deployment time by 80%." Each PoC aims to answer specific questions and gather real data. *See the Proof of Concept – PoC (TF06)* pattern.
- *Reporting and storytelling:* The lab doesn't just code in isolation. It must regularly share findings—both successes and failures—through well-structured reports or demos. These updates serve to educate the broader organization and show leadership the value of investing in emerging tech, as evidenced in the *Demo Your Ideas (TF07)* pattern.

The opposite of the Nordic financial institution is our first Cloud Native customer, HolidayCheck, a Swiss holiday booking website. We began working with HolidayCheck in 2014, before the term "Cloud Native" was even coined. At that time, Pini had just co-founded a consultancy called Container Solutions that focused on implementing Docker and related technologies.

When we started working with HolidayCheck, their main challenge was agility and their ability to deliver value to their customers quickly. As usual, there were a variety of issues. These included starting too many projects and not finishing many of them, which led to developer overload while delivering little value to customers. But we also jointly found that a high-load e-commerce website like HolidayCheck was a perfect fit for the upcoming container technologies.

It was clear this technology would provide a competitive advantage. We recognized that container technologies would allow them to scale horizontally, avoid the purchase of very expensive hardware and innovate very quickly by splitting the work into smaller components. The ability to schedule containers and dynamically provision them to the public cloud would also save on cloud costs and increase delivery agility.

Our first step was setting up a small, five to six person cross-functional team with representatives from a few key teams. The new research team reported to a senior manager who reported directly to the CTO. They were even situated in a separate room, detached from the rest of the teams. Their goal was to research all available technologies and see if containers, cloud, microservices, etc, would be a good fit for overcoming HolidayCheck's challenges. After just a few weeks of work, it was obvious that this was the correct direction. At this point a transformation could begin in earnest.

At that time, Kubernetes was not yet available. The main container orchestrator was an open-source tool called Mesos. There were many other technical challenges, but the most important ones were researched early on. Many quick PoCs were built and the results were presented to the leadership and the rest of the organization.

We'll come back to HolidayCheck later to explore how they managed the transformation and mature stages of this process.

The role of leadership

A pioneering lab lives or dies by its relationship with executive leaders. In large legacy settings, the lab leader often becomes a "rebel with a cause". They push boundaries but also need sponsorship from above. This champion should ideally be someone with a foot in both the technical and business worlds. They are a person who can speak to the bottom-line benefits of Cloud Native, yet also understand the intricacies of microservices or container orchestration.

There are several things the lab leader needs to do to support their team:

- *Empower the lab:* Give the lab enough rope to experiment, but also set clear milestones.
- *Shield the lab from bureaucracy:* Leadership must protect the lab from the many committees or processes that stifle innovation in the rest of the enterprise.
- *Celebrate small wins:* Each time the lab presents a working prototype or a data-driven recommendation, leadership should celebrate it. This positive reinforcement builds momentum and helps shift company culture, little by little.

There are several notable examples of pioneering teams that demonstrate the importance of autonomy and direct executive backing:

Lockheed Martin's Skunk Works

Created during world war two to rapidly develop advanced aircraft, Skunk Works had unprecedented autonomy and minimal red tape. Their high-impact successes, like the SR-71 Blackbird, are legendary.

Xerox PARC (Palo Alto Research Center)

Xerox gave PARC a broad mandate and significant funding to invent the future of computing, operating with considerable autonomy far from the corporate headquarters in Rochester, New York. This freedom allowed PARC scientists and engineers to generate a stunning array of foundational technologies that would define the personal computing era. Beyond the now-famous graphical user interface (GUI) and the mouse, PARC pioneered Ethernet networking, laser printing, the first personal computer (the Alto) which integrated these elements, object-oriented programming and the What You See Is What You Get (WYSIWYG) editor. It was a stunning demonstration of effective Pioneering mode, generating potentially transformative innovations.

However, Xerox itself ultimately failed to capitalize on these revolutionary breakthroughs, providing a stark case study in the *Innovator's Dilemma* and the challenges established companies face in embracing disruptive change. Several factors contributed to this strategic failure. Xerox's management, deeply entrenched in the lucrative copier business, struggled to recognize the market potential of personal computing, viewing PARC's work as disconnected from their core "toner head" focus. The company's B2B sales model, built around large equipment leases, was ill-suited for the emerging personal computer market. Internal bureaucracy, lack of strategic alignment between PARC and headquarters, and an inability to formulate viable business models for these new technologies, meant that inventions like the Alto (and its commercial successor, the expensive Xerox Star) languished internally.

Consequently, the door was left wide open for others. Visionaries like Steve Jobs readily grasped the potential during visits to PARC, leading Apple to successfully commercialize the GUI and mouse with the Lisa and Macintosh, fundamentally reshaping the industry. Microsoft similarly adopted GUI concepts for its Windows operating system. Ethernet became the foundation for networking companies like 3Com (co-founded by Ethernet inventor Robert Metcalfe).

Key figures from PARC went on to found Adobe, bringing technologies like PostScript to market and revolutionizing digital printing and graphics. In essence, while Xerox funded the invention, companies like Apple, Microsoft, 3Com and Adobe reaped the vast commercial rewards, building entire industries on the foundations laid at PARC. This underscores the critical lesson that inventing revolutionary technology is insufficient. Aligning those innovations with corporate strategy, market vision and the capability to execute is paramount for successful transformation.

The takeaway for Cloud Native transformations is clear: a pioneering team can find or invent amazing tech or discover powerful new workflows, but unless leadership is prepared to adopt and scale those learnings, the innovations can slip through the cracks.

Underground researchers

In many Waterfall-centric companies, there's a hidden cadre of developers or architects quietly tinkering with new technology. These people are attending meetups, reading books and testing small prototypes on personal machines. They might re-label these tasks as "bug fixes" or "performance reviews" in project trackers to avoid raising questions. If given official support and a mandate, these "underground researchers" often become the best candidates for the lab, bringing with them months or even years of suppressed insights, representing informal *Learn and Explore (TF01)* activities.

The shift towards transformation

Once the pioneering lab begins producing compelling evidence—like a functioning container-based prototype or data showing drastically reduced lead times—leadership can decide to move forward with a formal Cloud Native (or other) transformation. At that point, Step 0 concludes. The lab has shown the feasibility, built excitement and paved the way for more significant organizational changes. This compelling evidence, gathered through patterns like

Proof of Concept – PoC (TF06), provides the foundation needed to create a *Business Case (TF09)* required for a formal transformation decision. Future stages in the transformation journey will revolve around expanding those prototypes, integrating them with existing systems and eventually scaling to production environments. In other words, the baton passes from the Pioneering mode to the next phases of Bridge-Building, Scaling and Optimizing.

Knowing when Step 0 ends

Pioneering mode naturally wraps up when the organization's leadership recognizes the benefits of the new technology, organizational or business model changes and commits to an actionable roadmap. At that juncture, the lab's primary mission shifts from open-ended exploration to more structured transformation. That doesn't mean the lab needs to be disbanded though. Instead, it can continue exploring next-level or future technologies (like advanced AI or edge computing) once Cloud Native becomes mainstream within the company. This commitment signals that the outputs from *Proof of Concept – PoC (TF06)* and *Demo Your Ideas (TF07)* have successfully supported the *Business Case (TF09)* pattern, concluding the primary mission of this Pioneering phase.

Step 0 is crucial because it makes the unknowns known in a safe, cost-effective way. It liberates a small group to experiment without risking the business' core operations. Ultimately, that's how large, entrenched enterprises begin to pivot from legacy Waterfall systems towards a more adaptive, modern and future-proof tech strategy. By respecting the research lab's autonomy and embracing the Pioneering mode, businesses can chart a clear path into their next wave of innovation—whether that wave is Cloud Native, AI Native or beyond.

Step 1: Make the decision for Cloud Native transformation

Imagine an organization that has run smoothly for years under a predictable, incremental model. Products mature gracefully, customers receive periodic updates, costs gradually decrease and compliance or regulatory changes are folded into the workflow without drama. The enterprise has a Horizon 3 team off to one side, researching intriguing new technologies—yet day-to-day life remains firmly anchored in the established routine. Sooner or later, a truly transformational idea emerges from that pioneering team. This is an idea that promises not just an incremental tweak but a major step-change in how the entire business operates.

Deciding whether to embrace that idea—specifically for our purposes, transitioning to a Cloud Native model—is never a trivial task. Cloud Native transformations are fundamentally disruptive, demanding new architecture, reorganization and cultural shifts that can last years. They can also unlock dramatic improvements in speed, scalability, cost savings or market reach. Step 1 is all about making that high-stakes call: do we go all in? Making this high-stakes call requires a strong and compelling business case.

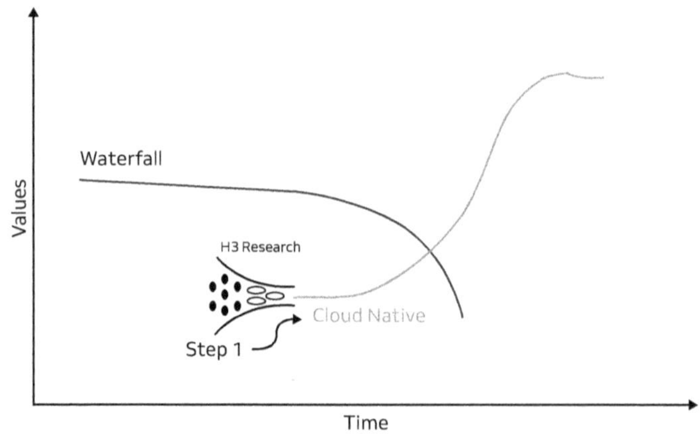

Figure 10: *Step 1—Decision to transform the organization*

From incremental to transformational

Before we explore how to make the Cloud Native transformation decision, let's clarify why it stands apart from more familiar changes.

Many new ideas from a Horizon 3 pioneering team end up in routine releases. These are incremental improvements, rather than anything transformational. A new mobile app? Potentially big for customers, but in most cases it's built on existing APIs without forcing the entire organization to overhaul processes. Or maybe your research group recommended adopting a newer database system or a slick CI tool. Even if those require a hefty investment, they rarely trigger full corporate restructuring.

In contrast, replatforming from a monolithic architecture to microservices, and adopting Kubernetes and dozens of tools around it at a large scale, can't happen without shaking up the rest of the company. Because of Conway's

Law, a new architecture demands new *Team Topologies*. That, in turn, spurs changes to budgets, HR policies, success metrics and culture. This is how a "technical upgrade" becomes an organizational revolution.

These transformations are so significant that they can cause two to three years of upheaval before the real benefits arrive. No matter how appealing Cloud Native might seem, it has to be weighed against real-world business priorities—especially if the company could keep thriving with minimal changes for a few more years. Mistaking such a profound shift for a simple upgrade falls into the *Incremental Facade (AP04)* anti-pattern, failing to recognize the need for *Holistic Transformation (TF35)* later on.

The leadership decision

Given the magnitude of a Cloud Native overhaul, the decision requires clear *Executive Commitment (TF11)* from the highest levels and cannot be a purely technical choice. It *must* be a strategic leadership decision. Even the most enthusiastic engineering team will struggle if they try to push a massive architecture shift without executive buy-in. This is, therefore, what an engineering team needs to consider:

- *Size of impact:* Transformations are so big they inevitably affect the entire enterprise—engineering, product management, HR, sales, marketing, operations and more. One department's plans can't go forward alone.

- *Risk and reward:* The potential gains—like faster releases, global scalability or substantially lower operational costs—must overshadow the disruptions. This careful weighing of potential gains against significant disruption is the core of the *Business Case (TF09)* pattern. Leadership must acknowledge that productivity often declines in the first year or two as teams learn new tools, restructure and tackle unexpected complexities.
- *Business case:* A genuine business case is indispensable. Relying solely on "the competition is doing it" or "Gartner says it's hot" sets you up for buyer's remorse. Leaders need realistic return on investment (ROI) projections, not inflated promises or overlooked costs. They must understand the time frames for recouping the initial investment—both in money and staff focus.
- *Correct timing:* Even if Cloud Native is beneficial, the decision might be premature if a company has other fires to put out or bigger short-term opportunities to chase. Sometimes building a quick mobile frontend or adding modern features on top of the monolith can buy time until leadership is ready for the more disruptive shift. Successfully navigating this requires avoiding both the *Strategic Inertia (AP01)* and *Bleeding Edge Gamble (AP02)* pitfalls.

In short, starting a Cloud Native transformation is more than a technical milestone. It's a company-wide pivot. This means it requires a compelling rationale and the unwavering support of top leaders.

Common decision pitfalls

Despite the best intentions, organizations often make mistakes when deciding whether (and when) to go Cloud Native. The most common of these mistakes are (contact us to help with an in-depth assessment before you commit: wavesofinnovation@re-cinq.com):

- *Underestimating transformation scope:* It's easy to view Kubernetes or microservices as "just another technical layer." Teams dive in, only to discover they need new DevOps processes, a different QA approach, team reshuffling due to architectural changes, revised budgeting for on-demand cloud resources and more. Without high-level backing and coordination, such partial transformations turn messy. This leads to "Frankenstein" systems that combine old Waterfall structures with half-baked microservices. This is a classic manifestation of the *Incremental Facade (AP04)* anti-pattern.
- *Skipping research and preparation:* Some executives get excited about Cloud Native but don't consult the pioneering team's findings. In some cases they don't give the pioneering team a chance to do thorough PoCs. This leads to transformations driven by hype, not data. As a result, the same old processes and tools are forced on to new architectures, with predictable chaos. This often happens when the outputs from Pioneering patterns like *Learn and Explore (TF01)* and *Proof of Concept – PoC (TF06) are ignored.*
- *No business case:* If leadership can't articulate concrete benefits (productivity gains, improved

speed to market, cost reductions or improved security/compliance) that outweigh the disruption, the transformation may fail because the big shift lacks obvious, measurable payoff.

- *Delaying too long:* Sometimes an organization is so entrenched in its old ways that it doesn't realize how quickly it's slipping behind competitors adopting cloud-based or microservices approaches. By the time leadership decides to transform, it might be too late to maintain market relevance, succumbing to the *Strategic Inertia (AP01)* pitfall.

Key takeaways

- **Pioneering mode is essential:** A dedicated research lab, operating in Pioneering mode, is crucial for exploring new technologies like Cloud Native *before* committing to a full-scale transformation. This minimizes risk and builds a foundation of knowledge.
- **Autonomy and protection:** The research lab needs autonomy to experiment, a dedicated (but limited) budget and protection from existing organizational bureaucracy.
- **Focus on PoCs:** The lab's success should be measured by tangible PoCs that demonstrate the potential benefits of the new technology.
- **Leadership sponsorship is critical:** A transformation champion—*Appoint Transformation Champion (TF12)*—and an executive sponsor—*Executive Commitment (TF11)*—are needed to advocate for the initiative, secure resources and drive organizational change.

- **Transformational, not just incremental:** Cloud Native transformation is not just a technology upgrade. It requires changes to team structures, processes, culture and business models.
- **Business case is mandatory:** A clear business case, outlining costs, benefits, risks and ROI, is essential for making an informed decision. Don't rely on hype.
- **Avoid common pitfalls:** Underestimating the scope of change, skipping research, lacking a business case and delaying too long are common mistakes that can derail a transformation.

Making the right decision is crucial. Scan the QR code to use our online assessment and pattern cards, which are designed to help you map your current state and build a powerful business case for transformation.

Chapter 5

Transformation

The journey into Cloud Native transformation truly begins now. Following the successful completion of Step 0 (Pioneering), where the initial explorations *(Learn and Explore (TF01))* and a series of focused PoCs successfully managed to *Proof of Concept – PoC (TF06)* and *Demo Your Ideas (TF07)* highlight the potential benefits, the critical decision in Step 1 was made. Leadership reviewed the *Business Case (TF09)*, committed to the transformation with *Executive Commitment (TF11)* and succeeded to *Appoint Transformation Champion (TF12)* to guide the effort.

With this executive backing and clear mandate, we are ready to start the hands-on work of the transformation. This next phase, Step 2, plunges us into the crucial modes of **Bootstrapping & Bridge-Building**. It begins when you decide to Form the *Core Team (TF13)*. These are the people tasked with constructing the initial foundation—a

Minimum Viable Platform (*Thinnest Viable Platform (TF19)*) while simultaneously ensuring essential connections are built back to the existing legacy systems (using *Bridge the Old World (TF22)*). This isn't about scaling widely yet. It's about establishing the first, vital foothold in the new Cloud Native reality (map out this crucial MVP phase with your team using our pattern cards workshop: https://re-cinq.com/patterns).

Step 2: Bootstrapping & Bridge-Building mode—Starting the transformation

Once your leadership has greenlit a Cloud Native transformation, the real work begins. In this stage, a small, empowered core team lays the groundwork for the future architecture, while connecting to the old system so the organization doesn't stall or fracture. Think of it as constructing the foundation of a new house while still living in your old one—you can't demolish everything overnight.

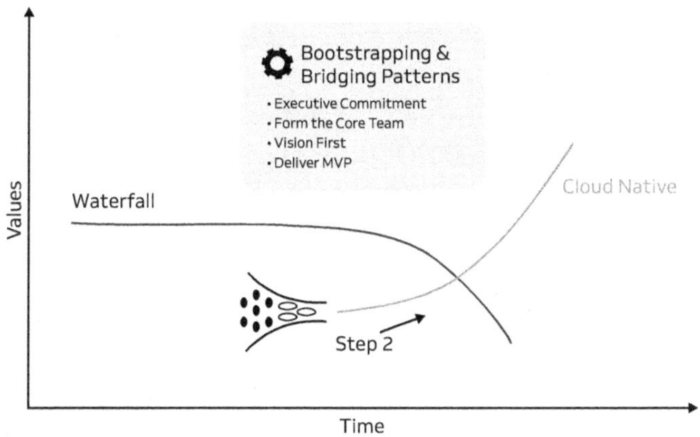

Figure 11: *Step 2—Starting the transformation*

Start small and build an MVP

An MVP typically refers to a minimal version of a new product. In a transformation context, it's the "thin slice" of your eventual Cloud Native platform. An MVP in this context will have foundational CI/CD pipelines, container orchestration, minimal security and compliance integrations, and perhaps one or two critical business services deployed. An MVP is invaluable because:

- *It's usable:* Teams can start migrating or building features on it, even if it's rudimentary. You gather real-world feedback as you build. Are your pipelines too slow? Is your container orchestration stable enough? This process of learning through creation is central to the *Research Through Action (TF16)* pattern.
- *It exposes gaps:* If your MVP can't handle certain features or fails compliance checks, you discover those shortcomings early. This beats rolling out a complex system and finding major issues after large-scale adoption.
- *It's adaptable:* You avoid prematurely optimizing or overengineering. Decisions can remain fluid. By staying small, the MVP invites incremental refinement and fosters learning. The aim is to *Deliver the MVP (TF18)*—the Minimum Viable Product—keeping it lean by applying the *Thinnest Viable Platform (TF19)* approach and ensuring it provides just enough value to start gathering feedback.

Building the MVP

When it comes to building your MVP, it's important to ensure it doesn't get too big. But it's equally important that it shows a clear trajectory for transforming the organization. The following three areas are the most important to consider at this stage:

- *Focus on core services:* The MVP might include a single microservice or a small cluster of them. Remember, it only needs to be enough to prove that your container setup, networking, monitoring and deployment processes work smoothly. Pick something moderately complex but not mission-critical as your first pilot.
- *Lightweight tooling:* Avoid a tangle of advanced solutions early on. Start with basic CI/CD, a standard container registry, automated tests and minimal secrets management. The goal is to build a workable environment quickly.
- *Bridging the legacy:* If you can't connect to existing data or systems, you're just building in a silo—doomed to remain niche. Begin with read-only integrations or "facade" services that unify old and new. Over time, you can deepen those bridges to handle more data flow, authentication and update legacy records.

One of our past customers, a British financial institution with 40-year-old legacy systems written in Cobol, decided to adopt Cloud Native. After a lot of convincing and multiple failed attempts at Cloud Native transformation, they finally succeeded. The first issue was that almost all revenue-mission-critical applications were highly monolithic, brittle, on-prem and very difficult to change. But all the customer data and functionality was there. So, while it would have been easy to build a new cloud setup and introduce some microservices, without connecting them to the legacy world, it would have brought very little value. This approach was unlikely to lead to meaningful adoption.

Therefore, a critical part of the MVP application architecture was an API running on-prem and exposing the data and some of the functionality of the original legacy systems. It was critical to build those APIs in a highly secure, compliant and resilient way, as they effectively became part of the core financial system. But the new applications were much easier to develop in a sandbox with mockups of the production data.

This way, the company was able to prove the value and viability of new technologies and make those new MVPs revenue-generating before making them part of its core system.

MVP Architecture

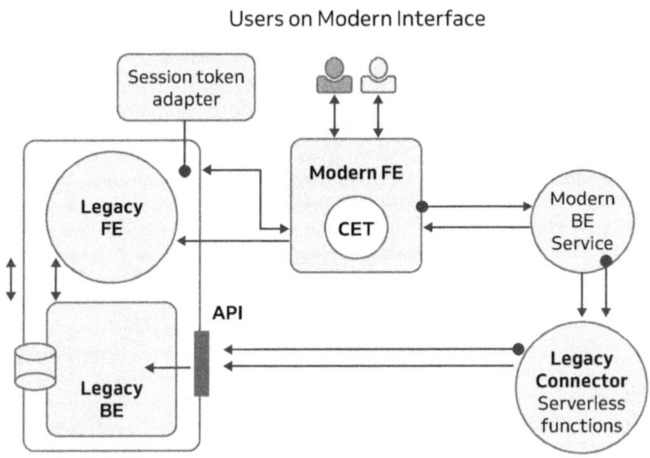

Figure 12: *MVP architecture*

Similarly, the company began investing in the Cloud Native platform's MVP to prepare for scaling up and onboarding additional teams. The platform was initially a thin slice with only basic functionality. However, it provided a strong foundation for future development. It not only enabled automated provisioning of landing zones in the cloud, and development and production environments, but also introduced CI/CD automation, agile development processes, basic scaling mechanisms and more.

Step 1:

Build first version of Dev Platform

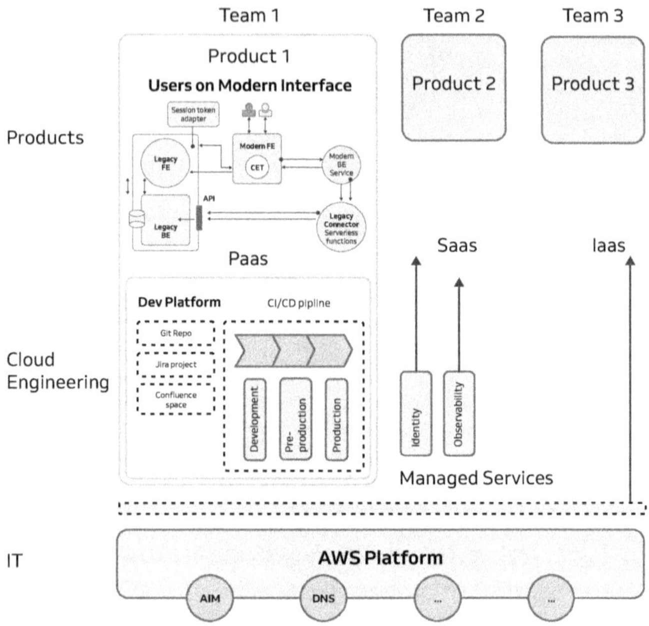

Figure 13: *The foundation for scaling*

The transformation champion

Leading such an effort requires a transformation champion. This is someone with transformational leadership skills and a clear vision, strong cross-functional relationships and enough technical grounding to make architectural calls. In many cases, this champion is promoted from the research lab team (Step 0). That person has already spent months—or even years—experimenting with new architectures, cloud platforms or container solutions. They're eager to move from a pioneering mindset to building tangible solutions. This individual, embodying the *Appoint Transformation Champion (TF12)* pattern decided upon in Step 1, is crucial for leading the newly F*ormed Core Team (TF13)*.

However, be wary. The transformation champion must shift from the freewheeling, boundary-pushing style of a researcher to a more structured approach that also includes the other people working at the department or company. Now they must define and enforce processes, set architectural guidelines and unify a stable foundation. Conversely, if someone from the "old guard" leads, there's a risk of replicating existing structures and stifling the transformation. As Albert Einstein famously said: "You cannot solve a problem with the same mind that created it."

Bootstrapping & Bridge-Building mode: Laying the foundation

In the Bootstrapping & Bridge-Building mode, two main things happen simultaneously:

1. *Bootstrapping:* You form the minimal platform, from container orchestration to pipeline automation, that future teams can rely on. This is about building robust fundamentals. Think of this like the supporting walls and the location of windows and doors in a home renovation. Decisions made here affect every step that follows, so it's vital to do them thoughtfully. The first involves the *Form the Core Team (TF13)*, executing the *Deliver the MVP (TF18)* and *Thinnest Viable Platform (TF19)* patterns.

The second focuses entirely on the *Bridge the Old World (TF22)* pattern to ensure connectivity.

2. *Bridge-Building:* The new Cloud Native environment must interact seamlessly with legacy systems, both technologically and organizationally. Integration layers, facades or anti-corruption patterns ensure data flows without forcing immediate rewrites of entire legacy modules.

Similarities and differences from Pioneering mode

Pioneering mode (Step 0) also used small, agile teams with freedom to experiment, but their focus was on *discovery*. They were testing to see if something *could* work, not guaranteeing it would become the corporate standard. By contrast, Bootstrapping & Bridge-Building mode is about delivering *production-grade fundamentals*. While you still move fast and remain open to new ideas, the stakes are higher. This is where you're laying the real pillars of your future Cloud Native ecosystem. The focus shifts firmly to *Deliver the MVP (TF18)* and *Thinnest Viable Platform (TF19)*, underpinned by the *Executive Commitment (TF11)* secured earlier.

One of the biggest mistakes organizations make is pulling too many people off legacy projects too soon. Yes, you're excited about microservices, containers and new architectures, but your existing systems still serve customers and bring in revenue. If you reassign the old teams prematurely, you could sabotage stability and frustrate loyal clients. Until the new MVP is ready, the majority of your staff should keep working on the legacy environment. They know their domain best and can continue rolling out small but meaningful updates. Meanwhile, a small core team remains dedicated to building the MVP and bridging solutions. This approach reduces friction between the old and new worlds.

Avoid an early "Legacy 2.0"

Another mistake is flooding the new environment with too many newcomers before it's mature. If architecture decisions aren't settled or your pipeline is half-baked, each additional person or team tries to fill in gaps with their own solutions. You end up with disjointed, half-formed microservices that replicate legacy sprawl—but in a container form. That's the worst of both worlds, a "Legacy 2.0" that you'll later have to untangle.

This is why we recommend keeping the initial Cloud Native environment sparse. The best engineers from your pioneering or core architecture teams can sculpt its basic shape. Once the minimal processes and guidelines are in place, you can onboard more teams in a controlled manner (plan your scaling and onboarding strategy with our pattern cards workshop: https://re-cinq.com/patterns).

Key activities in Bootstrapping & Bridge-Building mode

To give the Bootstrapping & Bridge-Building stage of the process the best chance of succeeding and setting your organization up for a relatively smooth transition to Cloud Native, focus on the following key activities. As with building the MVP, the key is not to overstretch here. Remember, slow and steady wins the race.

- *Thinnest platform setup:* Use minimal container orchestration (e.g. a basic Kubernetes cluster), plus a simple CI/CD pipeline. Don't incorporate a million plug-ins or advanced features yet. Use the pattern *Delayed Automation (TF20)* and wait until the team knows exactly what problems they need to solve.
- *Basic onboarding:* Document how a developer pushes code, how a microservice is built and deployed, how logs are accessed and how to request new namespaces or secrets. That's your quickstart manual for future teams, so it should be reasonably clear. It will be improved as onboarding goes on.
- *Strong connectors to legacy:* Build proxies or middle-tier services that talk to legacy databases or services, applying the *Bridge the Old World (TF22)* pattern. This reflects the *Adaptability over Efficiency (TF17)* pattern suitable for this stage that lets you replace or re-factor them gradually. This approach means you can start migrating modules piece by piece rather than performing a risky "big bang" rewrite.
- *Incremental architecture decisions:* You won't finalize everything in this stage—things can still evolve. But the basics around microservice boundaries, monitoring and service discovery do need to be defined. If each new microservice picks a random approach, you lose the standardization that makes Cloud Native manageable.

Timing and scale

A typical small organization might spend three to six months in Bootstrapping & Bridge-Building mode before it's ready to onboard additional product teams. Enterprises spend six to 12 months in this stage. During this time, the core group finalizes MVP-level architecture, tests a few microservices in a near-production environment and refines the bridging to legacy systems. After that, the transformation can accelerate—but these first months are crucial. Rushing them can cripple your entire Cloud Native journey, leading to chaos down the road. This period allows the *Form the Core Team (TF13)* sufficient time to *Deliver the MVP (TF18)* and *Thinnest Viable Platform (TF19)*, and establish functional integrations via *Bridge the Old World (TF22)*, often facilitated by *Staged Funding (TF23)* tied to milestones (contact the authors for a deeper insight and their own experience with transformational projects: wavesofinnovation@re-cinq.com).

Stage finish conditions

You'll know you're ready to move on from Bootstrapping & Bridge-Building mode when:

- *A minimal Cloud Native platform exists:* There's a stable cluster or environment with basic CI/CD and observability in place, signifying successful application of *Deliver the MVP (TF18)* and *Thinnest Viable Platform (TF19)*.
- *At least one service or microservice is running:* Even if it's not mission-critical, it proves the pipeline and architecture actually work end to end.

- *Bridge to legacy is functional:* Data and features can flow between old and new systems, validating the *Bridge the Old World (TF22)* implementation. You don't have to replicate *every* legacy feature, but the fundamentals must be integrated.
- *Clear onboarding guidelines:* New teams can join without guesswork. They know how to deploy code, maintain logs, follow security policies, etc.
- *Transformation champion is empowered:* This individual (along with a small leadership group) is steering the technical direction, ensuring that the platform remains cohesive and that bridging tasks stay on track. This demonstrates continued *Executive Commitment (TF11)* and effective leadership from the *Appointed Transformation Champion (TF12)*.

Once these conditions are met, your Cloud Native foundation is solid enough to support the next wave of teams—and the next stage of transformation. You'll be able to scale your approach, migrating more services and bringing in new product teams without descending into chaos.

Bootstrapping & Bridge-Building is the pivotal stage where Cloud Native progress transitions from theory to tangible reality. The core team sets up a minimal environment, proves it with one or two live microservices and ensures integration with the legacy stack. Meanwhile, the rest of the business continues to run smoothly in its existing processes. Done right, this stage establishes the vital architectural and organizational pillars on which your broader transformation will flourish. By starting small, championing the right leadership and carefully bridging old and new, you pave the way for a successful, scalable future.

Step 3: Scaling and Retiring—Onboard teams and sunset legacy

Congratulations—you've built a Cloud Native MVP and tested it with a small core group of pioneers! Now it's time to expand. The next challenge is scaling up. This involves migrating legacy teams and components on to the new platform in a systematic way. At the same time, you are retiring parts of the old environment. These two modes, Scaling and Retiring, often work hand in hand. As you welcome more teams into the new world, you free them up to decommission what's no longer needed from the old one. This careful balance between building up and tearing down is essential for any Cloud Native transformation to deliver full benefits.

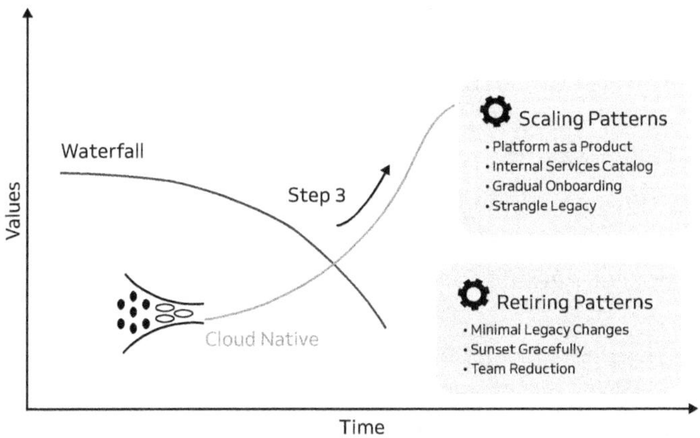

Figure 14: *Step 3—Scaling Cloud Native and Retiring Waterfall*

Onboard the first few teams

Once you have a stable Cloud Native environment, you need to nurture it. This happens in two ways through the Scaling and Retiring modes:

1. Introducing other teams to your Cloud Native setup (Scaling).

2. Updating the new environment while slowly decommissioning the old one (Retiring).

From a technical perspective, this means any new functionality goes to Cloud Native and any fresh features or major updates happen in the new environment. Over time, the existing legacy code should only receive necessary fixes or minor changes.

But what is perhaps more important is getting others onboard and using your Cloud Native environment. The original core team, which created the MVP, should partner with the early adopters in your organization. They help refine the new platform's processes—CI/CD pipelines, container orchestration, observability tools—and document the migration steps for future teams. This collaborative refinement helps *Build the Right Thing (TF29)* by incorporating early feedback and starts developing the resources needed for a *Dev Starter Pack (TF26)*.

This requires a shift in gear. While you're onboarding the first teams, your core team should focus on refining what they have in the Cloud Native environment, rather than adding to it. There will be opportunities to build it out in the future, but it's important to consolidate first. Think of this as a process of laying strong foundations.

During this period, you can generate early wins. As these first teams demonstrate faster deployments or improved developer experience, it builds confidence across the organization. If the platform falls short of their needs, you catch those issues before you attempt to scale further, saving time, money and many headaches.

The risks of premature scaling

A common pitfall is trying to onboard *too many* teams *too fast*, which creates its own problems. The most common issues we see are:

- *Platform overload:* If the MVP isn't solid, each new team exposes more weaknesses. The core team can't keep up with bug fixes, feature requests and platform improvements simultaneously.
- *Frankenstein solutions:* Without standardized patterns or enough support from the platform team, newly onboarded groups might hack together their own "quick fixes". The result is a patchwork of half-baked approaches.
- *Legacy 2.0:* Rushing everyone on to the new platform can recreate monolithic sprawl—just with containers. The underlying architecture, processes and cultural attitudes remain unchanged, turning "Cloud Native" into a frustrating buzzword rather than a real improvement.

To avoid this, ensure your MVP is robust, your core team is not overextended and you onboard only a handful of teams at first. This deliberate pace allows you to scale "the right thing" rather than replicate early mistakes. These issues often stem from failing to adequately *Prepare for Scale (TF30)* or executing *Gradual Onboarding (TF32)* too hastily, leading to the *Premature Scaling (AP11)* anti-pattern.

Dealing with technical debt

In the rush to prove the MVP, you likely took shortcuts—accumulating some technical debt. That's normal. But continuing to skip best practices or quality checks as you scale will mean the new environment can snowball into catastrophic complexity. Instead, take the time to deal with technical debt at an early stage rather than allowing it to compound. Addressing this debt is a key part of the *Prepare for Scale (TF30)* pattern. The following three steps may sound obvious, but it's remarkable how often they are overlooked.

1. *Pause, pay down:* Before onboarding the next wave of teams, set aside time to re-factor or fix underlying issues.

2. *Automate and document:* Invest in clear, repeatable processes for setting up new microservices, linking to external systems or performing security scans. Every minute you spend documenting and automating now saves hours later.

3. *Maintain vision:* Remember the original architectural intentions. Bad early decisions might be repeated

by *every new service* if you don't course-correct promptly.

A quote widely attributed to Bill Gates suggests: "Automation applied to an efficient operation will magnify the efficiency. Automation applied to an inefficient operation will magnify the inefficiency." In Cloud Native, the same principle holds: if you scale a flawed foundation, you simply replicate its flaws at greater volume.

A less-than-successful transformation example comes from one of our customers in Germany, a supermarket chain. They began introducing Cloud Native technologies, including Kubernetes, CI/CD pipelines and standardized software component builds and delivery about two years before our engagement. However, only a small fraction of the over 100 development and operations teams adopted the new workflow. The dedicated platform team worked hard but struggled with adoption and new functionality development.

Our assessment uncovered two primary issues. First, the platform's rigidity and specific workflows required significant application re-factoring or new platform functionality for any deviation from standards. This limited flexibility and self-service for the development teams. Second, premature scaling occurred, in part because the expectations of the development team regarding the initial platform capabilities were not effectively managed. It's crucial for development teams to understand that a platform, especially an MVP, is an evolving product and will not possess its full intended functionality from the outset. Setting realistic expectations and ensuring ongoing resources for platform development are essential to avoid overwhelming the platform team and hindering adoption. Despite its size, the team lacked time to invest in new platform functionality.

The inflexibility, premature scaling and lack of self-service turned the platform team into a bottleneck. The result was dissatisfaction among using teams, resistance from others, shadow IT creation, alternative delivery platforms in many development teams and legacy remaining the primary software development structure. Despite investing in Cloud Native and treating it as a transformational change, the company failed to follow the adoption process to achieve maximum value from the new technologies.

Team structures and knowledge transfer

Alongside the technology side of scaling, you also need to design how teams work. There are three main areas to consider here:

- *Platform team:* By now, your core team is likely morphing into or spawning a platform team who are dedicated to maintaining and evolving the new Cloud Native environment. This reflects the *Establish Platform Team (TF25)* pattern, ideally managed with a *Platform as a Product (TF24)* mindset. They handle IaC, the CI/CD pipeline, monitoring, self-service tooling and the overall developer experience.
- *Team Topologies:* Frameworks like *Team Topologies* guide how to structure squads around microservices. Applying principles like *Team*

Topologies and the *Reverse Conway Maneuver (TF31)* ensures a consistent, scalable architecture. Meanwhile, defining clear interaction modes relates to *Establish Team Communication APIs (TF38)*. In this setup, "stream-aligned" teams own end-to-end features, "platform" teams provide internal tools, "complex subsystems" teams work on narrowly specialized projects and "enabling" teams help with specialized skills. This ensures a consistent, scalable architecture without bureaucratic bottlenecks.
- *Cross-pollination:* Core team members often embed within newly onboarded product teams, spreading expertise and culture "mouth to mouth", not just via documentation. This immediate immersion helps new teams pick up best practices quickly and anchors them to the original vision.

To see how this can play out in the real world, let's return to HolidayCheck. The company's initiative progressed as the pioneering team concluded their research on different options and presented their findings to the leadership team. The CTO accepted these findings and presented a compelling business case to the executive team. This business case highlighted the significant competitive advantage that could be achieved through enhanced engineering productivity and agility.

Following this, the transformation began in earnest. The initial team, which had been working independently on PoCs and research, transitioned into the core team. This core team was tasked with constructing the actual MVP of the Cloud Native platform. Their objective was to develop a basic version of the platform within three to four months and re-factor a relatively self-contained function into a limited number of production-ready microservices. The ops manager, who had initially championed the introduction of containers and spearheaded the pioneering initiative, assumed the role of transformation champion. The CTO continued their support as the executive sponsor of the Cloud Native transformation.

But, as we're sure you're aware, not all Cloud Native transformations go so smoothly. Earlier, we mentioned the UK financial institution we worked with that had its legacy systems written in Cobol. Stage 3 was where they hit a significant roadblock, despite having successfully established a research team that was driven by a motivated champion and supported by the CTO.

More specifically, the transformation faltered when the CTO sought executive buy-in. The Cobol core application, though 40 years old, remained functional and supported a profitable business—a "Golden Goose". While everyone acknowledged its unsustainability and inability to fully support modern customer experiences, the risk was deemed too high. The CTO's attempts to implement parts of the new application were met with resistance from legacy teams. Value stream mapping revealed that 27 people had to approve every production change. This highlighted the organization's entrenched resistance to change and its prioritization of security and compliance above all else. It was like something straight out of the Dilbert comic.

In a *Dilbert* comic strip, Mordac, the Preventer of Information Services, one of the strip characters, famously said: *"Security is more important than usability"* and *"In a perfect world, no one would be able to use anything."*

Retire the first legacy components

Why retiring matters

As critical as building up the new system is, *retiring* old components is just as vital. If you indefinitely maintain legacy in parallel with the new platform, you end up paying for double the infrastructure, security patches and staff expertise. Worse, the old environment can remain a crutch, preventing full commitment to the new approach. The result is a half-migrated, half-stagnant system that saps resources without delivering the real benefits of Cloud Native. Failing to actively decommission creates the *Neglecting the Legacy Anchor (AP08)* anti-pattern and prevents the organization from fully realizing the gains or applying the *Free Up Resources (TF57)* pattern effectively.

The strangler pattern

A common technique, representing the *Strangle Legacy (TF33)* pattern, is the strangler approach. Here you identify a specific chunk of legacy functionality—maybe a service or a module—and replicate it in the new environment. Once the new microservice is running, you divert traffic from the old module and then disable it altogether. Over time, piece by piece, you strangle the entire legacy system until it's small enough to decommission. Here's what that looks like in practice:

1. *Select a manageable component:* Don't aim to kill the entire monolith in one shot. Pick something contained—like a reporting service or certain APIs.

2. *Redirect traffic:* Use proxies or gateways to route requests from the old environment to the new service.

3. *Monitor and decommission:* If all goes well, remove that chunk from the legacy environment entirely. It's a huge morale booster to "bin" a legacy module in an official ceremony—everyone sees tangible progress. This methodical approach leads towards the *Sunset Gracefully (TF58)* pattern for the targeted component.

Overcoming resistance

Legacy systems can be clingy. They often contain hidden functionalities that certain customers or internal stakeholders rely on—like an archaic FTP interface or specialized data export. Some teams may be reluctant to give up what they know, or a few big customers might run older processes.

Clear communication with the customers is key. Alert users early, set realistic decommission deadlines and offer alternatives. Executive backing is also essential. The leadership sponsor must endorse the retirement plan, preventing holdouts from stalling the migration indefinitely. If customers rely on old features, work with them to shift to newer, more secure and more efficient alternatives. This might require mini-transformations within those customer organizations, but it can also deepen the partnership.

If you don't actively retire components, your Cloud Native transformation may stall. If you avoid retiring your legacy system, your technology will devolve into a sprawling dual environment that still demands significant time and money to maintain—undercutting many of the benefits you hoped to achieve.

The sales and marketing angle

Beyond the technical side, consider how removing old systems and ramping up new ones affects sales, marketing and customer care.

Some features might be temporarily unavailable or require re-learning. Sales teams accustomed to selling the old product need training on the new platform's value proposition. If the old product is sold via traditional licensing but the new product is subscription-based, your sales team may resist the new approach if their commissions aren't adjusted accordingly. Legacy customers might need help transitioning to a new interface or workflow. The key to overcoming these obstacles is to provide straightforward documentation, support channels and transitional grace periods.

A successful transformation aligns *every* stakeholder—technical and non-technical—so that retirements don't catch anyone off guard. Success requires thinking about the *Holistic Transformation (TF35)*, encompassing technology, process, culture and business impact.

Stage finish conditions

You'll know Step 3 is complete when:

- Several teams are actively building and deploying on the Cloud Native platform without major disruptions, showing success in the initial phases of *Gradual Onboarding (TF32)*.
- Key architectural problems discovered by these early adopters are either solved or have clear action plans, reflecting effective use of *Build the Right Thing (TF29)*.
- The first legacy components have been fully retired, verifying that you can decommission old modules safely. This also demonstrates that *Strangle Legacy (TF33)* and *Sunset Gracefully (TF58)* can be executed safely.
- Team structures—including the platform team (*Establish Platform Team (TF25)*) and other Team Topologies structures (*Reverse Conway Maneuver (TF31)*)—are in place and stable enough to handle more load.
- Documentation and onboarding are sufficiently mature that new teams can join without heroic one-off interventions. You can show maturity in optimizing the onboarding by investing in a *Dev Starter Pack (TF26)*.

Reaching this stage confirms you've transcended the realm of prototypes and pilot projects. You're now in a position to continue scaling to more teams—and more customers—while simultaneously chipping away at the remaining legacy codebase. By proving the Cloud

Native environment can handle real workloads and systematically retire old components, you demonstrate that the transformation has genuine momentum and a clear path to success.

Step 4: Scaling and Optimizing—Expanding across the enterprise and fine-tuning the system

By the time you reach this step you've moved beyond an initial Cloud Native MVP, onboarded a few teams and started retiring select legacy components. Now comes the growth stage—the large-scale rollout of new practices and architecture across more teams, more applications and more business units. This expansion goes hand in hand with an Optimizing mindset, ensuring that what you build doesn't become the next messy monolith. This stage focuses on completing the *Gradual Onboarding (TF32)* across the organization while heavily emphasizing *Continuous Optimization (TF42)*.

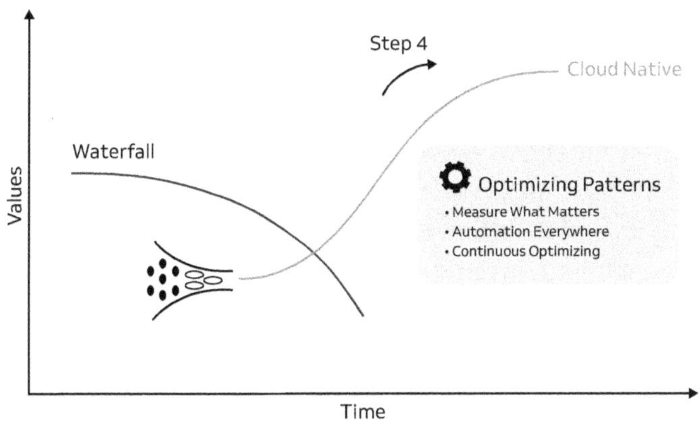

Figure 15: *Step 4—Finishing the transformation*

At the core of a successful scaling effort is a *platform*. Think of a platform as a service layer that handles 80–90% of the routine tasks in case of IDPs. We're talking about infrastructure provisioning, CI/CD, logging, observability and security. When these tasks are taken care of, your engineering teams can focus on value creation. Managing this platform effectively often involves adopting a *Platform as a Product (TF24)* mindset. As Gregor Hohpe describes in his work on platform strategies, there are various kinds of platforms:[8]

- *IDPs:* Where container orchestration, pipelines, monitoring and self-service tooling converge to give developers a frictionless path to production.
- *Business platforms:* These expose core capabilities as APIs for internal and external partners—think of payments, identity or supply chain features.
- *Data platforms:* For handling data ingestion, storage, transformation and analytics at scale.
- *Integration platforms:* For managing event buses or messaging layers that unify microservices with legacy systems.

Each type of platform can save development teams from reinventing the wheel. However, building or evolving these platforms is not trivial. You need solid architecture, robust security and a *Platform as a Product (TF24)* mindset, where you treat your internal teams as customers.

8 Hohpe, G. (2024) Platform Strategy. *Innovation Through Harmonization*. Leanpub.

Scaling: The organization-wide rollout

After successfully onboarding a handful of teams in Step 3, you're likely ready for broader adoption. To ensure that this part of your Scaling mode goes to plan, we recommend our clients take the following approach:

- *Create an onboarding plan:* Identify which teams will migrate next. This strategic approach to *Gradual Onboarding (TF32)* may decide to *Lift and Shift at the End (TF40)* for some stable legacy components. Some older legacy components may remain untouched for months or years if they're stable and rarely updated—perhaps you can "lift and shift" them to the cloud in virtual machines. Others, especially if they change often or cause frequent headaches, should be moved sooner to the new environment.
- *Train and educate:* Each newly onboarded team must learn how your platform works. Maturing the *Dev Starter Pack (TF26)* resources is key here. That means understanding how to use container orchestration, what your CI/CD pipeline expects and how to handle logging and monitoring. Having comprehensive documentation, tutorials or internal workshops can smooth this process. If the platform team is swamped with support tickets, that's a sign you might need better self-service tooling or a more systematic approach to knowledge sharing.
- *Iterate and improve:* Every team that joins will have unique requirements—some might need specialized data pipelines or unusual networking setups. The platform team must decide which requests to

incorporate globally and which are too specialized, pushing the requesting team to handle them on their own. Striking this balance is crucial to avoid "platform bloat" while also maintaining broad utility.

Avoiding overload

During Scaling mode, the platform team faces an onslaught of tasks: onboarding new teams, adding features, fixing bugs and dealing with load spikes as more traffic migrates. If you start with a well-architected MVP and robust automation, you'll handle the influx more gracefully. If not, you could slip into a vicious cycle—band-aid fixes, mounting technical debt and endless firefighting.

Automation is critical. The more you automate environment creation, security scans or capacity management, the fewer manual tasks you'll have and the more *consistent* your outcomes will be. The platform team can then focus on *real* improvements rather than repetitive requests. Robust automation *(Automation Everywhere (TF39))* is critical to successfully *Prepare for Scale (TF30)* and avoid overwhelming the platform team.

To see how this can be done well, let's return to HolidayCheck. Here, we witnessed the process of the Pioneering, Bootstrapping & Bridge-Building modes with a strong core team that delivered a small but high-quality MVP. When those steps were complete, the transformation team was ready to scale.

First, three teams were selected to onboard, based on their motivation for innovation and relatively independent self-contained components. These three teams were onboarded during an offsite in an old water tower that had been refurbished into a co-working space. It was three days of intense work. By the end, all three teams delivered their applications to production on Cloud Native. Before "the water tower offsite", the relevant teams went through intense training on technologies and their implementation at HolidayCheck.

The water tower offsite was so successful that it became the name of an exercise. The rest of the legacy teams went through training and "water tower workshops", gradually re-factoring old applications and moving them to the Cloud Native platform.

The core team gradually went back to their original teams to reinforce the new culture and bring technical expertise.

But this wasn't just a one-off exercise. When we met with HolidayCheck a few years later, they had already replaced their original Cloud Native stack based on Mesos with a new one based on Kubernetes. HolidayCheck didn't just *adopt* Cloud Native; they acquired the *capability* to change and transform.

Optimizing: Fine-tuning the engine

Scaling mode typically sparks a sudden jump in costs and complexity—more services, more data, more compute resources. Optimizing mode counters this by focusing on reducing waste, enhancing performance and embedding a culture of continuous improvement. There are several ways to optimize:

- *Cost awareness and FinOps:* The cloud makes spinning up new environments, VMs or serverless functions trivial. This can lead to runaway bills if not monitored. Frameworks like FinOps combine financial and operational metrics, letting engineering teams see usage and costs in near real time. This practice helps teams *Measure What Matters (TF36)* regarding financial efficiency. This fosters data-driven decisions like shutting down idle resources or resizing over-provisioned instances.
- *Performance tuning:* As more users hit your microservices, you'll discover bottlenecks—like slow database queries or CPU-thirsty processes. Tools for distributed tracing, load testing and performance monitoring guide teams to fix these issues methodically. This relies heavily on effective *Cultivate Observability (TF48)* tooling and practices.
- *Security and compliance:* Rapid expansion shouldn't mean holes in security. Automated compliance checks and scanning pipelines, along with minimal but enforced security guardrails, help ensure you don't compromise safety for speed. Incorporating *Automation Everywhere (TF39)* for checks is vital.

When you make resources easier and cheaper to access, usage can skyrocket rather than stabilize. That's Jevons Paradox: ironically, improvements in *efficiency* often spur more *consumption*. In the case of Cloud Native, once teams know they can spin up new test clusters effortlessly, they might do so more frequently. That's not inherently bad—experimentation can lead to innovation—but it also demands robust cost controls and a proactive mindset to avoid ballooning expenses.

The culture of quality v the culture of chaos

In a large-scale transformation, you can't rely solely on top-down mandates to keep systems well-structured. The organizational culture matters immensely. In our experience, organizations become obsessed with one of three things. This obsession dictates the company's culture:

- *Feature obsession:* Some companies fixate on delivering new functionality. As a result they always push non-functional tasks—like documentation or code quality—down the priority list. This leads to a snowball of technical debt, confusion and slow progress down the road.
- *Rules obsession:* Others bury every request under committees, approvals and volumes of paperwork. While this may reduce short-term risk, it slows innovation and frustrates talented developers who want to iterate quickly.
- *Quality obsession:* Successful Cloud Native transformations align with a "growth mindset" (the belief that intelligence and personal abilities can be improved with effort and learning). This means they are constantly scanning for improvements, automating tasks, refining pipelines and encouraging teams to do small, frequent re-factoring. Under this mindset, teams take pride in robust, well-monitored systems. They see cost

reduction and operational excellence as part of good engineering, not separate chores dictated from above.

A quality obsession yields the best results in the long run—both for velocity and stability. It nurtures a workplace where continuous improvement is embedded. This is an environment where new features can be delivered swiftly on top of a solid foundation, not hacked into a chaotic tangle. This culture supports *Continuous Optimization (TF42)* and encourages *Data-Driven Decision Making (TF37)*.

A great example comes from Admiral John Richardson's foreword to the book *Wiring the Winning Organization* by Gene Kim and Steven J. Spear.[9] He recounts his experience commanding a nuclear submarine, where even minor issues could compound into life-threatening disasters. This fostered a culture obsessed with quality, where every crew member was empowered to fix small problems immediately, resulting in the submarine becoming the best in the US Navy. In contrast, organizations obsessed with new features or rigid rule-following often defer addressing minor issues. In the process they accumulate technical debt that eventually leads to critical failures. The lesson is that a quality-driven culture leads to high performance.

9 Kim, G. and Spear, S.J. (2023) *Wiring the Winning Organization: Liberating Our Collective Greatness through Slowification, Simplification, and Amplification.* IT Revolution.

As more teams relocate to the new platform, make sure you keep retiring pieces of the old environment. Otherwise, you'll maintain parallel systems indefinitely, doubling costs and complicating everyone's workflow. For stable but rarely changing legacy components, consider "lift and shift" or delayed migration if rewriting them makes little sense. Over time, aim to reduce the legacy footprint to near zero, completing the *Strangle Legacy (TF33)* process and applying *Sunset Gracefully (TF58)* to the final components. You can potentially use *Lift and Shift at the End (TF40)* for non-critical parts.

Stage finish conditions

You know you've completed Step 4 when you can see:

- *Organization-wide adoption:* A majority of your product teams deploy microservices or services on the new Cloud Native platform, marking the successful completion of *Gradual Onboarding (TF32)*. Legacy holdouts are limited to specialized or rarely updated modules.
- *Robust IDP:* The platform handles the needs of numerous teams without meltdown. Automation is extensive, scaling is predictable and the platform team isn't drowning in support tickets. This demonstrates mature *Platform as a Product (TF24)* practices and effective *Enable Self-Service (TF47)* capabilities.
- *Optimized costs and performance:* There's a systematic approach (FinOps or similar) to cost control. Major performance bottlenecks are addressed proactively, achieved through *Measure*

What Matters (TF36) and prioritizing *Efficiency over Adaptability (TF43)*. Teams have the tools and metrics to deliver consistent, efficient services.

- *Cultural shift:* People across the company understand and appreciate the value of continuous improvement. Rather than clinging to old ways, teams embrace re-factoring, cost optimization and knowledge sharing as routine habits. This reflects ingrained *Continuous Optimization (TF42)* and progress towards becoming a *Foster Learning Organization (TF53)*, not emergency measures.
- Reaching these conditions signifies that the main disruptive phase is over, allowing the organization to *Finish the Transformation (TF41)* and pivot fully to ongoing improvement.

Once you've reached this level, your Cloud Native ecosystem is no longer a special project: it's the *new normal*. Your organization reaps the benefits of agility and resilience, while scaling up or down with relative ease. By embedding optimization into daily practices, you avoid letting cost or complexity spiral out of control. This paves the way for ongoing innovation and high performance in the years to come.

Key takeaways

- **MVP and gradual expansion:** Start with an MVP Cloud Native platform, rigorously test it with a small core team and *then* onboard additional teams incrementally. This minimizes risk and allows for course correction.

- **Bridge, don't just build:** Create robust connections between the new Cloud Native environment and existing legacy systems. This enables a phased migration, avoids disruption and allows you to leverage existing assets.
- **Dedicated leadership and team structure:** Appoint a transformation champion and establish clear team structures (using principles like *Team Topologies*) to support the new architecture and ways of working.
- **Automate, optimize and retire:** Embrace automation to scale efficiently. Continuously optimize for cost and performance (using practices like FinOps). Actively retire legacy components to avoid maintaining parallel systems.
- **Culture of continuous improvement:** Foster a culture that values quality, proactive problem-solving and ongoing learning. This is essential for long-term success and adaptability.

Navigating the hands-on stages of transformation requires a clear guide. Scan the QR code to access our complete library of transformation patterns and learn more about our hands-on cards workshop to steer your team's journey.

Chapter 6

New Maturity and Next Wave

Step 5: Optimizing and Innovating—Maintain quality and deliver rapid incremental innovation

After years of laying the foundation, migrating teams and retiring old components, you've reached a new mature state. Cloud Native is now embedded in your organization's day-to-day operations. At this point, you no longer worry about scaling from a handful of microservices to dozens or even hundreds—your architecture, platform and culture are largely set. But transformation never *truly* ends. It transitions into a steady rhythm of optimizing and innovating. This stage signifies the successful completion of the main disruptive phase *(Finish the Transformation (TF41))* and a pivot towards embedding *Continuous*

Optimization (TF42) and fostering *Nurture Incremental Innovation (TF49)* as the new normal.

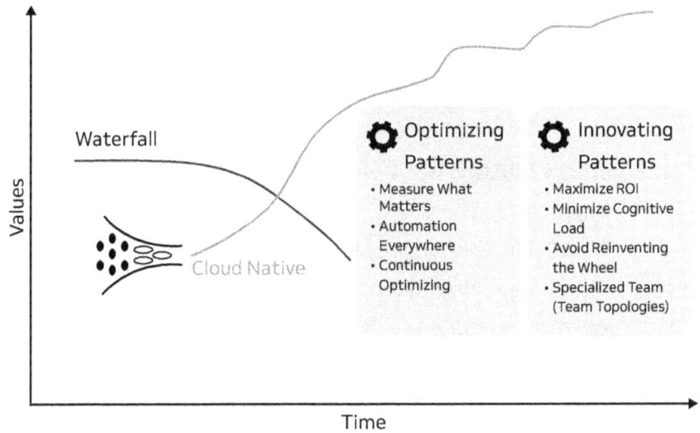

Figure 16: *Step 5—Continuous improvement and incremental innovation*

As the new status quo takes shape, the big changes to architecture, team structures and culture are behind you. You'll find most teams have adjusted to the new platform. Processes and practices that were once in flux have stabilized.

This is when your teams can settle into a routine. Technical teams will be back in a cycle of maintaining systems and delivering customer value. The question now is: will they keep polishing the product and remain open to new ideas, or stagnate until the next big disruption forces another massive overhaul?

At this stage, if your transformation was done right, you used those multiple years of upheaval to reshape the culture—favoring quality, continuous improvement and a growth mindset. If not, you risk sliding back into old habits. This presents as overly focusing on features, ignoring mounting tech debt and creating the same problems you tried to solve. Sustaining success requires embedding *Continuous Optimization (TF42)* into the culture and the pattern *Foster Learning Organization (TF53).*

Maintaining a culture of quality

Gene Kim and Steven Spear spotlighted organizational models that revolve around continuous improvement and resolving problems quickly in **Wiring the Winning Organization**. The essence is:

- *Slowification:* Make it easier for individuals and teams to see, investigate and fix problems.
- *Simplification:* Keep everything as modular and transparent as possible, so problems themselves are easier to spot and correct.
- *Amplification:* Ensure issues get escalated and resolved. Don't leave lingering defects or allow the "broken windows effect" to take hold, because neglecting small problems leads to larger problems.

The organizational model presented in *Wiring the Winning Organization* revolves around continuous improvement and quick problem resolution. This model promotes a culture of quality where issues are identified and resolved efficiently, preventing lingering defects and maintaining a high-performance environment.

Continuous optimization

In Cloud Native terms, this means you *never* stop optimizing. In practice, this involves the following activities:

- *Technical debt repayment:* Even when systems seem stable, there's always a backlog of small fixes, re-factorings or updates to modernize code. Allocating at least 20% of engineering time for upkeep helps prevent the slow decay of quality. This disciplined upkeep is a core part of *Continuous Optimization (TF42)*.
- *Automation and tooling:* Each team's routines—build pipelines, testing, environment provisioning—should be automated wherever it's cost-effective. This reflects the ongoing application of *Automation Everywhere (TF39)*. This reduces "toil", a concept borrowed from Google's Site Reliability Engineering (SRE), which recommends devoting up to half the team's time to eliminating repetitive, manual tasks. This means that developers can spend their time on creative and innovative tasks instead of repetitive, mundane work.
- *Preventive maintenance:* Just like property owners must repaint walls and clean gutters, software teams must keep dependencies current, security patches applied and documentation up to date. Regularly scheduled "maintenance sprints" can pay massive dividends over the long term, contributing to overall *Continuous Optimization (TF42)*.
- *Platform build-up:* As certain features or integrations mature, it may be worth packaging them into your internal platform—freeing dev

teams from reinventing the wheel *(Avoid Reinventing the Wheel (TF46))*. This enhances the platform's ability to *Minimize Cognitive Load (TF45)* and *Enable Self-Service (TF47)*. A small platform team curates these components, ensuring each is robust and easy to support.

Without a sustained approach to these areas, organizations risk adopting the "broken windows" syndrome: once a few small issues are ignored, more pile up, eventually crippling productivity and quality.

One of our recent customers in the Netherlands found themselves in exactly this situation. Although they had strong development and platform teams, they realized that their system was wasteful. We entered their story through the sustainability angle. We found that the demands on hardware were very consistent, with a few short spikes a day. However, because the platform relied on an older version of Rancher, a distribution of Kubernetes, autoscaling wasn't available. As a result, cloud resources were typically overprovisioned, delivering four or five times more than what was needed.

Additionally, most VMs in the cloud were larger than required, simply to avoid performance issues. Very little was optimized. Testing environments were automatically created and rarely used, but kept for weeks. There were other similar issues related to a lack of attention to optimization. This led to much higher carbon emissions due to wasted resources, as well as a higher cost of cloud computing. The reason they hadn't looked at it much was because it had happened slowly, one small step at a time. The development teams were much more focused on delivering new features. Another issue was that the cloud provider had sold them reserved capacity for three years, eliminating incremental cost pressure.

But cost and carbon emissions weren't the only factors they needed to consider. The lack of optimization wasn't just in overprovisioning. Using larger VMs and other similar quick solutions masked the real issues and led to continuously degrading software quality and slower delivery of value. In the end, despite prioritizing feature delivery over cost and emissions, they didn't achieve that either.

The required changes were not trivial, but they were also not very complicated. Upgrading their systems, systematically reducing waste and educating engineers to prioritize quality led to a quick turnaround. The real question in a scenario such as this is not how easy it is to build a new platform, but how easy it is to change the culture to prevent the same situation from recurring in a year or two.

A great way to achieve continuous optimization is to use SRE principles of toil reduction. Toil (manual, repetitive IT tasks) keeps engineers from strategic work. SRE aims to reduce toil through automation and proactive measures. SRE teams often split their time 50/50 between operational work and engineering work focused on toil reduction. This is managed through error budgets (acceptable downtime) and toil budgets (limits on manual tasks), ensuring continuous improvement of system reliability and efficiency.

Innovating mode: driving customer value

While Optimizing mode keeps your house in order, Innovating mode pushes your product and business model forward. This mode leverages the established platform to *Maximize ROI (TF44)* through new value creation. Now that you have a stable Cloud Native base, you can:

- *Develop new features rapidly:* Freed from monolithic constraints, teams can release incremental changes without tangling every new feature in massive code merges. This agility allows teams to *Nurture Incremental Innovation (TF49)* effectively. The faster feedback loops give you a competitive edge.
- *Explore emerging tech:* Service meshes, AI/ML, edge computing or serverless might be your *next* wave of disruption. Because your platform is already container-based and microservices-driven, adopting new tech becomes less daunting. That said, it still requires planning. This links back to the need for ongoing, low-level *Learn and Explore (TF1)* even in mature phases.
- *Stay agile in the market:* Customers' needs shift continuously, and your competitors are also innovating. Your new architecture and processes let you respond with minimal friction, delivering new capabilities while maintaining uptime and reliability, often guided by a *Dynamic Strategy (TF54)*.

Balancing optimization and innovation

Innovation = customer value. This is where you grow revenue, win market share or out-compete rivals. It often captures leadership attention.

Optimization = sustainability. Without it, the cost, complexity and technical debt overshadow any new features you introduce. Developers get bogged down in old problems and frustration mounts.

A healthy organization devotes most of its development capacity to innovation, with a consistent slice—maybe 30–40%—allocated to maintenance and continuous improvement, including technical debt cleanup or cost-saving measures. This ensures you don't regress into the heroic or bureaucratic cultures that hamper progress. Finding this balance between *Continuous Optimization (TF42)* and *Nurture Incremental Innovation (TF49)* is key to sustainable high performance.

Stewart Brand's classic book, *How Buildings Learn*,[10] shows how structures evolve over time. Buildings have various layers: site, structure, skin, services, space plan and stuff—each with a different rate of change. The deeper layers (structure) change rarely, while the upper layers (stuff) can change almost daily. Translating this to software:

---

10 Brand, S. (1995) *How Buildings Learn: What Happens After They're Built* (paperback)

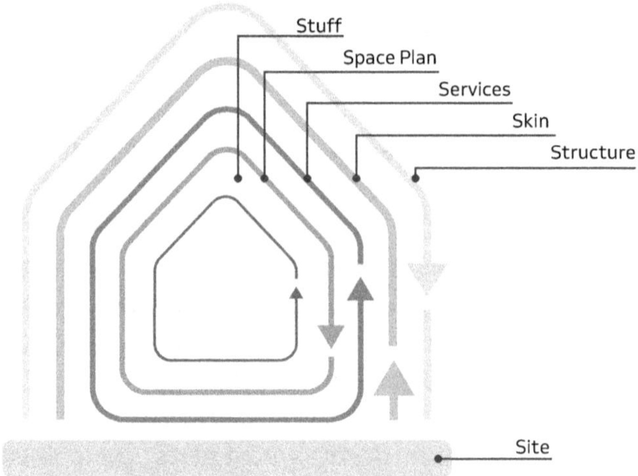

Figure 17: *How structures evolve*[11]

- *Structure:* This represents your core architecture—microservices v monolith, language choices, container v serverless. Changing this is as disruptive as tearing down load-bearing walls in a house.
- *Services:* These are platform components (CI/CD, logging, cloud environment). They evolve periodically but not daily.
- *Space plan:* The boundaries and organization of microservices. These can shift when needed but require care because each microservice aligns with a specific team (Conway's Law).
- *Stuff:* The daily churn—datasets, configurations, frontend design elements, small feature changes.

---

11 Brand, S. (1995) *How Buildings Learn: What Happens After They're Built* (paperback)

This is where frequent innovation happens with minimal overhead.

When your architecture is flexible and well-designed, small changes occur in the "stuff" layer, incurring little friction. Larger re-architectures in the "structure" or "services" layers should remain relatively rare, but still possible if planned thoughtfully. A mature platform helps *Minimize Surface of Innovation (TF51)*, allowing teams to focus changes primarily in the "stuff" layer.

It's crucial to understand that early architectural decisions made during a transformation can restrict innovation later on. The core team building the MVP is essentially laying the foundation and structure of your future software development house. Often, a misplaced "supporting wall" can prevent you from achieving your desired results.

A personal example is Pini's Dutch rowhouse with a rectangular floor plan. A supporting wall in the middle divides most of the ground floor between the living room and the corridor/kitchen. When they moved in, Pini's wife wanted a kitchen island to divide the space between the kitchen and the living room. Unfortunately, the supporting wall made this change possible but very expensive. It wasn't just about removing a divider, but adding a pole, replacing the floor and other costly investments, making the change impractical.

Similar "supporting walls" exist in software. Of course, the foundation is even harder to change. Early Cloud Native decisions on orchestration, data storage, architecture (monolith v microservices v serverless), networking and observability can become limiting factors later.

Beware of "transformation over" mindset

A common pitfall is declaring victory once the big reorganization ends and the new platform is widely in use. People may think: "We're done. Let's coast." But there is a real risk of stagnation. This is when neglected improvements or cost optimizations allow overheads to accumulate. There is also always the looming threat of future disruption. Another radical shift—possibly around AI—could demand a fresh wave of transformation. If you let your culture become rigid, you'll face the same struggles anew. True maturity involves ongoing *Continuous Optimization (TF42)* and vigilance *(Periodic Checkups (TF55), Dynamic Strategy (TF54))*.

Long-term success hinges on *continuously* refining your architecture, processes and skill sets so the next disruption isn't a crisis—it's just another step in your evolution.

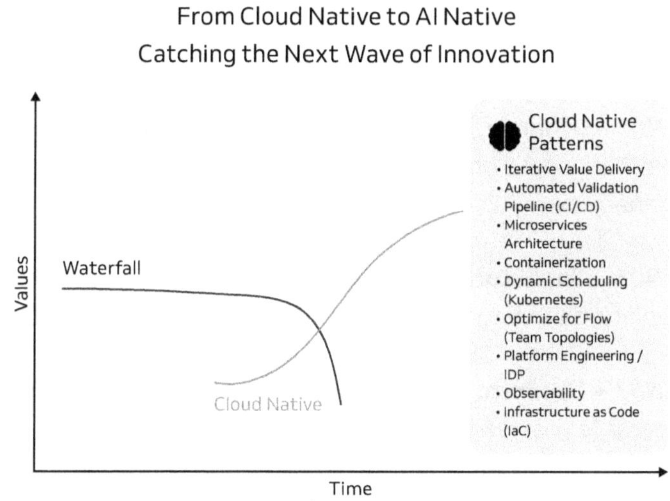

Figure 18: *Cloud Native maturity patterns*

Agile/Cloud Native patterns

If you recognize these patterns from your daily work, then your organization is likely operating within an Agile/Cloud Native paradigm (browse all patterns online: https://re-cinq.com/patterns).

CN01 – Iterative Value Delivery: Deliver working software frequently in small, valuable increments.

CN02 – Automated Validation Pipeline (CI/CD): Implement automated CI/CD for build, test and release preparation.

CN03 – Microservices Architecture: Break systems into small, autonomous, independently deployable services.

CN04 – Containerization: Package applications with dependencies into isolated, portable container units.

CN05 – Dynamic Scheduling (Kubernetes): Use platforms like Kubernetes to automate containerized application management.

CN06 – Immutable Infrastructure: Deploy changes by replacing existing instances with new immutable artifacts.

CN07 – Optimize for Flow (Team Topologies): Structure teams (e.g. stream-aligned) for fast value delivery.

CN08 – Platform Engineering/IDP: Provide automated, self-service capabilities via an IDP.

CN09 – Observability: Design systems for detailed telemetry (logs, metrics, traces) for insight.

CN10 – Design for Failure: Apply patterns (timeouts, retries, circuit breakers) for resilience.

CN11 – Infrastructure as Code (IaC): Define and manage infrastructure using declarative, version-controlled code.

CN12 – Service Discovery: Implement dynamic mechanisms for services to locate each other.

CN13 – API Gateway: Provide a unified entry point for external clients accessing microservices.

CN14 – Sidecar: Deploy auxiliary containers for decoupled infrastructure concerns.

CN15 – Service Mesh: Use a dedicated layer for managing service-to-service communication reliably.

CN16 – Database per Service: Each microservice manages its own dedicated, private database.

CN17 – Event-Driven Architecture: Structure system communication around asynchronous events for decoupling.

CN18 – Immutable Infrastructure Rollouts: Deploy changes by replacing entire sets of immutable instances.

CN19 – Feature Flags/Toggles: Decouple code deployment from feature release using controllable flags.

CN20 – GitOps: Manage infrastructure and applications declaratively using Git as truth.

CN21 – Blue-Green/Canary/Rolling Releases: Employ strategies for safe, low-downtime application deployments.

CN22 – Circuit Breaker: Prevent cascading failures by temporarily halting calls to failing services.

Stage finish conditions

You'll know you've completed Step 5 when:

- *All teams are in a steady state:* They no longer need major transformations to function. Instead, they perform ongoing optimization and incremental innovations as part of normal operations, demonstrating mature *Continuous Optimization (TF42).*

- *A culture of quality prevails:* Engineers fix problems as they find them. They automate tasks, manage tech debt responsibly and embrace continuous improvement as a shared value, indicating a successful *Foster Learning Organization (TF53)* culture.
- *You see innovative feature delivery:* Customers see regular updates that solve *real* problems, rather than sporadic or drawn-out releases, showing effective *Nurture Incremental Innovation (TF49).* Business stakeholders appreciate the agility gained from Cloud Native.
- *You achieve sustainable costs and efficiency:* Resource usage, team bandwidth and maintenance efforts are kept in check. There's a healthy feedback loop (like FinOps) to keep finances aligned with technical growth, achieved through *Measure What Matters (TF36)* and *Efficiency over Adaptability (TF43).*
- *You are prepared for the next disruption:* You've built an organization that can spot and adapt to looming changes—whether it's a new technology wave or a shift in market demands—without repeating the same painful process from scratch, enabled by adopting a *Dynamic Strategy (TF54).*

Reaching this final step solidifies the Cloud Native transformation and sets you up for enduring success. Teams function smoothly, delivering rapid, high-quality features in an environment where constant improvement is the norm. That doesn't mean you'll *never* face another massive overhaul—innovation is relentless—but you'll face it from a position of strength. You're now in a strong position, underpinned by a robust architecture, a proven culture of excellence and the adaptability to pivot when opportunity or threat emerges.

Step 6: Pioneering mode—Looking ahead to the next disruption (AI Native?)

After reaching a new mature state—where your organization routinely optimizes and innovates within a stable Cloud Native environment—it might *feel* like a final victory. But true technology leaders know that complacency invites obsolescence. As the world evolves, new disruptions inevitably arise. Once again, you need a dedicated Pioneering mode to spot and assess radical shifts *before* your competitors seize the advantage. This involves re-engaging the patterns associated with Pioneering mode, primarily *Learn and Explore (TF01)*, often through a dedicated *Skunk Works Team (TF02)*.

This returns us to where we began the transformation journey: a small, empowered pioneering team or "labs" group. Initially, they sparked interest in Cloud Native. Now, with that transformation essentially finished, their role is to scout the *next* big wave—perhaps AI or AI Native (we will explore the differences in the following chapters), or any gamechanging innovation that requires major changes in architecture, organizational structure and business strategy.

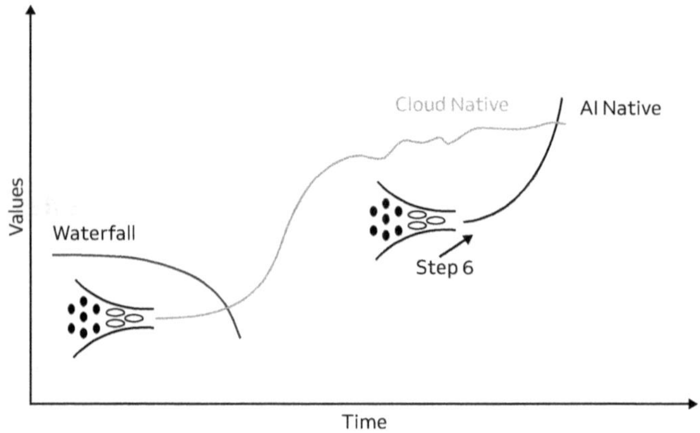

Figure 19: Step 6—Looking for new disruptive ideas

Returning to Pioneering mode even when your Cloud Native solution has reached maturity is important for several reasons:

- *Avoiding dual transformations:* The book *Zone to Win* reminds us that organizations should never undertake two large-scale transformations simultaneously.[12] It splits focus, confuses employees and dilutes resources. When you were in the intense struggle of a Cloud Native overhaul, the pioneering team could only maintain a low profile, providing small updates but avoiding any major new disruptive initiative. This respects the principle that attempting multiple large transformations concurrently often leads to failure, allowing the

12 Moore, G.A. (2015) *Zone to Win: Organizing to Compete in an Age of Disruption*. Diversion Books.

organization to focus after having applied *Finish the Transformation (TF41)* to the Cloud Native journey.

- *Continuous discovery:* Now that your Cloud Native transformation is done—or at least stable—it's time to ramp up deeper, more experimental research again. This is the practical application of *Learn and Explore (TF01)*, enabled by the stability achieved in the previous phase. This ensures you're not blindsided by shifts in technology or market demands.
- *Future-proofing:* Even the most successful Cloud Native environment can grow outdated if the industry pivots to a new paradigm—like advanced AI, quantum computing or something entirely unforeseen. Having a pioneering team that's *constantly* exploring these possibilities puts you ahead of the curve. This proactive exploration (*Learn and Explore (TF01)*) helps *Test Hard Things First (TF05), protecting* business against unforeseen disruptions.

The birth of the "next Docker"—is AI that trigger?

When Docker exploded in popularity around 2013–2014, containers were *not* a new invention. Solaris Zones and LXC containers had existed for years. But Docker packaged them in a way that resonated with mainstream developers, kickstarting an entire ecosystem—microservices, Kubernetes, the Cloud Native Computing Foundation and more.

AI is following a similar pattern. Neural networks and LLMs have been around for decades, but ChatGPT brought them into the public consciousness, demonstrating how powerful and versatile they can be when combined with user-friendly interfaces. Just as Docker's layered images and repositories simplified container distribution, ChatGPT made AI accessible for everyday tasks. Now, an entire ecosystem is springing up around generative AI. This includes specialized models, new frameworks, MLOps pipelines, data governance solutions, etc. Understanding this emerging ecosystem requires focused *Learn and Explore (TF01)* efforts.

Pioneering mode is exactly where your organization can test these waters. Is generative AI relevant for your customer interactions, product recommendations, code auto-generation, data analytics or something else entirely? Before you commit to a new transformation, you *must* investigate feasibility, ROI and risk.

Once again you need a team in Pioneering mode to help you understand and navigate the changing landscape. The team will need to *Proof of Concept – PoC (TF06)* for specific AI use cases and begin exploring the *Business Case (TF09)* for potential future adoption. As before, this team will take on the following:

- *Autonomy:* Just as it did before your Cloud Native journey, the pioneering team needs enough autonomy to explore radical ideas freely, a hallmark of the *Skunk Works Team (TF02)* pattern. This might involve separate budgets, looser timelines and fewer constraints from existing operational requirements.
- *Regular updates:* The rest of the organization should be aware of ongoing research but *not* be disrupted

by it. A monthly or quarterly "labs demo" can help leadership understand new AI or other emerging tech findings without forcing widespread immediate change. Using *Demo Your Ideas (TF07)* keeps stakeholders informed.

- *Business case exploration:* The pioneering team isn't just "tinkering". They also think about whether adopting AI or another big innovation might trigger the *next* transformation. They contribute findings that will inform the eventual *Business Case (TF09)* decision. They estimate the scale of organizational changes needed and weigh them against potential benefits and risks.
- *Avoiding premature launches:* If leadership senses something big on the horizon while you're still in the tail end of the *previous* transformation, it must either wait or be extremely small-scale. Otherwise, you risk the chaos of running two transformations at once.

Balancing maturity and radical innovation

In a mature Cloud Native enterprise, most of the workforce is focused on optimizing daily operations or innovating new features for customers. They're *not* looking to upend fundamental structures again—especially after living through a multi-year transformation. That's why you can't let *everyone* chase the new wave immediately.

Instead, the pioneering team remains a dedicated, small group who can go deep into AI or other emerging paradigms without derailing normal business. If their results prove truly revolutionary—like your original

Cloud Native push—then leadership might eventually green-light a new transformation. But that only happens after the existing environment has fully stabilized *and* the new approach has a compelling business case. This requires the pioneering *(Skunk Works Team (RF02))* team to operate effectively in its *Sandbox Environment (TF04)*, successfully *Proof of Concept – PoC (TF06)* and contribute to the *Business Case (9)*.

Common pitfalls if you abandon Pioneering mode

It's important to maintain the cycle you went through for your Cloud Native transformation. If you abandon Pioneering mode and disband your pioneering team, you face several risks, including:

- *Slow response to market changes:* By the time a competitor leverages the new technology to disrupt your market, you're scrambling to catch up. This is a consequence of neglecting *Learn and Explore (TF01)*. Without prior research, you're forced into a hasty transformation under crisis conditions.
- *Continuous minor improvements with no major leaps:* The organization drifts into a comfortable loop: incremental updates without leaps in capability. Over time, your product or service might become "good enough" but you are never a market leader. This makes you vulnerable to big leaps by others.
- *Misinterpreting radical shifts as minor:* If you lack a dedicated team to deeply assess new tech, you risk trivializing something that might require an entirely different architecture. This leads to a piecemeal approach—adopting a "cool feature"

here or there—only to realize too late that *genuine* transformation was necessary. This often happens because *Learn and Explore (TF01)* and *Proof of Concept – PoC (TF06)* were not rigorously applied.

The next wave: AI (... and beyond?)

All signs indicate that AI, particularly generative AI, has the potential to be as disruptive as Cloud Native was a decade ago—or even more so. Examples that are already emerging as we write this include:

- *Automated code generation:* AI assistants can write or review code, drastically speeding up development and reducing errors if integrated well into CI/CD pipelines.
- *New product possibilities:* Personalized user experiences, advanced analytics, predictive maintenance or real-time natural language interaction that redefines your customer's journey.
- *Team structures:* AI-driven projects require data scientists, MLOps engineers, domain experts and specialized GPU infrastructures. That may demand a different organizational layout—mirroring the microservices shift that once reorganized your dev teams.

None of this implies your entire enterprise should pivot to AI *tomorrow*. But ignoring these trends is risky. If the pioneering team invests time in testing AI-based prototypes—like GPT-driven customer support or AI code review—they'll know if there's real promise. They also might find minimal ROI for your particular industry, which is equally valuable information. That knowledge ultimately informs leadership on whether a second major transformation is worthwhile.

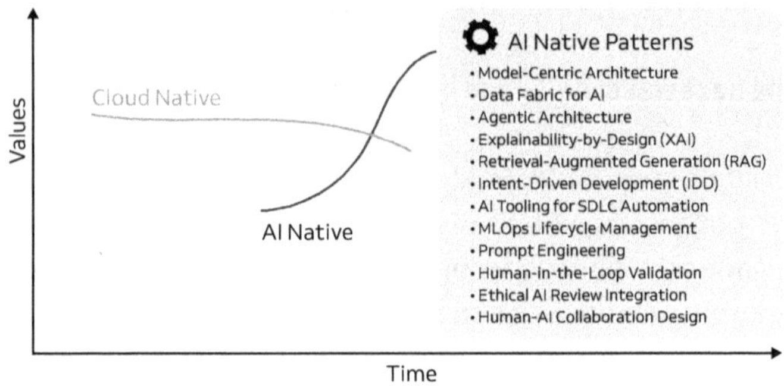

Figure 20: *AI Native maturity patterns (speculative)*

Stage finish conditions

Step 6 concludes when:

- *A small, autonomous pioneering team exists:* They regularly explore advanced technologies—potential next-wave disruptions—and keep leadership informed.
- *The organization is not triggering multiple transformations:* The Cloud Native transformation is declared finished, or close enough.
- *Continuous improvement is non-negotiable:* Even after a successful Cloud Native transformation, ongoing optimization, innovation and technical debt management are essential for sustained success. This is not a "one and done" project.
- *You've cultivated a culture of quality:* Embed practices that prioritize proactive problem-solving,

simplification and rapid feedback loops. This prevents technical debt from accumulating and ensures long-term system health.

- *You're balancing stability and exploration:* Maintain a stable core platform while simultaneously dedicating resources to exploring emerging technologies (like AI Native) through a dedicated pioneering effort.
- *You understand system layers and change rates:* Recognize that different parts of your architecture (infrastructure, services, applications) will evolve at different speeds. Plan accordingly and avoid premature optimization or rigid structures.
- *You're preparing for the next wave (AI Native):* Learn from past transformations (like Cloud Native). AI, particularly generative AI, has the potential to be deeply disruptive, so continuous learning and adaptation are crucial.

Key takeaways

- **Sustain and innovate:** Once a transformation stabilizes, the focus must shift to a dual mode of continuous optimization to maintain quality and efficiency, alongside incremental innovation to keep delivering value to customers.
- **A culture of quality is essential:** To avoid regressing, organizations must embed a culture of quality where continuous improvement, proactive problem-solving and managing technical debt are normal, ongoing activities, not afterthoughts.

- **Balance optimization and innovation:** A healthy organization allocates significant capacity to innovation while consistently dedicating resources (e.g. 30–40%) to maintenance, optimization and technical debt cleanup to ensure long-term sustainability and speed.
- **Re-engage in Pioneering for the next wave:** After one transformation concludes, it is critical to re-engage a "Pioneering mode" to explore the next major disruption, such as AI Native, to avoid being caught off guard.
- **Avoid dual transformations:** An organization should only focus on one major transformation at a time. While the primary transformation is underway, pioneering for the next wave should remain a low-profile, exploratory effort.
- **AI as the next disruptive wave:** AI, particularly generative AI, shows signs of being the next major transformative wave, similar to how Docker and Kubernetes catalyzed the Cloud Native shift. Organizations must start exploring its implications through dedicated, low-risk pioneering efforts.

Reaching this stage of maturity marks the successful conclusion of the primary transformation, but not the end of the journey. The focus now shifts to a dual mandate: sustainably reaping the benefits of the current Cloud Native paradigm through continuous optimization and incremental innovation, while simultaneously restarting the cycle of exploration to prepare for the next disruptive wave on the horizon, such as AI Native.

Mastering this balance—between stabilizing the present and pioneering the future—is the hallmark of a truly resilient and adaptive organization. This is one that is prepared not just to ride a single wave of innovation, but to navigate the ever-changing tides of technology successfully.

You've achieved Cloud Native maturity—what's next? Scan the QR code to take the AI Native Assessment and subscribe to our newsletter to prepare for the next wave of innovation before it arrives.

Part III

Beyond the Cloud–Lessons, Stability and the AI Frontier

In this final part, we consolidate the learnings from the Cloud Native journey and look towards the horizon. We will begin by examining the common costly mistakes and pitfalls organizations encounter when "going Cloud Native", offering insights to avoid derailing transformation efforts. We then explore how to sustain a mature Cloud Native environment, focusing on critical factors like platform engineering, cultural change, leadership, budgeting strategies and the often-overlooked aspect of environmental sustainability.

The focus then shifts to the next major wave: AI Native. We will chart these uncharted waters, discussing what an AI Native transformation might entail, its core ideas and the unique challenges it presents, learning from our Cloud Native experiences. Finally, we will present case studies to illustrate these concepts in real-world scenarios, helping you understand how to balance current transformations while preparing for the next.

Chapter 7

The Costly Mistakes of Going Cloud Native

Cloud Native promises faster development, easier scaling and improved efficiency. Yet, many organizations stumble, failing to achieve these benefits—or worse, wasting vast resources. This chapter explores the common mistakes (anti-patterns) that derail Cloud Native efforts, offering insights to steer your transformation towards success (use our pattern cards workshop to identify and navigate these pitfalls as a team: https://re-cinq.com/patterns).

The following are the main anti-patterns we see in our work with our clients:

- The cost of being too late—*Strategic Inertia (AP01).*
- The cost of being too early—*Bleeding Edge Gamble (AP02).*

- Never finishing the transformation—*Perpetual Transition (AP03).*
- Treating disruptive change as incremental—*Incremental Facade (AP04).*
- The illusion of control and the cost of over-planning—*Illusion of Control (AP06).*
- The shadow IT problem—*Unmanaged Shadow IT Proliferation (AP07).*
- Waste and sustainability impact—*Uncontrolled Cloud Costs (AP24)* and *Environmental Impact Neglect (AP36).*

1. Cost of being too late: Missing the transformative wave

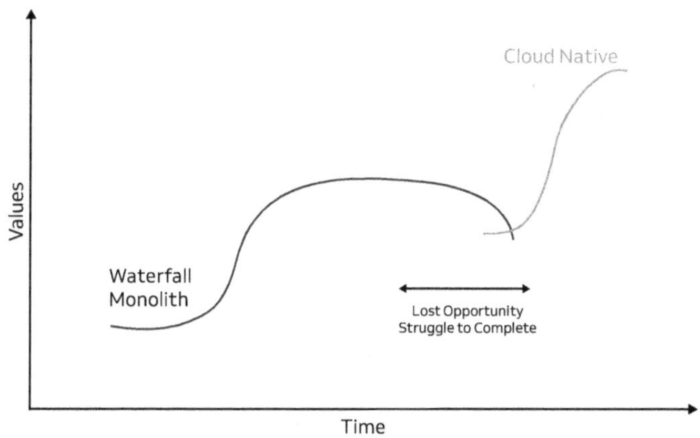

Figure 21: *The cost of being too late*

Ignoring the challenger disruption

In the fast-moving tech world, timing is everything. Delaying adoption of transformative technology can leave organizations scrambling to catch up, much like stagecoach companies once dismissed early automobiles. This scenario exemplifies the **pitfall: *Strategic Inertia (AP01)***.

- *Relevant solution patterns:* Proactive *Learn and Explore (TF01)*, establishing a Skunk Works Team (TF02). Using *Proof of Concept – PoC (TF06)* and *Demo Your Ideas (TF07)* to build urgency. Developing a *Business Case (TF09)* case sooner and maintaining a *Dynamic Strategy (TF54)*.

In the modern banking scene, challenger banks (Starling, Monzo, N26) exploited Cloud Native practices and Agile cultures to disrupt industry giants. Traditional banks that hesitated to modernize have lost market share—and been forced into costly, chaotic transformations later on.

The danger of waiting often seems minor at first. A small dip in market share or a fledgling startup adopting Cloud Native might appear non-threatening. But small, compounding changes can balloon into massive shifts. By the time the legacy players grasp the *real* threat, agile newcomers have momentum, investment and a modern tech stack that scales quickly.

Grassroots transformation

When leadership ignores new trends, enthusiastic developers often try to modernize from the bottom up. If leadership remains aloof, top engineering talent leaves to join more forward-looking companies. Middle management must become a bridge that allows teams to experiment while aligning the timing and approach to business strategy.

> **Key takeaway**
>
> Being too late can be catastrophic. Proactive, well-timed decisions are crucial to avoid losing market share and facing frantic, expensive catch-up attempts.

2. Cost of being too early: Navigating the bleeding edge

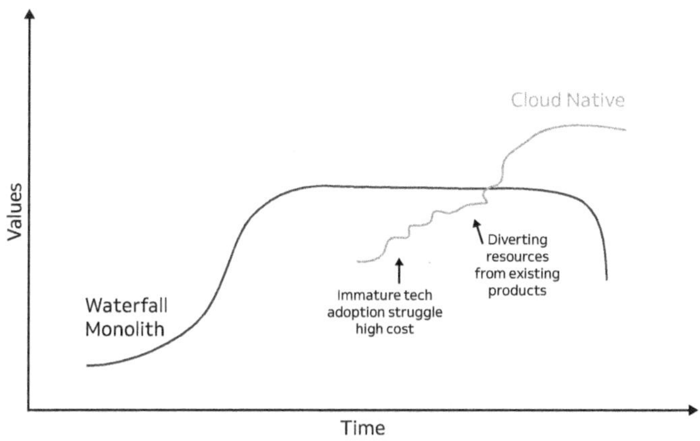

Figure 22: *The cost of being too early*

Premature adoption risks

Although being late is disastrous, jumping *too soon* also poses dangers. Early versions of Kubernetes (2017–2019) lacked mature tooling to support stable operations across areas like logging, security, networking and monitoring. Organizations adopting it prematurely often faced operational instability. Organizations that rushed in found themselves grappling with instability, shortages of skilled engineers and incomplete best practices. This often harmed their existing business while chasing unproven tech. This highlights the **pitfall: *Bleeding Edge Gamble (AP02)***.

- *Relevant solution patterns:* Thorough *Learn and Explore (TF01)*, using *Proof of Concept – PoC (TF06).* Applying *Test Hard Things First (TF5)* by testing hard things first in sandboxes, leveraging *Research Through Action (TF16)* and ensuring designs prioritize *Adaptability over Efficiency (TF17).*

The ecosystem factor

A technology's success depends on a supportive ecosystem: reliable tooling, available expertise, proven patterns. Think of a digital camera in the 1980s—few personal computers and an immature ecosystem limited consumer interest. The same logic applies to Cloud Native. Organizations that jumped in 2014 faced countless complexities, whereas by 2025 the ecosystem is largely mature and mainstream.

AI as the next frontier

Today, Cloud Native is stable enough that adopting it "too early" is unlikely. AI, on the other hand, stands at the cusp of major breakthroughs but is still evolving. For many businesses, diving headlong into AI might be akin to those early days of Docker—exciting but fraught with incomplete tools, steep learning curves and ambiguous ROI.

> **Key takeaway**
>
> Organizations must weigh maturity and market readiness before plunging into new tech. Even the best ideas fail when deployed prematurely.

3. Never finishing the transformation: Lost in the clouds

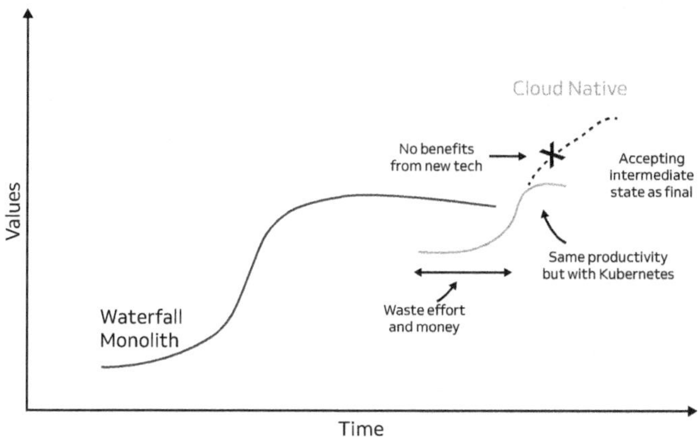

Figure 23: *Never finishing the transformation*

Endless change fatigue

One of the most pervasive traps is *never ending* a Cloud Native transformation. Companies remain in permanent upheaval—constant sprints, tool churn, reorgs—without reaching a stable, efficient baseline. It's like renovating a house forever while living in it: disruptive, expensive and exhausting. This state is the **anti-pattern: *Perpetual Transition (AP03)***.

- *Relevant solution patterns:* Clearly articulate the *Vision First (TF14)* including a target state. Diligently *Measure What Matters (TF36)* to track progress towards completion. Formally apply the *Finish the Transformation (TF41)* pattern by defining exit criteria.

Illusion of progress

Teams may appear busy, but real productivity is elusive. The organization cycles through new features, half-implemented tools and countless stand-ups without anything new to discuss and with little tangible improvement in performance or cost. There's a relentless cycle of:

- *Tool churn:* Adopting the "next hot thing" with no stable maturity.
- *Role confusion:* Repeated reassignments, blurred responsibilities.
- *Never-ending rework:* Each wave of changes disrupts prior progress.

All the while, actual business goals—serving customers, delivering stable solutions—take a back seat.

Defining a target state

To avoid endless transformation, the enterprise must identify a clear target. This includes specifying the stable architecture, standard delivery pipelines and how microservices or platforms are structured. Once 80–90% of systems meet that state, you can declare the transformation "done". Teams can then pivot to a normal optimization and innovation cycle.

> **Key takeaway**
>
> Cloud Native's true power comes from balancing agility with efficiency. A stable, mature state is essential. Ongoing micro-adjustments can continue once the main transformation is declared complete.

4. Treating disruptive change as incremental improvement

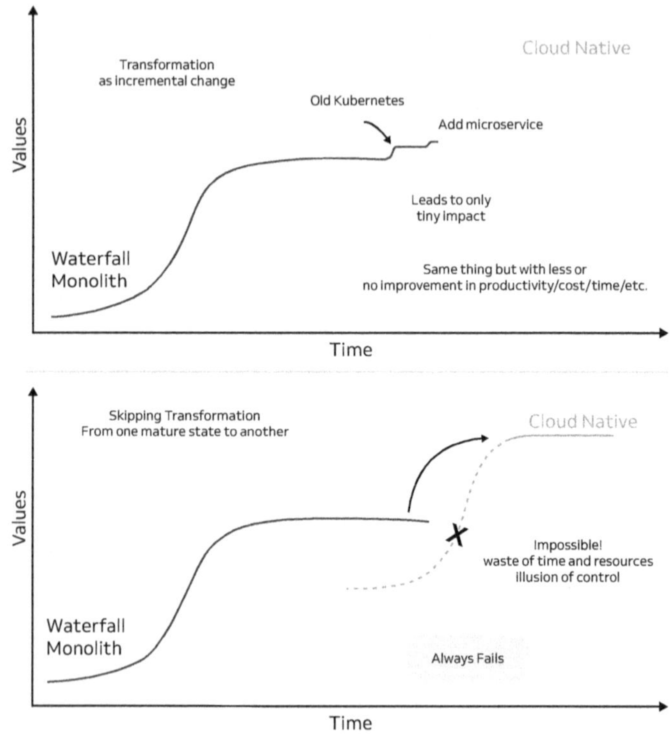

Figure 24: *Treating disruptive change as incremental improvement*

Cloud Native isn't "just another project"

A lethal mistake is viewing Cloud Native as a routine IT upgrade—akin to adopting a new database or code library. In reality, microservices and DevOps break from legacy Waterfall structures. Conway's Law ensures architecture and organizational design are interlinked. In other words, you can't modernize one without reshaping the other.

Treating it otherwise is the **anti-pattern: *Incremental Facade (AP04)***.

- *Relevant solution patterns:* Embracing *Holistic Transformation (TF35)*. Having leadership *Articulate the Vision (TF14)* and provide *Visible Sponsorship (TF11)*. Working to *Cultivate Psychological Safety (TF15)* for new ways of working and aiming to *Foster Learning Organization (TF53)*.

Cargo cult adoptions

This parallels GM's attempt to mimic Toyota's production system by copying superficial tools (Kanban and Andon cords) without embracing the deep cultural shifts. Similarly, some organizations install Kubernetes or microservices but keep top-down project structures, multi-month release cycles or bureaucratic gating. They check a "Cloud Native" box but don't transform.

The result is disillusionment and minimal benefit. This phenomenon is the **anti-pattern: *Cargo Cult Adoption (AP05)***. A cargo cult means mindlessly imitating successful practices without understanding the underlying principles that make them work.

- *Relevant solution patterns:* Embracing *Holistic Transformation (TF35)*. Having leadership *Vision First (TF14)* and providing *Executive Commitment (TF11)*. Working to *Cultivate Psychological Safety (TF15)* for new ways of working and aiming to *Foster Learning Organization (TF53)*.

Culture, processes and technology must evolve in tandem. Cross-functional teams, continuous delivery mindsets and flattened hierarchies are non-negotiable. Just layering containers on to Waterfall processes yields a fragile system.

Key takeaway

Disruptive changes demand disruptive approaches. Half-measures or cargo-cult imitations lead to poor outcomes and wasted effort.

5. The illusion of control and the cost of over-planning

Explorer v taxi driver

Cloud Native transformations are initially voyages into the unknown—akin to an explorer forging new paths. Organizations trying to script every detail upfront (the "taxi driver" approach) inevitably fail, because they don't yet know the terrain. Overly rigid roadmaps lead to missed opportunities and hamper adaptation. This describes the **pitfall: *Illusion of Control (AP06)***.

- *Relevant solution patterns:* Emphasizing *Research Through Action (TF16)*. Ensuring designs deliver *Adaptability over Efficiency (TF17)*. Delivering value iteratively via *Iterative Value Delivery (CN01)* and adopting a *Dynamic Strategy (TF54)*.

A significant challenge for leadership during transformation is managing the organization's expectation for certainty. Stakeholders, accustomed to predictable planning cycles, may demand detailed roadmaps and answers to all foreseeable questions upfront. It falls upon leadership to communicate effectively that in transformative endeavors, particularly those involving disruptive technologies, such comprehensive foresight is often impossible. This communication should frame the embrace of uncertainty not as a lack of preparation, but as a deliberate adoption of agility. Acknowledging the unknowns and committing to an emergent strategy, guided by iterative learning and feedback loops, signals a mature understanding that each organization's journey through the transformation landscape will necessarily differ and require adaptation.

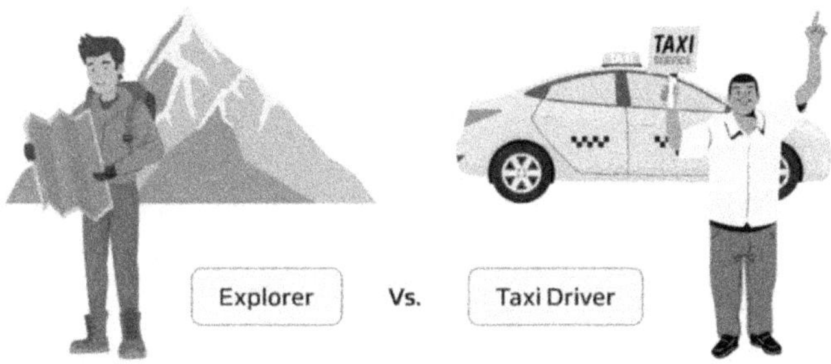

Figure 25: *Explorer v taxi driver*

Emergent strategy

As the transformation matures and best practices solidify, planning can become more structured. But early on, emergent strategy—iterative goal setting, feedback loops, continuous learning—proves far more practical. Leaders must embrace uncertainty. Overcoming the fear of not controlling every variable is essential for success.

Key takeaway

Let teams explore the early transformation phases. Later, a "taxi driver" approach with standardized routes is valuable once you truly know the territory.

6. The shadow IT problem: Fast experiments v company standards

The allure of quick progress

When official processes slow innovation, managers and dev teams often spin up shadow IT—buying cloud resources with personal credit cards or using a free-tier platform. They bypass bureaucracy, move fast and deliver PoCs. At first, these "underground" solutions are cheap, ephemeral and seemingly beneficial.

However, as pilot projects grow, ops teams are forced to support unvetted solutions. Different teams pick different configurations, tooling or even different cloud providers. The result is a sprawling ecosystem of "mini-platforms", each poorly documented and lacking standardization. Overburdened ops or platform teams scramble to maintain them all, leading to chaos. This outcome results from the **anti-pattern: *Unmanaged Shadow IT Proliferation (AP07)***.

- *Relevant solution patterns:* Treating the official offering using *Platform as a Product (TF24)* principles. Providing effective *Enable Self-Service (TF47)* and *Dev Starter Pack (TF26)*. Offering sanctioned ways to experiment via *Reduce Cost of Experimentation (TF03)* and providing a *Sandbox Environment (TF04)*.

Balancing speed and standards

Exploring new tech in the early stages can be invaluable. But once a system edges towards production, the enterprise must unify around stable architecture, security policies and cost controls. The key is to delineate an official path for adopting new tools so shadow IT experiments don't balloon into unmanageable operational nightmares.

One practical mechanism for managing this transition from promising experiment to integrated standard involves establishing clear, pre-agreed KPIs. For instance, defining a specific threshold—such as reaching a certain number of active users (e.g. 10,000), achieving specific stability or performance metrics, or demonstrating quantifiable efficiency gains—can serve as an objective trigger. Once such a threshold is met, the experimental service or tool automatically enters a defined process for formal review. This is followed by integration into the standard platform (if deemed appropriate) and adherence to all relevant company policies regarding security, compliance and operational support. This provides autonomy for initial exploration while ensuring successful innovations are eventually brought into the governed ecosystem.

> **Key takeaway**
>
> Shadow IT can catalyze innovation but quickly becomes a burden if not integrated into a governed, standardized platform once it matures beyond small experiments.

7. Waste and sustainability impact: The environmental cost of inefficiency

Improperly managed Cloud Native can drive up operational costs—and the environmental toll. Quick-scaling microservices or ephemeral clusters are easily spun up but often left idle. While the cloud *can* be more eco-friendly than on-prem hosting, wasteful usage, overprovisioning and indefinite resource sprawl add up. This inefficiency often manifests as the **pitfalls: *Uncontrolled Cloud Costs (AP24)*** and ***Environmental Impact Neglect (AP36)***.

- *Relevant solution patterns:* Implementing practices to *Measure What Matters (TF36)* (FinOps/GreenOps). Fostering *Continuous Optimization (TF42)*. Focusing on *Efficiency over Adaptability (TF43)* in mature stages. Leveraging *Automation Everywhere (TF39)* for resource management.

FinOps and GreenOps

A robust FinOps practice ensures financial accountability for resource usage, while GreenOps focuses on sustainability. Both revolve around monitoring real usage, turning off unneeded resources and designing for minimal overheads. Incorporating these from the start fosters cost savings *and* less environmental impact.

> **Key takeaway**
>
> Cloud Native done well can be both economical and green. But ignoring usage patterns creates cost bloat and harms the planet.

Additional pitfalls to watch out for

Although these are the main pitfalls, this list is far from exhaustive. Here are some other frequent mistakes to be aware of:

- ***Blind Leap (AP30)*** *(lack of research):* Adopting Cloud Native without research leads to ill-fitting tech choices. Failure to apply *Learn and Explore (TF01)* and *Proof of Concept – PoC (TF06)* leads to this outcome.
- ***Post-Transformation Stagnation (AP31):*** Failing to continually optimize allows technical debt to creep back in. Failure to apply *Continuous Optimization (TF42)* and a *Dynamic Strategy (TF54)* can cause this.

- ***Accidental Transformation (AP32):*** An unplanned approach that wastes resources and lacks clear objectives. Signs are a lack of *Vision First (TF14)* and *Business Case (TF09)*.
- ***Grand Canyon Jump (AP09)*** *(skipping Bootstrapping):* Re-platforming everything in one giant leap leads to integration challenges. This can be mitigated by Deliver the MVP *(18)* and *Bridge the Old World (22)*.
- ***Tower of Babel (AP10)*** *(separate independent efforts):* Different teams use different stacks, causing duplication. This is mitigated by the patterns *Vision First (TF14), Executive Commitment (TF11)* and *Reference Architecture (TF27)*.
- ***Premature Scaling (AP11):*** Scaling without well-defined platforms leads to inconsistent processes. This is mitigated by the *Prepare for Scale (TF30)* and *Gradual Onboarding (TF32)* patterns.
- ***Neglecting Legacy Anchor (AP08):*** Never fully decommissioning old systems slows innovation. You can mitigate this with the *Strangle Legacy (TF33)* and *Sunset Gracefully (TF58)* patterns.
- ***Uncontrolled Cloud Costs (AP24):*** Scaling haphazardly skyrockets costs with no optimization. To reduce this risk, use *Measure What Matters (TF36)* and *Continuous Optimization (TF42)*.
- ***Nanoservices Proliferation (AP26)*** *microservice maze:* Over-splitting services makes them too complex to manage. You can tackle this with sound architectural principles (e.g. bounded contexts) and *Reference Architecture (TF27)*.
- ***Conway Conundrum (AP33):*** Ignoring the link between team structure and software architecture. This is mitigated by applying *Reverse Conway*

Maneuver (TF31) and *Establish Team Communication APIs (TF38)*.

- ***Budget Blunder (AP12):*** Using the wrong metrics or success criteria. You can avoid this pitfall with *Measure What Matters (TF36)*.
- ***Cloud Native Skills Gap (AP29):*** Failing to invest in upskilling or recruiting. This can be managed by applying *Finance Topologies (TF10)* correctly.
- ***Security Blind Spot (AP28):*** Rushing to adopt containers without robust security. This is mitigated by the *Foster Learning Organization (TF53)* pattern, as well as training and targeted hiring.
- ***Shiny Object Syndrome (AP34):*** Constantly chasing the latest tool and ignoring fit. Reduce this risk by adopting *Platform as a Product (TF24)*, governance and *Best Tool for the Task (TF21)*.
- **Culture Clash (AP35):** Planting Cloud Native methods in a hierarchical culture. Failure to apply *Holistic Transformation (TF35)* and *Cultivate Psychological Safety (TF15)* are the main causes of this pitfall.

Real-world case studies

Starling Bank: A Cloud Native triumph

Starling Bank built a fully functional Cloud Native platform in about a year. The key to their success was a "You Build It, You Run It" DevOps culture, continuous delivery and microservices (or "miniservices"). The bank's agile leadership allowed them to outmaneuver large incumbents. They intentionally balanced speed with robust design. In practice this looks like a minimal core architecture, chaos engineering to ensure resilience and strong DevOps ownership. This synergy of technology, culture and leadership turned Starling into a FinTech heavyweight.

The high street bank that missed the mark

A large, established UK bank, attempting to replicate Starling Bank's success, launched its own fully Cloud Native digital bank. However, despite significant investment, the project failed and was ultimately shut down, wasting an estimated £30 million. Several key factors contributed to this failure. First, the bank overstaffed the project from the beginning, assembling massive teams without a coherent product direction. This led to confusion and unnecessary complexity. Imposing a rigid, top-down Waterfall management style only compounded their issues. They were left with inflexible plans and timelines that completely ignored the iterative, feedback-driven nature of DevOps. This was a classic example of cargo cult technology adoption. They blindly copied actions without understanding them. This meant they implemented Kubernetes, microservices and other advanced tools while retaining the old bureaucratic processes and infrequent release cycles. Finally, low developer ownership meant engineers felt powerless and disengaged. The bank never cultivated the agile "You Build It, You Run It" mindset essential for success in a Cloud Native environment. The final result was a bloated, underwhelming product with minimal market traction.

Avoiding the common pitfalls

Cloud Native transformations are not simple IT projects. They entail a fundamental re-evaluation of architecture, culture, processes and leadership approaches. The pitfalls described in this chapter reflect deeper organizational dysfunctions rather than mere technical missteps.

Key takeaways

- **Timing matters:** Too late, and you're obsolete. Too early, and you risk immature tech.
- **Commit to the whole:** Disruptive transformations demand leadership commitment, cultural changes and cross-functional collaboration.
- **Define and achieve a target state:** Avoid endless churn by clarifying what "done" looks like.
- **Balance exploration with stabilization:** Start with an explorer's mindset, then shift to structured, repeatable practices.
- **Mind costs and environment:** Cloud *can* be a cost-saver and greener—if you manage resources efficiently.
- **Learn from success and failure:** Starling Bank soared with the right cultural and technical blend. A large high street bank sank because it only mimicked tools, not the underlying ethos.

Ultimately, Cloud Native is a powerful enabler for agility and resilience. Yet, as these pitfalls make clear, it can also devolve into chaos and waste if not approached thoughtfully. By heeding these warnings and tackling both the technical *and* cultural dimensions, organizations can harness Cloud Native's full promise—and avoid paying the steep price of transformation gone awry.

Want to avoid these common and costly pitfalls? Scan the QR code to access our patterns library and learn how our cards workshop can help your team identify and navigate around damaging anti-patterns.

Chapter 8

Sustaining Cloud Native: Culture, Leadership, Finance and the Planet

As Cloud Native projects scale, maintaining agility and preventing fragmentation becomes a critical challenge. Development teams must, therefore, focus on building adaptable systems *and* fostering the creation of stable, reusable components. This demands not just technical skill, but effective innovation management and a strategic approach to platform development. Sustaining success requires embedding *Continuous Optimization (TF42)* and supporting *Nurture Incremental Innovation (TF49)*. We've seen first-hand how seemingly small inefficiencies, when multiplied across a growing organization, can grind progress to a halt.

An IDP, when executed effectively, is far more than a simple toolkit. It represents the operational backbone of a thriving Cloud Native strategy. It's the very mechanism that enables faster, more reliable software delivery while simultaneously reducing the cognitive load on development teams *(Minimize Cognitive Load (TF45))*. As we've established, platform engineering directly addresses fundamental business requirements, such as delighting customers, quickly responding to evolving market conditions and accelerating time to market. This is all achieved by streamlining the development workflow and cultivating a widespread culture of automation *(Automation Everywhere (TF39))*.

From experimentation to standardization: a necessary evolution

Early-stage project development often benefits from a degree of freedom, allowing teams to explore a diverse landscape of tools and technologies. We've seen it work, but only in the short term. However, as projects mature and scale, an unrestrained proliferation of tools inevitably leads to escalating complexity, inconsistencies and a significant burden of technical debt. A disciplined, strategic approach becomes paramount. This necessitates a carefully managed transition from ad hoc solutions to standardized, reusable platform components. This is *not* about stifling innovation; it is about using and directing it effectively. Development teams should retain the freedom to explore, but within clearly defined boundaries and with a transparent understanding of the implications.

The decision to introduce *any* new tool or technology should always be preceded by a rigorous cost-benefit analysis. Does this new tool offer a demonstrably superior solution to a specific problem, compared to the existing, standardized components of the platform? Does its projected benefit outweigh the long-term costs associated with integration, ongoing maintenance and potential security vulnerabilities? Those experimental components that prove genuinely successful and gain widespread adoption should be prioritized for seamless integration into the central platform. This crucial process ensures they become fully supported, first-class citizens of the platform ecosystem, benefiting from its inherent resilience, robust security posture and streamlined maintainability. This integration process helps *Avoid Reinventing the Wheel (TF46)* and solidifies the *Reference Architecture (TF27).*

In such a culture, development teams retain the freedom to experiment with new tools and ideas in their own sandboxes and can even take those ideas to production. However, they must understand that they will be solely responsible for supporting those tools in a production environment. These new ideas can only be scaled to other teams once all central platform requirements are implemented and ownership is accepted by the platform team. This creates a tradeoff.

Teams have the freedom to choose the right tool but must support it themselves, or they can use readily available tools provided by the central platform. This approach allows for freedom while maintaining reasonable standards. In most cases, a single team, recognizing the significant benefits of a tool, introduces it into their environment and develops it to production quality. The tool can then be handed over to the platform team for proper maintenance and support, making it available to the rest of the organization.

The Cloud Native IDP: product thinking for internal success

The most effective IDPs are those that embody the *Platform as a Product (TF24)* pattern, where they are conceived, built and managed as *products*, not as internal projects. This fundamental shift in perspective is crucial. In this model, developers are the platform's valued customers. This means their needs and experiences must be paramount, driving the platform's evolution and roadmap. Embracing a product mindset requires several key practices.

A clearly defined roadmap is essential. This outlines the platform's future trajectory and prioritizes new features based on their anticipated business value and direct feedback gathered from developer users. Continuous feedback loops—incorporating regular surveys, interactive feedback sessions and the meticulous analysis of platform usage data—are critical for understanding developer pain points and identifying areas ripe for improvement. The platform should evolve incrementally, with new features released frequently and subsequently refined based on real-world usage patterns and direct feedback.

A cornerstone of this approach is the concept of the "paved path". The platform should provide pre-approved, thoroughly documented and easy-to-follow workflows for common development tasks. This simplifies processes, ensures consistency across teams and minimizes the potential for errors. This "paved path" approach helps *Minimize Cognitive Load (TF45)* and is a key aspect of effective *Enable Self-Service (TF47)*. It encompasses self-service access to infrastructure resources and automated CI/CD pipelines. Usually this means leveraging the GitOps principles suggesting managing infrastructure and applications declaratively using Git as the single source of truth for automated deployments.

A dedicated platform team is indispensable. This team assumes full ownership of the platform's operational health, ongoing maintenance and continuous evolution. They function as the platform's dedicated product owners, advocating for the needs of the developer community and ensuring the platform remains tightly aligned with the overarching business objectives. This team requires a diverse and specialized skill set, encompassing deep infrastructure expertise, strong software development capabilities and solid product management acumen. It's not just about technical skills. It's about understanding and serving the needs of the internal "customer"—the development teams. This reflects the *Establish Platform Team (TF25)* pattern, which is crucial for managing the platform effectively.

Avoiding common pitfalls: the dual threats of bottlenecks and shadow IT

In numerous organizations we've seen how poorly designed or inadequately managed platforms can rapidly transform into a significant bottleneck. Ironically, this hinders development velocity instead of accelerating it. If the platform team becomes an unavoidable gatekeeper for every minor change, lacking the necessary automation and self-service capabilities, developers will inevitably encounter frustrating delays. This situation creates a powerful incentive for the emergence of shadow IT. Shadow IT introduces a cascade of serious risks, including potential security vulnerabilities, compliance violations and a significant increase in overall operational complexity and technical debt.

To effectively combat the allure of shadow IT, the platform must be inherently responsive, addressing developer needs and requests promptly and efficiently. It must be flexible and provide designated sandboxes and controlled environments that encourage experimentation with new technologies in a safe and managed manner. It must be transparent, offering clear and comprehensive documentation that highlights both the advantages of using the platform and the inherent risks of circumventing it. And, fundamentally, it must be easy and enjoyable to use, with excellent documentation and support.

A frustrating platform *will* be bypassed. Avoiding the *Platform as Bottleneck (AP25)* and *Unmanaged Shadow IT Proliferation (AP07)* anti-patterns requires diligent application of the *Platform as a Product (TF24)* and *Enable Self-Service (TF47)* principles (get help with your platform strategy by contacting the authors: wavesofinnovation@re-cinq.com).

Building a truly effective IDP is not about imposing rigid restrictions or stifling creativity. It's about providing a well-engineered, supportive and empowering environment that enables developers to move quickly, confidently and securely. This process creates a "well-oiled factory" for software delivery. This is an environment where innovation flourishes within a framework of established best practices and operational excellence. The platform is not a static entity. It's a living, evolving product. As a result it requires continuous investment, careful adaptation and an unwavering focus on delivering an exceptional developer experience.

The goal of good platforms is to consolidate all the stable, infrequently changing functionality and systematically improve its quality in terms of non-functional requirements. These include performance, resilience, security, compliance, sustainability, observability, usability and others. The platform's role is to eliminate 80–90% of developers' work on routine tasks, allowing them to obtain that functionality seamlessly and effortlessly.

Today, development teams only need to touch 10–20% of the overall application code to innovate and create new functionality. This is the source of agility. Development teams become ten times more efficient and effective, focusing on actual features and relying on the platform teams for everything else. This also increases the quality and consistency of the platform, and allows for non-linear scaling of innovation without a massive increase in team size. By allowing application teams to *Minimize Surface of Innovation (TF51)*, the platform enables efficient scaling.

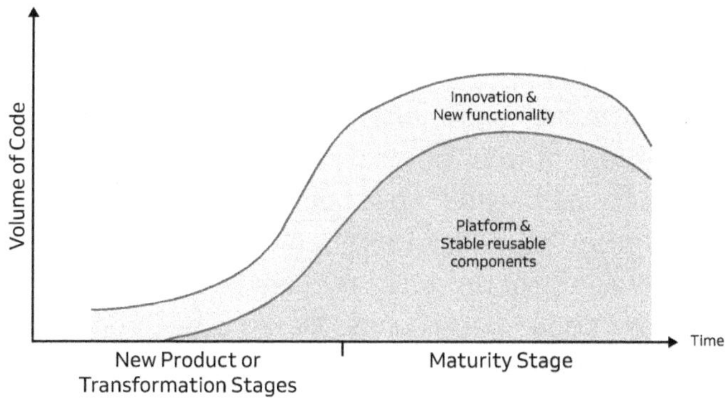

Figure 26: *An effective IDP*

Cultural change

Organizations often realize that culture—the shared attitudes and behaviors of everyone involved—directly shapes their outcomes. In Chapter 5, we highlighted three cultural extremes: an obsession with new features, an obsession with rules and an obsession with quality. Shifting from one culture to another isn't as simple as issuing a memo. It requires consistent actions over time, because organizational culture is the sum of all habits across all people. As Daniel Coyle states in *The Culture Code: The Secrets of Highly Successful Groups*, culture is not something you *are*, it's something you *do*.[13] Shifting towards a culture of quality requires ongoing effort, reflecting *Holistic Transformation (TF35)* principles aimed at becoming a *Foster Learning Organization (TF53)*.

13 Coyle, D. (2018) *The Culture Code: The Secrets of Highly Successful Groups*. Random House.

Old habits die hard

Many cultural change initiatives falter because they rely on old methods to create new mindsets. Leaders might declare they're "Agile" or "Cloud Native", but if they impose those ideas through the same top-down, bureaucratic structures, the outcome is often the same old organization—just running Kubernetes. People cling to familiar routines, resisting changes that seem risky or too big a departure from their norm. It's similar to trying to lose weight. Most people know what to do (eat less, exercise more) but often lack the discipline, especially when the status quo is easier.

The majority wins

Culture is determined by the majority's habits. If you have only a small core of innovators within a large, tradition-bound enterprise, those innovators can feel like they're "fighting windmills". Their small successes rarely spread unless they gain real traction and executive support. Top-down cultural mandates often lead to surface-level compliance rather than genuine transformation. People pretend to adopt new practices while quietly continuing the old.

The key is to grow the new culture in a protected environment, like a small cross-functional team that's shielded from the old processes. This core group can choose its own tools, define fresh ways of working and solidify new habits over three to six months. Carefully select the early adopters—people eager to embrace change. Once they've built momentum and proven success, they gradually onboard other teams. Importantly, the new culture should remain dominant in that separate space, never flooded by a massive influx of legacy thinkers. Only after the new culture is strong and stable can more hesitant groups join.

For example, a previous client (a Danish financial services company) successfully implemented a significant cultural shift by starting with a small, dedicated team. This team pioneered new ways of working and demonstrated success, gradually influencing the broader organization. However, it's crucial that such initiatives have strong executive support to ensure widespread adoption.

With each small win, the core culture expands. By the time you reach a critical mass or "tipping point", the new practices feel normal. Others see tangible successes—faster releases, reduced technical debt, happier developers—and become more receptive to adopting the same methods. This approach contrasts sharply with an "all-at-once" transformation, which typically fails under the weight of inertia and skepticism. Successfully nurturing this shift requires leadership to *Cultivate Psychological Safety (TF15)* for the new ways of working.

Empower, don't mandate

True cultural change focuses on *empowerment*, not mere compliance. Leaders protect the early teams, nurture their experiments and celebrate their wins. They minimize the friction of old processes. Instead of forcing reluctant participants to change immediately, they let motivated teams pave the way, documenting successes that provide a compelling case for broader adoption. This aligns with the principle that lasting change often requires a movement, not just a mandate, as highlighted in several *Harvard Business Review* articles.[14 15]

The key is to shift the center of organizational gravity from the old culture to the new one. Organizations often allow new teams to grow and create new habits, but instead of relying on them to lead the future, managers force these Cloud Native teams to go to production using old processes. They may also put gatekeepers in place who come from the legacy world and want to protect their old ways of working.

You can't overhaul culture by decree. You *must* grow it. Start with a small, enthusiastic team (or teams), give them the freedom to form new habits and ensure they don't get overwhelmed by the old status quo. Over time, as more people join these successful pockets of culture, what began as a tiny pocket of change can spread across the entire organization.

We witnessed this scenario unfold at a major financial institution in the UK. Their newly formed, Cloud Native team, hand-picked by the CTO and operating somewhat

---

14 Kotter, J.P .(1995) "Leading change: Why transformation efforts fail," *Harvard Business Review.* Available at: https://hbr.org/1995/05/leading-change-why-transformation-efforts-fail-2.

15 Soule, S. and Walker, B. (2017) "Changing company culture requires a movement, not a mandate," *Harvard Business Review.* Available at: https://hbr.org/2017/06/changing-company-culture-requires-a-movement-not-a-mandate.

independently in a sandbox environment, built a fully functional platform. They'd cultivated the right culture and produced a genuinely impressive implementation. However, when it came time to deploy to production, they were forced to navigate the *same* approval process used for their 40-year-old Cobol core application. This was a process that, unbelievably, required sign-off from *27* individuals. Needless to say, those deployments never saw the light of day.

Leadership

At its core, leadership shapes every aspect of an organization's success or failure—particularly during a transformation. Even the best technical blueprints or Agile methodologies falter if leaders don't steer the enterprise towards a clear goal. From hiring practices and team structures, to cultural norms and financial decisions, leadership choices permeate every level. Consistent *Executive Sponsorship (TF11)* remains vital even in mature phases.

Organizational v technical leadership

Leadership in a transformation spans both organizational and technical dimensions.

Organizational leaders define the overarching vision and strategy. They decide whether to invest in modern practices, set timelines for change and create an environment that fosters or stifles innovation.

Technical leaders, such as architects or engineering managers, shape the practical roadmap. They choose architectures (monolith v microservices), pick core tools (Kubernetes v other platforms) and ensure the technical health of the organization.

When these two spheres are aligned, transformations progress smoothly. If they diverge—say, those at the top demand Cloud Native while engineering lacks the freedom or expertise to implement it—you get half-baked solutions and wasted effort.

Management styles and the balance of power

Transformations often highlight the management style of an organization. A rigid, top-down approach can impose sweeping changes without input from frontline teams, triggering resentment or "checkbox compliance". Conversely, an entirely bottom-up culture might lack direction, leading to inconsistent decisions and a "hero culture", where a few key individuals shoulder all responsibilities in a patchwork environment. The best models blend both.

In this ideal scenario you have a top-down vision that is articulated via clear goals from senior leaders. These might be goals like delivering features twice as fast or reducing operational costs by 30%. Meanwhile, you have bottom-up execution also taking place. That allows teams to propose *how* to meet those goals, harnessing their first-hand knowledge of current systems. This balance ensures decisions aren't purely theoretical but remain grounded in real capabilities. This requires leadership to effectively

Vision First (TF14) while empowering teams *(Specialized Teams (TF50))*.

Goal setting and accountability

Well-defined goals give focus. They prevent the transformation from drifting into endless tool experimentation. Leaders should keep teams accountable with meaningful metrics—for instance, measuring deployment frequency, mean time to recover or cost per transaction. If these indicators don't improve, leaders step in to remove obstacles or adjust the plan. Equally important is celebrating incremental successes, which signals that progress is real and encourages continued buy-in. This depends on the ability to *Measure What Matters (TF36)* effectively.

Financial and market leadership

At a macro level, leaders decide how to fund the transformation and handle risk. They might allocate special transformation budgets, offer short-term incentives for milestone achievements or pivot their market strategy to leverage new capabilities (e.g. adopting a subscription model instead of traditional licenses). Financial oversight ensures the transformation doesn't become a black hole of spending. Moreover, having market leadership means understanding how modern technology can differentiate the company. Leaders who effectively champion this narrative—internally and externally—bring everyone on board, from developers to investors to customers.

The transformation leader

A dedicated transformation leader typically orchestrates the biggest shifts. This person, often a senior executive or someone with deep organizational clout, must balance the freedom to break old structures with the discipline to avoid anarchy. By knowing when to allow experimentation and when to enforce standards, they prevent "wild west" scenarios that devolve into constant firefighting.

Instead, they strive for a systematic move towards maturity and stability, where the entire organization reaps the benefits of agility without sacrificing reliability. For example, at HolidayCheck, the operations manager championed the initial introduction of containers and later became the transformation champion. In this role, they bridged the gap between technical innovation and organizational change.

Leading a transformation isn't about merely approving a new tool. It demands setting a unified vision, enabling teams to carry it out and ensuring the organization's culture, structure and finances all reinforce that goal. Whether driving major reorganizations, establishing new budgets or championing the next wave of technology, leadership ultimately decides whether a transformation yields real results—or ends as yet another unrealized "big idea".

Budgeting for transformation

Budgeting, or applying appropriate *Finance Topologies (TF10)*, often seems like a routine administrative task. But it can be a powerful strategic lever that shapes how an organization invests in innovation and transformation. The key insight is that budgets don't just track costs; they also influence team structure, incentives and technology choices. By aligning budgets with specific innovation needs, leaders can ensure smoother progress along the Cloud Native journey.

Budgetary decisions directly impact team formation and, consequently, the evolution of their systems. A generous budget might enable rapid expansion, while a constrained one forces lean teams to prioritize ruthlessly. These choices, often made far from the code itself, indirectly dictate architectural outcomes—what gets built, how it's managed and which tools become standard. Therefore, extending Conway's Law, we can see that budgets define organizational structure, which in turn shapes technical architecture. Financial realities, then, are a powerful, often overlooked, influence on technical decisions. *Finance topologies* are, in a very real sense, a reflection of *Team Topologies*.

Budgeting for mature operations

Established, mature operations aim for stability, predictability and efficiency. Rolling budgets tied to revenue allow teams to plan confidently over the long term. This consistency helps them refine processes, minimize costs and stay aligned with well-known business needs. However, a stable budget can become *too* rigid, making it difficult to pivot quickly if the market shifts or new requirements emerge. The advantage—predictability—can become a limitation.

Budgeting for innovation (labs)

Research-oriented labs need a separate, consistent budget that's *not* tied to immediate returns or short-term profits. Operating like a university grant, this funding covers radical exploration. Lab teams must keep experiments cheap, quick and simple, encouraging a lean approach rather than adopting a "throw money at it" mindset. A typical model might allocate 1–5% (depending on the size of the company and the market conditions) of the annual budget to these high-risk, high-reward initiatives. Success is measured in learning and future readiness, not near-term revenue.

Budgeting for transformation

Transformations—like a move to Cloud Native—are inherently uncertain and milestone-driven. Traditional rolling budgets can stifle progress by imposing rigid structures too early or letting failing projects drag on due to sunk costs. Instead, a startup-style approach fits best: staged funding that unlocks more resources once key goals are met. Think seed rounds (PoC), Series A (MVP with real customers and revenue) and Series B (scaling). This keeps the organization accountable—if milestones aren't reached, funds can be redirected. It also recognizes transformations are a long-term investment, where the ROI generally appears *only after* scaling and early maturity.

The CFO's role and avoiding misalignment

The CFO is crucial in orchestrating these budget strategies. They must grasp the unique tempo of labs,

Agile transformations and lean operations to ensure each initiative gets the right type of funding. Otherwise, misaligned budgets—like dumping massive funds into a transformation too early or starving a labs team of funding—undermine the entire effort. Tying budgets to clear goals, using appropriate success metrics and avoiding the "sunk cost fallacy" help maintain focus. Failure to align funding models correctly leads to the *Budget Blunder (AP12)* pitfall.

A topological approach to budgeting recognizes that each realm—mature, innovation and transformation—demands its own financial model. By treating budgeting as a strategic tool rather than a rote exercise, organizations can better harness innovation, adapt to change and drive operational excellence.

Sustainability

It's often easy to dismiss sustainability as an abstract or altruistic concern, especially in a market economy driven primarily by profit. Yet sustainability metrics can serve as a surprisingly effective proxy for operational efficiency. By closely monitoring how resources—compute, energy, hardware—are consumed, organizations can spot and reduce inefficiencies that might otherwise remain hidden behind discounts or complex pricing deals. Using sustainability metrics can offer a clearer way to *Measure What Matters (TF36)* regarding efficiency.

Beyond cost alone

Many see cost as the simplest measure of resource use. But cost is subject to distortions: vendors offer short-term discounts in exchange for multi-year contracts, making it appear that an over-allocated environment is "affordable". In reality, the organization might be paying for resources it doesn't need and locking itself into a rigid commitment. So, while cost does matter, it can be misleading if looked at in isolation.

Sustainability as a clarity lens

Unlike cost, sustainability metrics—like carbon footprint, energy usage or resource wastage—are harder to mask with deals or vendor lock-ins (but still possible with carbon offsets and other greenwashing techniques). If development teams frequently spin up large VMs that remain idle, your carbon emissions (and electricity bill) reveal the waste, even if a cloud vendor discount has made the monthly invoice look tolerable.

Moreover, sustainability metrics can galvanize teams. Engineers often get excited about optimizing performance and resource use when they align with both financial *and* environmental goals. Publicly tracking a service's carbon impact can spark friendly competition and creative problem-solving that might not occur if the only objective were to shave a few dollars off the cloud bill.

Aligning efficiency and environmental responsibility

Adopting autoscaling, ephemeral environments and serverless architectures can simultaneously reduce costs *and* carbon footprint. These strategies allocate resources only when they're needed, shrinking periods of idle capacity. Similarly, thoughtful scheduling—such as shutting down non-critical environments during off-hours—also cuts both costs and emissions, contributing to both *Continuous Optimization (TF42)* and *Efficiency over Adaptability (TF43)*.

Driving operational excellence

In essence, sustainability metrics help expose operational flaws that a discounted vendor contract could obscure. For instance:

- *Overprovisioning:* When teams assume "we're paying for it anyway", they might allocate ten CPUs for a service that only needs two. Sustainability metrics highlight the discrepancy, driving a conversation about right-sizing.
- *Resource lifecycle:* Outdated servers or unneeded VMs might languish indefinitely. Carbon usage data can highlight these zombie workloads, prompting timely deprovisioning or archiving.
- *Cultural impact:* Regularly discussing sustainability fosters a mindset of continuous improvement and meticulous resource management, similar to a DevOps culture that tracks deployment frequency or time to recovery. This fosters *Continuous*

Optimization (TF42) and supports *Data-Driven Decision Making (TF37)*.

Therefore, embracing sustainability practices isn't just a green initiative. It's a tangible way to refine operations and expose hidden inefficiencies. By using sustainability metrics alongside cost, organizations gain a more honest view of resource consumption, encouraging responsible architecture choices and longer-term thinking. While pure profit motives typically guide market decisions, sustainability provides a sharper lens that reveals where the system can be truly optimized—benefiting both the bottom line and the planet.

Key takeaways

- **Platform as a product:** Treat your internal developer platform as a product with developers as its customers. This mindset fosters a focus on usability, maintainability and continuous improvement, driving developer productivity and system consistency.
- **Strategic standardization:** Balance initial experimentation with a strategic move towards standardization as projects mature. This prevents fragmentation, reduces technical debt and ensures long-term maintainability.
- **Empowered teams, aligned leadership:** A successful Cloud Native transformation requires both empowered, autonomous teams, *and* aligned organizational and technical leadership providing a

clear strategic direction. This combines top-down vision with bottom-up expertise.

- **Finance shapes architecture:** Budgetary decisions profoundly influence team structures and, consequently, the technical architecture of systems. Aligning financial strategies (finance topologies) with development needs is crucial.
- **Continuous, sustainable improvement:** Foster a culture of continuous improvement and optimization, focusing on both speed and efficiency. View sustainability metrics as a tool for identifying and reducing operational waste, leading to long-term cost savings and resilience. Embrace iteration and adaptation as ongoing practices.

Sustaining a mature platform is an ongoing effort. Scan the QR code to visit the Waves of Innovation hub for a wealth of resources, including podcast episodes and articles on fostering the right culture and strategies for long-term success.

Chapter 9

AI Native—Charting the Uncharted Waters of the Next Transformation

Now our journey through IT innovation moves beyond the shores of Cloud Native, shaped by containers, microservices, dynamic scheduling and DevOps culture. Here we must turn our gaze to the next significant surge forming on the horizon: **AI Native** (check your readiness with the AI Native Assessment: https://re-cinq.com/ai-native-assessment).

This represents more than incremental improvement or just adding smart features; it heralds a potential **Intelligence Revolution**, focused on augmenting and automating *cognitive* power, thinking, deciding and creating—much as the Industrial Revolution augmented *muscle* power with machine power. If the engine was the key invention then, AI models fuelled by vast data are the "cognitive engines" now.

Looking even further, merging this AI "brain power" with advanced robotics' "muscle power" could ignite a **Cyber-Physical Revolution**, enabling intelligent machines to act autonomously in our physical world.

In essence, **AI Native refers to systems and architectures designed fundamentally around AI/ML capabilities, where autonomy is not an add-on but a core component (Model-Centric Architecture (AIN01)) driving behavior, learning and adaptation (Self-Evolving Systems (AIN25)), deeply integrated with data.** This shift requires careful navigation, as misunderstandings and potential pitfalls are common, echoing mistakes made in previous transformations.

To truly grasp the potential scale of the AI Native transformation, it helps to compare it more deeply with the Industrial Revolution. The Industrial Revolution was fundamentally about **augmenting and replacing muscle power**. Humans and animals have limits to their physical strength and endurance. The invention of the engine, whether steam or internal combustion, broke through those limits, allowing us to build machines like tractors, cranes and assembly lines that perform physical work far beyond biological capacity. This revolutionized agriculture, manufacturing and transportation.

The AI Native wave, or **Intelligence Revolution**, targets a different domain: **cognitive powe**r. Just as muscles have limits, so do human brains in terms of processing speed, memory recall, pattern recognition in massive datasets and sustained focus on complex calculations. AI models, like LLMs or neural networks, are the "engines" of this new revolution. They process information and perform cognitive tasks (analyzing data, making predictions, generating text or images, understanding language) at a scale and speed vastly exceeding human capability. This shift is already transforming fields driven by information, like science, finance and media.

Looking further ahead, we can envisage the **Cyber-Physical Revolution**. This involves creating autonomous systems and machines that can both *think* and *act* in the physical world.

Examples range from self-driving cars navigating complex streets and smart industrial robots adapting tasks on a factory floor, to service robots delivering goods or assisting in healthcare, and exploration robots making decisions on distant planets. This fusion promises to automate not just specific tasks, but entire complex processes involving both cognitive and physical work. It will fundamentally alter industries reliant on physical interaction and complex decision-making.

Understanding this progression, from muscle power augmentation to cognitive power scaling, and potentially to integrated autonomous systems, helps frame the profound nature of the AI Native transformation we are just beginning to navigate.

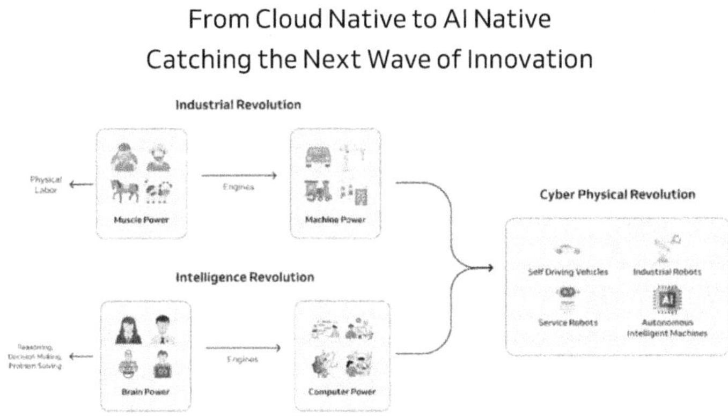

Figure 27: *From Industrial Revolution to Cyber-Physical Revolution*

However, approaching this new AI Native wave requires caution and a clear head. Much is still unknown. The technology is evolving rapidly, the best ways to use it are still being discovered and its full impact is hard to predict. A recent conversation with a company interested in AI highlights the common misunderstandings and potential pitfalls.

This company's leaders wanted to use AI in their call center, primarily to cut costs. Their plan was simple: buy an AI chatbot that a vendor promised would magically solve their problems and save money by replacing many human agents. This immediately sounded familiar, echoing mistakes made in the early Cloud Native days. Many companies then thought buying tools like Docker or Kubernetes was enough. They saw containers as just "faster virtual machines", missing the deeper changes needed.

As we've already explored, Cloud Native success required a big transformation. It involved changing system design to microservices, adopting new management tools, forming new kinds of teams (like those in *Team Topologies*) and fundamentally altering how developers worked (You Build It, You Run It). It was about changing architecture, organization, processes and culture together.

When we looked closer at the call center plan, it became clear the AI chatbot couldn't simply replace people. It could handle basic questions, but complex ones required very specific instructions or "prompts". A direct complex question often led to an error or hallucination. The human agents would need to break down problems, guide the agent and check its answers. This meant their jobs weren't disappearing. They were changing into prompt engineers, needing entirely new skills like *Prompt Engineering (AIN13)*.

The real issue wasn't just buying a tool. It was the need for upskilling and reskilling the workforce, and redesigning the whole customer service process. This mistake, treating a huge potential change like a simple upgrade, is a common trap, as we saw earlier with the *Incremental Facade (AP04)* anti-pattern. Furthermore, focusing only on cost savings (the *AI for Cost Reduction Only (AP43)* anti-pattern) ignored the possibility that higher efficiency might lead to *more* calls (Jevons Paradox). It also missed the bigger opportunity: using AI to help the human agents become *more* productive, handle harder problems and provide better service (*Human-AI Collaboration Design (AIN19)*). Achieving that requires a real transformation, affecting technology, people and how work gets done. That's the true challenge and promise of the AI Native wave.

Understanding AI Native: core ideas and why it's a big change

What makes AI Native a truly transformational change, potentially on a par with the move from Waterfall to Cloud Native? The key reason lies in its impact on architecture—the fundamental design of our software systems. The Cloud Native shift was driven by moving from single, large programs (monoliths) to collections of small, independent services (microservices) that could scale easily. This architectural change, as explained by Conway's Law (systems reflect team communication), forced companies to also change their organization, team structures (*Team Topologies*), processes (CI/CD, DevOps) and culture.

AI Native seems poised to drive similarly deep architectural changes, leading inevitably to related shifts in organization and process. While the final picture is still emerging, we can identify some early core ideas that seem central to AI Native, much like containers, microservices and dynamic scheduling were for Cloud Native.

First is the idea of **built-in AI and intelligence everywhere**. In AI Native systems, AI isn't an added feature. It's a fundamental part of the design from the beginning *(Model-Centric Architecture (AIN01))*. Autonomy is spread throughout the system, influencing how components behave and interact *(Agentic Architecture (AIN04))*. This also demands that it is trustworthy, reliable, secure, fair and understandable *(Explainability-by-Design (XAI) (AIN07), Ethical AI Review Integration (AIN18)* and *AI Trust Framework Integration (AIN21))*.

Second is a strong **focus on data**. AI systems run on data. Therefore, AI Native architectures treat high-quality, well-managed data as the most crucial element *(Data Fabric for AI (AI02))*. Ensuring data quality, consistency and fairness is essential for good AI performance. This requires excellent data management practices and avoiding the *Data Governance Failure (AP31)* pitfall. This requires *Data-as-a-Product (DaaP) (AIN20)* and consideration of ethical aspects by *Bias Mitigation Pipelines (AIN22)*.

Third is the principle of **always learning and adapting**. Unlike traditional software that only changes when updated, AI Native systems are designed to learn continuously from new data and user feedback. They can adapt and improve over time (Continuous Runtime Adaptation—*Self-Evolving Systems (AIN25)*).

Fourth, AI Native involves **AI automating itself**. This means AI isn't just part of the software. It's also used to manage the ML lifecycle through *MLOps Lifecycle Management (AIM12)* and *AI Tooling for SDLC Automation (AIN11)*. In doing so, it applies DevOps principles like automation, CI/CD and monitoring specifically to the unique needs of building, deploying and operating ML models. AI also enhances IT operations via **AIOps** (AI for IT Operations), enabling more intelligent monitoring and automation—ML Pipeline Orchestration (MLOps), Intelligent Operations (AIOps Enhanced).

Fifth, we see the potential **emergence of smart agents working together**. Future systems might consist of many AI "agents". In other words, different services that can sense, reason, act and collaborate to achieve complex goals autonomously *(Agentic Architecture (AIN04))*. Agentic AI is set to revolutionize business operations by integrating with existing company tools, thereby enhancing current technology investments rather than demanding complete overhauls. This approach can lessen the need for extensive staff training on entirely new software and reduce investment in redundant new tooling. However, companies will still need to invest in upskilling employees to effectively collaborate with and manage these AI agents, alongside strategic spending on the agentic AI technology itself and its integration (*Human-AI Collaboration Design (AIN19)*).

Let's explore two potentially foundational AI Native architectural patterns in more detail: **data-centric architecture** and **agentic architecture**.

A **data-centric architecture** represents a fundamental shift in perspective compared to typical Cloud Native approaches. In many microservice designs, data persistence is often secondary, managed within the boundaries of each service ("database per service"). The primary focus is on the service's logic and API. Data-centric architecture flips this. Data itself, particularly the high-quality, well-governed data needed to train and run AI models, becomes the central, enduring asset (*Data Fabric for AI (AIN02)* and *Data-as-a-Product (DaaP) (AIN20)*). Imagine an e-commerce platform: instead of focusing solely on the "order service" or "inventory service", a data-centric approach prioritizes creating a highly reliable, consistent and accessible "product data fabric" or "customer interaction stream".

Applications and AI models are then designed to consume from and contribute to this core data asset, adhering to its predefined structure and quality standards. The emphasis moves from manipulating data to fit application logic, towards building applications and AI models that leverage a fundamentally sound data ecosystem. This requires rigorous **systematic data quality focus** and robust **data provenance and lineage** tracking.

Consider the AI-powered gym example. This isn't just a gym with an added app. It embodies ***Model-Centric Architecture (AIN01)***. Sensors tracking user movements feed data directly into AI models analyzing form and performance in real time. The core value proposition *is* the AI—the personalized workout adjustments, the real-time virtual coaching feedback. The architecture is designed *around* this AI capability, likely involving edge computing for low latency, specialized models for movement analysis and a data architecture (*Data Fabric for AI (AIN02)*) optimized for continuous streams of sensor data and personalized user profiles. Removing the AI wouldn't just degrade a feature. It would remove the fundamental reason for the product's existence.

Building upon the capabilities of agentic AI, *Agentic Architecture (AIN04)* proposes a different way of structuring system components altogether. Instead of services defined purely by function (e.g. "payment service"), an agentic system might be composed of autonomous AI agents defined by their goals and capabilities (e.g. a "booking agent", a "payment negotiation agent" or a "fraud detection agent"). These agents could potentially perceive their environment (e.g. monitor incoming requests or market data), reason about actions, make plans and use tools (like calling external APIs, accessing internal databases or interfacing with existing enterprise software) to achieve their objectives. They may even collaborate with other agents.

Imagine a travel booking system where a "trip planning agent" interacts with "flight booking", "hotel booking" and "budget monitoring" agents to fulfill a complex user request. This contrasts sharply with microservices that typically execute predefined logic via fixed APIs. Agentic systems introduce possibilities for more dynamic, adaptive and goal-oriented *Self-Evolving Systems (AIN25)* system behavior. However, they also bring significant challenges in orchestration, governance and ensuring predictable outcomes.

Picture a complex logistics operation managed via an *Agentic Architecture (AIN04)*. A "dispatch agent" receives an urgent delivery request. It queries a "traffic prediction agent" and multiple "vehicle status agents" (representing autonomous delivery drones or trucks). Based on the predicted traffic, vehicle availability, fuel/charge levels and delivery priority, the dispatch agent negotiates task allocation with the vehicle status agents. A "route optimization agent" calculates the best path, considering real-time updates from the traffic prediction agent. A "customer notification agent" proactively informs the recipient of the estimated arrival time. Each agent acts semi-autonomously towards its goal, collaborating through potentially standardized protocols to fulfill the overarching delivery task efficiently and adaptively.

These principles suggest that AI Native systems might often use *Event-Driven AI Orchestration (AIN03)* designs to react quickly to changing information. They will rely on new kinds of databases optimized for AI, particularly vector databases (*Vector-First Knowledge Management (AIN06)*). These are designed specifically to store and efficiently query the high-dimensional vector embeddings that AI models use to represent meaning, enabling tasks like semantic search and retrieval crucial for applications like *Retrieval-Augmented Generation (RAG) (AIN09)*.

What's more, they must be built with *Explainability-by-Design (XAI) (AIN07)*, so humans can understand their decisions. This proactive approach is essential for tackling the "black box" problem (AI opacity) common in complex models, which otherwise undermines trust and complicates debugging. The transparency and inspectability offered by open-source models, including access to their weights, can significantly strengthen these XAI initiatives. In doing so, this makes it easier to build understandable and reliable systems. These fundamental architectural shifts will undoubtedly require new ways of organizing teams and work, driven once again by Conway's Law, which suggests that an organization's structure will eventually mirror the architecture of the system it designs.

The uncharted territory: we're just starting

It's vital to repeat: we are at the very beginning of the AI Native journey (subscribe to the Waves of Innovation newsletter to follow the developments as they happen: https://re-cinq.com/newsletter). Think about Cloud Native in 2014. Docker was new, Kubernetes was just appearing and the rich ecosystem of tools, platforms and best practices we have today didn't exist. Early adopters faced major hurdles. They were taking risks with unproven technology (the *Bleeding Edge Gamble (AP02)*). Tools were often unstable, clear guidance was lacking and finding people with the right skills was tough.

We face a similar situation now with AI Native. The potential seems huge, but we lack:

- *Mature technology:* Many AI tools and platforms are changing incredibly fast and may lack the stability and security needed for critical business systems (*AI Technological Immaturity (AP40)* pitfall).
- *Clear best practices:* We're still figuring out the best ways to design, build, test and operate AI Native systems reliably and ethically.
- *Needed skills:* There's a shortage of experts in AI (real ones, not the ones you find on LinkedIn), ML, MLOps, prompt engineering and applying AI ethically (AI skills gap).
- *Trust and understanding:* It's often hard to understand exactly *why* an AI makes a certain decision (the AI opacity or *"Black Box" Challenge (AP38) pitfall)*, making it difficult to fully trust or fix these systems.
- *Ethical frameworks:* We are still developing the rules and guidelines needed to ensure AI is used fairly and responsibly (*Ethical Misalignment & Amplified Bias (AP37)* pitfall).

The emerging "AI stack", while often built upon Cloud Native infrastructure, incorporates distinct layers specifically designed for AI workloads. The **compute layer** provides the raw power. It is increasingly reliant not just on standard CPUs but heavily reliant on specialized accelerators like GPUs and TPUs (Tensor Processing Units) optimized for the parallel computations common in AI model training and inference (*Specialized Compute Orchestration (AIN05)*). Access is often via scalable cloud services, but edge computing resources are also vital for real-time AI applications needing low latency. High-bandwidth, low-latency networking is crucial for connecting these resources, especially for distributed training (*Hybrid Edge-Cloud AI (AIN08)*).

The **data layer** is arguably the most critical and complex layer specific to AI. It handles everything from ingesting diverse data types (structured, unstructured) to storage (using traditional databases, data lakes or warehouses) and extensive preprocessing (cleaning, transforming, labeling). A key component here is the rise of **vector databases** (*Vector-First Knowledge Management (AIN06)*). These are specifically designed to handle the high-dimensional vector embeddings that AI models use to represent semantic meaning, enabling powerful similarity searches crucial for applications like recommendation systems and *Retrieval-Augmented Generation (RAG) (AIN09)*. Robust data security and governance are managed within this layer.

Above this sits the **machine learning (ML) frameworks layer**, providing the libraries and tools developers use to actually build models (e.g. TensorFlow, PyTorch, scikit-learn). The *MLOps Lifecycle Management (AIN12)* layer then provides the operational backbone, adapting DevOps principles to manage the unique lifecycle of models.

Its activities include tracking experiments, versioning models, automating training and deployment pipelines, and continuously monitoring performance and drift in production (*MLOps Lifecycle Management (AIN12)*). Finally, as AI systems become more complex, an *Event-Driven AI Orchestration (AIN03)* may be needed to manage workflows involving multiple interacting AI models or agents, handling dependencies, data flow and integration with external tools or APIs. This stack highlights the added complexity AI introduces beyond typical Cloud Native infrastructure management, particularly around data handling, specialized compute and model lifecycle automation.

Cloud Native practices matured over years as companies experimented, failed, learned and shared their knowledge. AI Native will likely follow the same path. The best practices will emerge from real-world experience. This means we need to embrace learning and experimentation—or a "build to learn" mindset.

This early stage also means our current ways of working might need to change. Methods like Agile, Scrum and Kanban helped manage software projects effectively in the Cloud Native world. Frameworks like *Team Topologies* provided useful models for organizing teams. But AI introduces such fundamental changes, especially the "time reversal" we'll discuss shortly, which means these methods might not be enough. We will likely need new methodologies specifically designed for developing software with AI.

Just as Agile emerged to address Waterfall's shortcomings, a successor framework might be needed for the AI Native era. Similarly, new organizational models and an evolution of *Team Topologies* will likely be needed to effectively structure human-AI collaboration. Expecting today's methods to work perfectly for tomorrow's AI-driven development is likely another form of the *Incremental Facade (AP04)* mistake.

The time reversal: when thinking takes longer than building

A key reason new methods are needed is the "time reversal" caused by AI. For decades, building software involved relatively quick planning followed by long, slow execution (coding, testing, deploying). Waterfall tried to perfect the plan upfront. Agile broke execution into smaller, manageable chunks. But in both cases, human *building* time was the main constraint.

AI Native flips this. AI can perform much of the building work—coding, testing, deploying—at incredible speeds, potentially reducing tasks that took weeks down to hours (*AI Tooling for SDLC Automation (AIN11)* and *AI-Generated Test Case Development (AIN16)*). When execution becomes lightning fast, the bottleneck shifts. The part that now takes the most human time and focus is the *thinking* work. In other words, deciding what to build, setting clear goals and constraints, ensuring ethical guidelines are met, guiding the AI effectively, observing the results and validating that the output is correct, safe and truly meets the need.

This "time reversal" has huge implications:

- *Humans guide, AI builds:* People focus less on writing every line of code and more on strategy, defining requirements (*Intent-Driven Development (IDD) (AIN10)*), overseeing the AI (*Human-in-the-Loop Validation (AIN14)*) and ensuring quality and ethical outcomes (*Human-AI Collaboration Design (AIN19)*).
- *Faster idea testing:* The ability to quickly turn ideas into working prototypes allows for much faster experimentation and learning. The cost of experimentation plummets (*AI-Driven Prototyping (AIN15)*).
- *New workflows needed:* Methods based on long building cycles, like two-week sprints, make less sense when AI builds in a day. We need new ways to structure the "thinking" work in very short, rapid cycles. Traditional project management frameworks like Scrum, with fixed-length sprints, were built around managing the *human execution bottleneck*. AI Native shifts the bottleneck dramatically towards *human guidance, validation and strategic intent*, demanding entirely different cadences and collaborative models.
- *Clear instructions are crucial:* Since AI does what you ask, giving clear, precise instructions (prompts) becomes a vital skill (*Prompt Engineering (AIN13)*). Checking the results carefully is just as important. Poor prompting leads to poor results requiring *Human-in-the-Loop Validation (AIN14)*.

This is like the Industrial Revolution freeing people from physical farm labor to focus on design, management and innovation. AI Native potentially frees people from routine coding and debugging to focus on the more strategic and creative aspects of software creation. The main job shifts from building to guiding.

Role of humans in the world of Cyber-Physical Revolution

As AI takes over more routine cognitive and potentially physical tasks, what becomes of the human role? The "time reversal" suggests a shift from *doing* to *guiding*, but the picture is more nuanced. Rather than widespread obsolescence, we can anticipate a transformation of human work. The focus will be on areas where human intelligence, creativity and values remain unique and essential. Based on current trends, several key human roles seem likely to become even *more* critical in an AI Native future:

- **Creators and innovators:** Humans will continue to be the source of truly novel ideas. Designing the next generation of AI algorithms, inventing new robotic forms and envisioning entirely new applications for these technologies relies on human creativity and curiosity, which AI currently cannot replicate.
- **Strategists and decision-makers:** Setting the overall direction, defining ethical boundaries, establishing policies for AI use and making high-stakes strategic decisions will remain firmly in the human domain. AI can provide analysis, but it lacks the moral reasoning, cultural context and

accountability needed for complex societal or business choices.

- **Supervisors and collaborators:** Humans will work *alongside* AI and robotic systems, monitoring their performance, ensuring safety, handling unexpected situations or edge cases where AI falters and providing the judgment needed to keep systems aligned with real-world goals. Think of doctors working with robotic surgical assistants or technicians maintaining autonomous systems.
- **Cultural and emotional contributors:** Activities demanding empathy, interpersonal connection, cultural understanding and emotional intelligence—such as therapy, teaching complex social skills, creating deeply resonant art or providing nuanced customer care—remain uniquely human strengths.
- **Explorers and pioneers:** Humans will continue to push boundaries, whether in scientific research, space exploration or developing new markets. AI and robotics will be powerful tools in these endeavors, but humans will provide the vision, set ambitious goals and interpret discoveries within the context of human experience.
- **Advocates and ethicists:** As AI becomes more powerful, ensuring it is used responsibly, fairly and safely becomes paramount. Humans will be essential as advocates for equitable policies, ethicists debating complex moral dilemmas (like autonomous weapons) and leaders addressing the societal impacts of automation, such as job displacement.

Of course, this transition brings challenges, notably the potential displacement of routine jobs and the critical need for widespread **upskilling and reskilling** to prepare the workforce for these new roles. Addressing the economic shifts and ensuring humans find purpose beyond traditional work will require careful societal planning. Ultimately, the AI Native future likely involves humans orchestrating, innovating and providing the moral compass for increasingly capable intelligent systems.

The Dunbar challenge and AI's potential impact

AI might also help us overcome a basic human limitation often related to the Dunbar number. This idea suggests people can only effectively manage a limited number of complex relationships or items, maybe around 150. In software, this could explain why systems with too many microservices become incredibly complex to manage, even with Cloud Native tools. Keeping track of all the interactions pushes our mental limits (*Nanoservice Proliferation (AP26)*). We need good platforms (*Platform as a Product (TF24)*) and clear rules (*Reference Architecture (TF27)*) just to cope. Our brains limit how much complexity we can handle and how fast we can react.

AI systems don't have these biological limits. An AI could potentially track millions of components and interactions simultaneously. It processes information vastly faster than humans. This leads to intriguing questions:

- *Can AI manage more complexity?* Could AI tools allow us to build and run systems with far more

interacting parts (services or agents) than is feasible today?
- *Will monoliths return?* Or could AI make large, single programs (monoliths) practical again by helping us understand, test and modify them safely?
- *Will new architectures emerge?* Perhaps AI enables entirely new software structures, like collaborating smart agents (*Agentic Architecture (AIN04)*) or self-adapting systems (*Self-Evolving Systems (AIN25)*)?

We don't have answers yet. But AI clearly challenges the human-based limits that influence our current software designs. Future AI Native architectures might be structured very differently.

Peeking over the horizon: a guess at the mature AI Native landscape

Predicting the future is difficult, especially with fast-moving technology. What follows is therefore presented as an educated guess—a speculative picture of how things *might* look when AI Native evolves. This is based on current trends and understanding, not a guaranteed forecast.

In architecture, we might see highly dynamic systems where AI agents form and reform connections as needed, orchestrated by a central AI (*Event-Driven AI Orchestration (AIN03)*). Data might flow through shared *Data Fabric for AI (AIN02)* using advanced *Vector-First Knowledge Management (AIN06)*, rather than being locked in service silos. *Explainability-by-Design (XAI) (AIN07)* could be built into communication protocols for real-time transparency and safety (*AI Trust Framework Integration (AIN21)*). Infrastructure (*Specialized Compute Orchestration (AIN05)* and *AI Tooling for SDLC Automation (AIN11)*) could optimize itself based on predicted workloads and energy costs, managed by enhanced AIOps. Agentic architectures might use standard protocols for complex collaboration.

Furthermore, AI might help overcome inherent human cognitive limitations, such as the Dunbar number suggesting limits on managing complexity (a challenge sometimes seen with microservice proliferation). **Could AI, unburdened by biological constraints, effectively manage systems with millions of interacting components or agents, enabling architectures far more intricate than feasible today (potentially revisiting monolithic structures with AI-aided comprehension or vastly scaling agentic architectures)?** This capability could fundamentally alter architectural assumptions influenced by human cognitive scale.

Regarding teams, the static Scrum or stream-aligned structures might evolve. Perhaps we'll see small, highly skilled "guidance pods" or small ad hoc teams focused on defining intent and validating AI outputs (*Intent-Driven Development (IDD) (AIN10), Human-in-the-Loop Validation (AIN14)* and *Human-AI Collaboration Design (AIN19)*). These pods might be assembled dynamically by AI based on the task at hand, following the task-based assembly concept and requiring people to be flexible across roles. Specialized roles focusing on AI ethics, security and validation could become standard (*Ethical AI Review Integration (AIN18)* and *Adversarial Defense Mechanisms (AIN23)*).

Internal platform teams would manage the core AI infrastructure and MLOps pipelines, providing the intelligent foundation (*MLOps Lifecycle Management (AIN12)*). This suggests the need for new organizational frameworks, a kind of "Team Topologies for AI" (*Agile AI Teams (AIN17)* and *Agentic DevOps Teams (AIN24)*).

Processes could become a continuous flow driven by *Intent-Driven Development (IDD) (AIN10)*. Humans define goals and constraints; AI executes in rapid micro-cycles. Validation (*Human-in-the-Loop Validation (AIN14)*) would be ongoing, not a separate phase. The MLOps lifecycle, from data prep (*MLOps Lifecycle Management (AIN12)*) to monitoring (continuous model monitoring and drift detection), could become highly automated.

Imagine a product manager wanting a new feature for their e-commerce site: displaying personalized product recommendations on the user's homepage. Instead of writing detailed specification documents for developers, they engage in *Intent-Driven Development (IDD) (AIN10)*. They might prompt an AI development assistant: "Generate a recommendation module for the homepage. Use collaborative filtering based on purchase history and browse data. Ensure recommendations exclude out-of-stock items and prioritize items with high ratings. Design the UI as a horizontally scrolling carousel with product images and prices. Generate Python code using our standard Flask framework and integrate with the existing user profile API."

The AI generates the initial code, tests and UI components. The product manager and a developer then review the output *(Human-in-the-Loop Validation (AIN14))*, perhaps providing feedback like: "Refine the algorithm to also consider items recently viewed but not purchased", iterating quickly until the feature meets their refined intent.

Delivery might become largely autonomous. AI could manage releases (*AI Tooling for SDLC Automation (AIN11)*), optimizing strategies like canary deployments and ensuring zero-downtime becomes the norm. Systems might even perform self-healing code fixes in production based on AI monitoring (*AI Tooling for SDLC Automation (AIN11)*), blurring the lines between deployment and operation (*Self-Evolving Systems (AIN25)*).

Observability would need to go beyond logs, metrics and traces. It would likely incorporate deep XAI dashboards to show *why* AI decisions were made. Automated root cause analysis would become standard. Monitoring for fairness, bias and ethical compliance (*Ethical AI Review Integration (AIN18)* and *Bias Mitigation Pipelines (AIN22)*) would be critical. AI might even predict failures before they happen.

Planning would shift entirely to the strategic level. Humans would focus on defining high-level intent, setting business and ethical constraints (cost, performance, fairness rules) and deciding on validation criteria. AI might assist with feasibility checks and resource estimation based on this high-level guidance.

The act of coding itself would transform. Prompt engineering becomes the primary human interface for creation. AI handles most code generation, re-factoring and optimization. Human coding might focus on truly novel algorithms or critical oversight functions. Debugging becomes about understanding AI failures (prompt issues? data bias? model limits?) using XAI tools.

The culture would likely emphasize extreme adaptability, continuous learning *(Foster Learning Organization (TF53))*, ethical responsibility *(Ethical AI Review Integration (AIN18))*, radical transparency enabled by *Explainability-by-Design (XAI) (AIN07)* and effective *Human-AI Collaboration Design (AIN19)*. The focus shifts from valuing manual effort to valuing effective guidance and strategic direction. In other words, steer, don't sweat.

Finally, a new methodology seems necessary. Something beyond Agile/Scrum is needed to structure work around intent definition, micro-cycle iteration, continuous validation and AI-mediated coordination, reflecting the fundamental "time reversal" AI introduces.

Again, this is just one possible picture of the future, a guess based on extending current trajectories. The reality will likely be shaped by unforeseen innovations and practical challenges.

Practical implementation: embracing transformation the AI Native way

Knowing AI Native is a major transformation demanding architectural, organizational and cultural shifts, how should companies approach it practically? Learning from Cloud Native's journey provides a valuable guide. First of all, you need a clear goal and a specific use case you want to address, otherwise the initiative falls short and lives in isolation. If you have identified the use case and the goal, a deliberate, phased approach focused on learning and adaptation is far more likely to succeed than a rushed, technology-focused effort (contact the authors to discuss your specific AI Native use case: wavesofinnovation@re-cinq.com).

The journey starts not with replacing systems but with establishing continuous pioneering. This means setting up a dedicated AI lab or *Skunk Works (TF02)* team, protected from day-to-day pressures. Their job is to *Learn and Explore (TF01)* AI tools, run small experiments in *Sandbox Environments (TF04)* to *Reduce the Cost of Experimentation (TF03)*, test risky ideas early (*Test Hard Things First (TF05)*) and build tangible *PoCs (TF06)* for the agreed use case.

If the exploration and learning lead to a positive result, the *Business Case (TF09)* can be clearly demonstrated and further investment requires appropriate, patient funding (*Finance Topologies (TF10)*). Alongside this technical exploration starts the crucial work of upskilling and reskilling the broader workforce in basic AI literacy and data concepts. Address the inevitable AI skills gap proactively.

Once leadership provides *Visible Sponsorship (TF11)* and appoints a *Transformation Champion (TF12)*, the Bootstrapping & Bridge-Building phase begins. *Form the Core Team (TF13)*—a dedicated, cross-functional group—to build the initial minimum viable AI product or platform component (*Thinnest Viable Platform (TF19), Deliver the*

MVP (TF18)). Ensure this team has *Psychological Safety (TF15)* to experiment and learn. Critically, they must Bridge the Old World (TF22) by creating integration points with existing legacy systems, enabling a gradual transition rather than an isolated experiment. Funding should be released in stages based on achieving milestones (*Staged Funding (TF23)*). Remember to prioritize *Adaptability over Efficiency (TF17)* in these early stages.

Scaling requires careful management. Avoid *Premature Scaling (AP11)* by *Gradual Onboarding (TF32)* of additional teams on to the new AI capabilities. This gradual approach can be applied for new tooling and services. It is equally valid when agentic AI is introduced to automate specific manual steps within existing business processes, where the core software tools used by staff remain unchanged. An example of such a scenario would be where agents might automate data entry between existing applications, generate standard reports from familiar systems or handle routine communications based on established templates. The transformation, while less disruptive as the tooling and ways of working mostly remains, still demands focused attention:

- *Staff training and preview:* This will require targeted staff training. The focus isn't on learning entirely new software. Instead it's on helping employees understand the agent's specific function, its impact on their individual workflow and the broader process, how to initiate or interact with the agent (if applicable), the new process flow and how to manage exceptions or situations the agent isn't designed to handle, including support channels. A "short preview" or pilot phase with the affected users is crucial for gathering feedback, building confidence and refining the agent before a full "going live".

- *Process adjustment:* While tools may not change, the process does. Manual steps are eliminated, potentially altering task sequences, timelines and role responsibilities. These process adjustments need to be clearly documented and communicated.
- *Cultural adaptation:* Employees need to adapt to working alongside AI agents, trusting their outputs and understanding their role as collaborators that free them up for higher-value tasks. This is a key component of cultural change.

This targeted approach to automation within existing toolsets, and indeed any AI Native component introduction, underscores that a *Holistic Transformation (TF35)* must address technology (the new agent or component), process (the modified workflow) and culture (the human-AI interaction and broader organizational shifts) changes concurrently. As these new AI Native components become stable, systematically decommission replaced legacy systems (*Strangle Legacy (TF33), Sunset Gracefully (TF58)*) while keeping essential older systems stable (*Protect the Core (TF34)*).

As adoption grows, mature the internal AI platform (*Platform as a Product (TF24), Establish Platform Team (TF25)*) focusing on platform user self-service *(Enable Self-Service (TF47))* and providing clear guidelines (*Reference Architectures (TF27), Internal Service Catalog (TF28)*).

Mature the MLOps practices by aiming for *Automation Everywhere (TF39)*.

Once the major transition stabilises, shift your focus to *Continuous Optimization (TF42)* (efficiency, cost, performance) and *Nurture Incremental Innovation (TF49)* by leveraging the new AI capabilities. *Foster a Learning Organization (TF53)* culture. Finally, formally *Finish the Transformation's (TF41)* disruptive phase to avoid *Perpetual Transition (AP03)*, then pivot to ongoing improvement while restarting the Pioneering mode for the *next* wave.

Addressing the unique challenges of AI Native transformation

While the transformation process shares similarities with Cloud Native, AI Native introduces unique and often more complex challenges that must be addressed proactively:

- *Ethics and bias:* Ensuring fairness and avoiding harmful bias (*Ethical Misalignment (AP37)*) is paramount. This requires robust *Bias Mitigation Pipelines (AIN22)*, *Ethical AI Review Integration (AIN18)*, adherence to *Trustworthy AI Frameworks (AIN21)* and fostering an ethical AI culture.
- *Data governance:* The critical dependence on data makes robust governance, quality control and provenance tracking essential but difficult (*Data Governance Failure (AP41)* mitigated by *Data Fabric for AI (AIN02)* and *Data-as-a-Product (DaaP) (AIN20)*).

- The "black box" nature of many AI models (*"Black Box" Challenge (AP38)*) hinders trust and makes debugging difficult, necessitating the integration of *Explainability-by-Design (XAI) (AIN07)*. Open-source models that provide access to their architecture and weights significantly aid explainability and build trust by enabling greater transparency, scrutiny and the application of diverse XAI techniques. While not a complete solution to the complexities of AI, this openness is a crucial step towards more understandable and reliable systems.
- *Security vulnerabilities:* AI systems are susceptible to new threats like adversarial attacks, requiring specific *Adversarial Defense Mechanisms (AIN23)* and a secure AI supply chain approach.
- *Technological volatility:* The rapid pace of AI innovation increases the risk of choosing immature or quickly outdated technologies (*AI Technological Immaturity (AP40)*).
- *Sustainability:* The high energy demands of AI necessitate a focus on efficiency and sustainable practices.
- *Human factors:* Overcoming cultural resistance, managing the AI skills gap, ensuring clear communication and avoiding automation complacency (where humans blindly trust AI) are critical organizational hurdles. The risk of *Naive Prompt Engineering (AP42)* leading to poor results is also significant.

Among the most critical challenges facing AI Native adoption is the complex issue of ethics, particularly algorithmic bias. The *Ethical Misalignment & Amplified Bias (AP37)* pitfall is a serious risk because AI systems, unlike traditional software, learn from data. If the data reflects historical inequities or societal biases (e.g. biased hiring data, skewed loan application data), the AI model will likely learn and potentially amplify these biases, leading to unfair or discriminatory outcomes.

An AI used for screening job applications might unfairly disadvantage candidates from certain backgrounds, or a facial recognition system might perform poorly on specific demographic groups, simply because the training data was not representative.

Addressing this requires more than just good intentions. It demands proactive, technical and procedural interventions woven throughout the development lifecycle. This is where patterns like *Bias Mitigation Pipelines (AIN22)* become essential. These involve integrating specific techniques to detect, measure and counteract bias. Strategies can include *pre-processing* (cleaning or re-sampling training data to improve fairness), *in-processing* (adjusting the model's learning algorithm itself to penalize biased outcomes) and *post-processing* (modifying the model's predictions after they are made to improve fairness). Ensuring diverse and representative datasets is fundamental. Techniques like careful feature engineering (choosing what data the AI sees), data augmentation (creating more balanced data), adversarial debiasing (training AI to be resistant to bias) and rigorous testing against multiple fairness metrics (like demographic parity or equalized odds) are part of the toolkit.

Furthermore, establishing an ethical AI culture with *Ethical AI Review Integration (AIN18)* is paramount. This involves training teams to recognize potential biases, using human-centered design approaches with diverse user input and implementing robust governance processes.

Emerging regulations, such as the EU AI Act, are also setting stricter requirements for fairness, transparency and accountability in high-risk AI systems. Adhering to *Trustworthy AI Frameworks (AIN21)* like those from the National Institute of Standards and Technology (NIST) or International Organization for Standardization (ISO) provides guidance for building systems that are not only powerful but also responsible. Ignoring these ethical dimensions doesn't just risk societal harm. It risks building systems that are unreliable, non-compliant and ultimately damaging to user trust and business reputation.

Successfully navigating these requires embedding patterns like *AI Trust Framework Integration (AIN21), Bias Mitigation Pipelines (AIN22)*, privacy-preserving AI techniques and *Human-in-the-Loop Validation (AIN14)* into the strategy from the very beginning.

The imperative of learning and experimentation: preparing for serendipity

Given the vast potential coupled with significant uncertainty, the most effective strategy for organizations today is one rooted in continuous learning, deliberate experimentation and proactive preparation. Passively waiting (*Strategic Inertia (AP01)*) is not a viable option.

Continuous pioneering remains the cornerstone. This means investing now in dedicated teams (*Skunk Works (TF02)*) tasked with exploring AI (*Learn and Explore (TF01)*). These teams can run controlled experiments (*PoCs – Validate Viability (TF06)*), making it cheaper and safer to try new things (*Reduce Cost of Experimentation (TF03), Sandbox Environments (TF04)*), actively upskilling the workforce and grappling with the ethical dimensions.

Lasting organizational change isn't achieved through sudden mandates. It's built incrementally. Consistent investment in these pioneering activities develops crucial "organizational muscle memory". Small groups learn, adapt and gradually diffuse knowledge and new practices. When AI Native technologies reach a critical maturity point or a key market opportunity emerges, an organization that has been actively learning and preparing will be far better positioned—culturally and technically—to respond effectively. It avoids the paralysis or chaotic reaction of being caught unprepared.

Deciding when to scale AI Native initiatives remains a delicate balancing act. Committing too early risks the *Bleeding Edge Gamble (AP02)*; waiting too long risks competitive irrelevance (*Strategic Inertia (AP01)*). The optimal path involves staying informed through continuous exploration, prioritizing initial projects based on clear strategic value and always starting small, iterating and learning from each step.

Therefore, the immediate focus should not be on deploying perfect, fully mature AI Native systems, which are likely still years away. Instead, the focus must be on the *process* of discovery and preparation. Learn the tools. Understand the techniques. Define best practices through practical experience. Experiment with business cases. Build internal knowledge and experience. This proactive engagement cultivates readiness. It fosters the conditions for serendipity—being prepared to recognize and seize opportunity when it unexpectedly arises.

By embracing learning and experimentation today, organizations position themselves not just to react to the AI Native wave, but to potentially shape its direction and ride it to future success.

Envisioning AI Native proficiency: the full Innovation Waves Maturity Matrix

As we venture into the AI Native paradigm—a shift promising to embed intelligence at the very core of our systems and processes—it's crucial to have a comprehensive framework for understanding what this new state of maturity entails. The journey from traditional, Waterfall-centric operations to a thriving Cloud Native ecosystem was complex. The path to AI Native proficiency will be even more so.

The key lesson from the Cloud Native transformation was the need for holistic development. Simply layering new tools on to old processes resulted in friction and failed expectations. True mastery requires concurrent advancement in technology, culture and process. This principle applies with even greater force to the AI Native wave. Adopting AI tools without fundamentally re-engineering how an organization operates will lead to "AI-washing" rather than genuine transformation—a classic *Incremental Facade (AP04)* anti-pattern where disruptive change is treated as a mere add-on.

To help visualize this profound evolution, the Innovation Waves Maturity Matrix has been expanded to define the characteristics of an organization that has achieved AI Native proficiency.

Maturity Category	Legacy: Waterfall	Current: Cloud Native	Next: AI Native
Culture & Leadership	Functional silos; command-and-control.	Cross-functional teams; DevOps culture.	AI-first mindset; human-AI teaming.
Product & Experience	Feature-focused; generic UX.	Data-informed stratgey; API-driven services.	AI at the product core; predictive and adaptive UX.
Development & Delivery	Manual processes; periodic, risky releases.	Automated CI/CD; rapid, iterative delivery.	AI-assisted SDLC; intent-driven development.
Architecture & Design	Monolithic applications; technology sprawl.	Microservices and containers; designed for scale.	Agentic architecture; decentralized intelligence.
Platform & Operations	Reactive monitoring; manual interventions.	infrastructure-as-Code; proactive self-services.	Predictive AIOps; self-adapting infrastructure.
Data & Intelligence	Siloed data; used for historical reports.	Centralized data lakes; foundational analytics.	Real-time data fabric; AI-triggered actions.
Trust & Security	Perimeter security; late-stage manual testing.	DevSecOps practices; Zero Trust models.	Predictive, AI-driven security; explainable AI (XAI)
Governance & Compliance	Manual governance, reactive compliance checks.	Policy-as-code; continous compliance.	Automated AI ethics; proactive risk management.
Sustainability	Basic carbon accounting; manual efficiency.	Cloud-optimized resource usage; green IT policies.	AI-optimized emissions; "Green AI" principles.

Figure 28: *Innovation Waves Maturity Matrix*

The AI Native stage: a new apex of maturity

The "Next: AI Native" column in the matrix represents a state where AI is not an auxiliary function but the central nervous system of digital products and operations. This stage is defined by the following characteristics across key domains:

- **Culture and leadership:** The paradigm shifts to an "AI-first mindset" where "human-AI teaming" is the default mode of operation, moving beyond the DevOps culture of Cloud Native.
- **Product and experience:** Strategy is no longer just data-informed but has AI at the product core. This enables a "predictive and adaptive UX" that anticipates user needs rather than just responding to them.
- **Development and delivery:** The process evolves from the automated CI/CD of Cloud Native to an "AI-assisted SDLC". This is characterized by "intent-driven development", where humans define goals and AI handles much of the implementation.
- **Architecture and design:** The shift is from microservices to "agentic architecture" and "decentralized intelligence", where autonomous AI components collaborate to achieve goals.
- **Platform and operations:** Operations become predictive rather than just proactive. "Predictive AIOps" and "self-adapting infrastructure" anticipate needs and automatically adjust resources.
- **Data and intelligence:** Data moves from centralized data lakes to a "real-time data fabric". Instead of

foundational analytics, the focus is on "AI-triggered actions" based on live data streams.
- **Trust and security:** Security evolves from proactive DevSecOps to "predictive, AI-driven security". A core component is "explainable AI (XAI)" to ensure trust in automated decisions.
- **Governance and compliance:** Manual or policy-as-code compliance is superseded by "automated AI ethics" and "proactive risk management", where AI itself helps govern its use.
- **Sustainability:** The focus shifts from cloud-optimized resource usage to "AI-optimized emissions" and the application of "green AI principles" to design more efficient models from the start.

Achieving this AI Native stage requires that all of these dimensions advance cohesively. An organization cannot, for example, deploy a sophisticated agentic architecture if its data is still siloed or its culture resists human-AI collaboration. The journey demands the same holistic commitment and balanced progress that characterized successful Cloud Native transformations. It needs to be guided by a clear vision of what this new state of maturity looks like.

AI Native patterns (speculative)

If your organization identifies with these patterns, it likely signifies significant progress towards the future of the AI Native paradigm. However, it's important to note that these patterns do not yet constitute fully tested and defined ecosystems, and should still be considered largely speculative and in an intermediate stage of development.

AIN01 – Model-Centric Architecture: Design systems with AI model as central decision-making component.

AIN02 – Data Fabric for AI: Unify data infrastructure for AI; automate ingestion and governance.

AIN03 – Event-Driven AI Orchestration: Trigger AI actions via asynchronous events for real-time responsiveness.

AIN04 – Agentic Architecture: Structure systems as autonomous, goal-driven AI agents performing tasks.

AIN05 – Specialized Compute Orchestration: Optimize AI hardware usage with domain-specific accelerators (GPUs, TPUs).

AIN06 – Vector-First Knowledge Management: Store and query embeddings in vector databases for semantic search.

AIN07 – Explainability-by-Design (XAI): Embed interpretability tools from outset for transparent AI decisions.

AIN08 – Hybrid Edge-Cloud AI: Distribute AI tasks between edge devices and cloud for balance.

AIN09 – Retrieval-Augmented Generation (RAG): Enhance generative AI with external knowledge retrieval for factual grounding.

AIN10 – Intent-Driven Development (IDD): Define system behavior via high-level intents; AI generates code.

AIN11 – AI Tooling for SDLC Automation: Use AI tools to automate tasks in software development.

AIN12 – MLOps Lifecycle Management: Apply DevOps principles to entire machine learning model lifecycle.

AIN13 – Prompt Engineering: Skillfully craft prompts to guide generative AI system outputs.

AIN14 – Human-in-the-Loop Validation: Integrate human expert review for critical AI outputs.

AIN15 – AI-Driven Prototyping: Use AI tools to rapidly create functional mockups/prototypes.

AIN16 – AI-Generated Test Case Development: Employ AI to automatically generate comprehensive software test cases.

AIN17 – Agile AI Teams: Adapt Agile methods for AI's iterative and experimental nature.

AIN18 – Ethical AI Review Integration: Integrate formal ethical reviews into AI system development lifecycle.

AIN19 – Human-AI Collaboration Design: Intentionally design workflows for symbiotic human-AI task completion.

AIN20 – Data-as-a-Product (DaaP): Manage key datasets as discoverable, reliable, reusable products.

AIN21 – AI Trust Framework Integration: Adopt external standards (NIST, ISO) for trustworthy AI development.

AIN22 – Bias Mitigation Pipelines: Implement pipeline stages to detect, measure and reduce AI bias.

AIN23 – Adversarial Defense Mechanisms: Incorporate defenses to protect AI systems from manipulative attacks.

AIN24 – Agentic DevOps Teams: Form specialized DevOps teams to support agentic AI architectures.

AIN25 – Self-Evolving Systems: Self-evolving systems learn continuously from new data and user feedback, adapting and improving over time.

Of course, AI Native will not be the last wave of innovation we experience, but we don't yet have an understanding of what the waves that will build behind AI Native will look like as we write this. This is why our ability to transform is the most critical and enduring capability we can develop.

Using the full matrix to chart your AI Native journey

This comprehensive matrix serves as a vital tool for organizations aspiring to catch the AI Native wave. It allows you to:

1. **Benchmark your current state holistically:** Assess where your organization stands, not just in its AI capabilities, but across all interconnected dimensions, from Cloud Native proficiency onwards.

2. **Define a coherent AI Native vision:** Understand what "good" looks like in an AI Native context across these ten dimensions, helping to create a more complete and integrated strategy.

3. **Identify critical gaps and priorities:** Highlight the specific areas that will require the most significant development and investment to move towards AI Nativity.

4. **Facilitate strategic dialogue:** Provide a shared language and framework for leaders, technologists and business units to discuss the implications and requirements of becoming AI Native.

5. **Guide iterative transformation:** Just as with Cloud Native, the journey to AI Native will be iterative. The matrix can help track progress and ensure that advancement remains balanced across the crucial dimensions, preventing the kind of "spikes" that hinder true transformation.

As we delve further into the specifics of the AI Native landscape and how to navigate its emergence, this matrix will serve as a valuable reference, helping to frame the challenges and opportunities that lie ahead. It underscores that consistent, holistic progress across all facets of the organization is the key to successfully riding each new wave of innovation.

Connecting back to transformation modes: the AI Native journey

As we contemplate the journey towards AI Native, it's useful to frame it within the **six modes of operation**—Pioneering, Bootstrapping & Bridge-Building, Scaling, Optimizing, Innovating and Retiring—that characterize major technological transformations (as discussed in Part II). It is highly likely that organizations successfully navigating the AI Native wave will need to traverse these same modes once again, applying hard-won lessons from their Cloud Native experiences while adapting to the unique demands of AI.

Currently, for most organizations, AI Native resides firmly in the **Pioneering** mode. The focus must be on exploration, learning, experimentation (PoCs), understanding feasibility and identifying potential value (*Learn and Explore (TF01), Proof of Concept – PoC (TF06)*). Rushing prematurely into large-scale implementation (**Scaling**) without robust foundations risks repeating the *Premature Scaling (AP11)* pitfalls encountered by some during the Cloud Native transition, but potentially with higher stakes given AI's complexities.

The **Bootstrapping & Bridge-Building** phase for AI Native will involve establishing foundational data infrastructure, core MLOps capabilities (*MLOps Lifecycle Management (AIN12)*), initial governance frameworks (*AI Trust Framework Integration (AIN21)*) and creating those first connections (*Bridge the Old World (TF22)*) between emerging AI systems and existing business processes or legacy data sources.

As specific AI Native solutions mature, organizations will enter the **Scaling** and **Optimizing** modes, focusing on wider adoption, establishing internal platforms (*Platform as a Product (TF24)* for AI), standardizing practices, managing costs (including significant compute costs), ensuring reliability and potentially retiring older, less intelligent systems (*Strangle Legacy (TF33)*). The **Innovating** mode will involve leveraging the mature AI Native capabilities for continuous improvement and generating novel features or insights.

Understanding that AI Native adoption is another transformational journey through these familiar modes helps set realistic expectations. It highlights the need for patience, iterative progress and strategic management. The goal now is not immediate, widespread AI Native deployment, but rather mastering the **Pioneering** mode effectively to build the knowledge, skills and readiness required to successfully navigate the subsequent stages when the technology and business cases fully align. Lessons from the Cloud Native transformation provide a valuable map, but charting the specific course for AI Native requires ongoing exploration and adaptation.

Key takeaways

- **AI Native requires true transformation:** AI Native is the next major wave after Cloud Native, demanding fundamental changes in architecture, organization, skills and culture—not just adding AI tools.
- **Architecture drives organizational change:** Like previous transformations, the shift towards

new AI-centric and data-centric architectures will necessitate corresponding changes in team structures and processes (Conway's Law).

- **Human role shifts to guidance:** AI drastically speeds up execution ("time reversal"), shifting human focus from manual implementation to defining intent, guiding AI (e.g. via prompt engineering) and validating outcomes ethically and functionally.
- **Early days demand new approaches:** We are in the nascent stages of AI Native (similar to Cloud Native circa 2014). Established methodologies (Agile/Scrum) and team structures (*Team Topologies*) will likely need significant adaptation or replacement.
- **Unique challenges must be addressed:** Successfully navigating AI Native requires proactively tackling distinct challenges related to data quality/bias, AI security, model explainability/trust, ethical governance and significant workforce upskilling.
- **Continuous pioneering is crucial:** Given the uncertainty, ongoing exploration, experimentation through PoCs and building internal knowledge are essential now to prepare the organization to recognize and seize AI Native opportunities later.

The AI Native wave is building. Scan the QR code to take our AI Native Assessment to see where you stand, and subscribe to our newsletter to follow the development of this new ecosystem with us.

Chapter 10

Case Studies

Case study: Kärcher's waves of innovation

A blueprint for transformation fuelled by the German principle of Nachdruck

A strategic analysis of Kärcher's waves of innovation with Leonhard Kerscher, Vice President of IT & Digital Transformation, and Benjamin Hermann, CEO of Zoi.

Introduction: the pattern of demolition

This is not a story about migrating to the cloud. It is a strategic blueprint for corporate reinvention. It's a lesson in how a global manufacturing company, famous for its world-class products, confronted the digital anarchy festering within its own walls and chose not to renovate, but to demolish.

The core of this blueprint is a German principle with no easy English equivalent: Nachdruck. It means relentless, insistent pressure. It is the strategic application of force to make change non-negotiable by making the past impossible to return to. This document deconstructs how Kärcher weaponized this principle to eliminate its technical debt, rewire its corporate DNA and build a repeatable engine for innovation. For any leader who feels their organization is being held hostage by its own legacy, [16] this is your playbook.

Part 1: Confronting the debt of success

The situation: An empire of anarchy

To understand Kärcher's revolution, you must first picture the crisis its own success had created. By 2023, the family-owned company had grown into a €3.294 billion global powerhouse with over 16,000 employees and 86% of its sales coming from outside Germany, but its IT was a different story. The landscape was a textbook case of historical growth: a fragmented confederation of digital fiefdoms.

"The environment was a patchwork of on-premises systems with limited global standards," admits Leonhard Kerscher. Each of the 82 countries Kärcher operates in had its "local heroes" solving local problems with limited business value. This created a chaotic and incompatible

16 ***AP08 - Neglecting the Legacy Anchor:*** Failing to manage/decommission legacy systems hinders transformation progress.

application landscape that actively sabotaged global initiatives and led to *Unmanaged Shadow IT Proliferation*.[17] "We had every file-sharing tool imaginable—Dropbox, Sharefile, OneDrive—each with a passionate local champion," Kerscher explains. This digital anarchy was a direct betrayal of the Kärcher brand, which stood for precision, power and reliability.

The simmering crisis first boiled over in their e-commerce operations. The first attempt at a global rollout was a "stark wake-up call". Running online stores from a German data center resulted in high latency and poor performance for international customers, especially those in places like Australia. The IT department, drowning in a "huge backlog of IT demands", was seen as a bottleneck. The symptom was a slow website. The disease was systemic fragmentation.

The journey began not with a grand, top-down mandate, but with a series of pioneering experiments driven by a small, determined group, a classic Pioneering mode. As early as 2012, to solve the pressing e-commerce issues, the team experimented with Amazon's content delivery network (CDN). The effect was an immediate and dramatic "wow moment" that served as a crucial *Proof of Concept*,[18] proving the value of the cloud in a tangible way. A year later, they built their "Kärcher Fleet" IoT solution from

17 ***AP07 - Unmanaged Shadow IT Proliferation:*** Uncontrolled independent IT solutions create chaos, risk and costs.

18 ***TF06 - Proof of Concept - PoC:*** Execute focused PoCs to validate or refute new concepts.

scratch on AWS, another successful "lighthouse project" that demonstrated the power of building innovative solutions directly in the cloud. [19]

These early successes were a bottom-up movement, born from necessity. But it was a challenging time, filled with skepticism. "We had plenty of people who made fun of us," Benjamin Hermann remembers, "because they thought it was a really stupid idea to do something in the cloud at that time." Resistance wasn't just internal. As late as 2018, application manufacturers were still insisting their software couldn't run in the cloud. Kerscher's team simply tried it themselves. "Never trust someone who's telling you it's not working," he advises. "We just installed it, and it was running."

Blueprint for leaders

1. **Conduct a brand-IT audit:** Map your internal technological capabilities directly against your public brand promises. A slow e-commerce site for a company known for power and efficiency is a critical disconnect. Use these contradictions as political capital.

2. **Identify your "local heroes":** Every fragmented organization has them—well-intentioned local managers who "solve" problems with unauthorized tools. Recognize that these heroes are often

19 ***TF16 – Research Through Action:*** Build MVP and bridges to uncover real-world challenges.

gatekeepers of complexity and a primary source of technical debt and security risks.[20]

3. **Don't waste a good failure:** When a public-facing system fails, resist the urge to simply patch it.[21] Frame it as irrefutable evidence that the entire underlying system is broken and requires fundamental, not incremental, change.

Part 2: The catalyst as a tool

The situation: A deadline as a gift

This state of managed decline was shattered in 2019. The catalyst arrived not as a strategic vision, but as an existential threat: their colocation data center provider was closing its facility. Kärcher had just seven months to migrate over 100 non-SAP applications and nearly 200 servers. A conventional organization would see this as a crisis. Kärcher's leadership recognized it as a gift.

The seven-month deadline was not a constraint; it was a tool that eliminated the possibility of endless debate and political maneuvering. It forced a single, binary choice that demanded *Executive Commitment*.[22] "We had a choice,"

20 ***AP07 - Unmanaged Shadow IT Proliferation:*** Uncontrolled independent IT solutions create chaos, risk and costs.

21 ***AP04 - Incremental Facade:*** Treating disruptive change as mere tool upgrades fails transformation.

22 ***TF11 - Executive Commitment:*** Secure active, visible executive backing for transformation priority.

Kerscher recalls: "find another data center and repeat the past, or seize the moment to make a revolutionary leap."

They chose to leap, shifting their strategy from "Cloud First", which they had adopted in 2016, to, effectively, "Cloud Only". They rejected the safe, simple "lift-and-shift" migration. Instead, with Zoi, a subsidiary Kärcher established to act as an Agile technology spearhead, they mandated a "great cleansing". This structure was a critical strategic move, a perfect *Skunk Works Team*[23] that allowed Kärcher to attract Cloud Native talent that prefers a startup culture, moving at a speed that would have been impossible within the main organization.

The mandate was to reinstall nearly every application, including their CRM system which moved to Azure (Dynamics 365), on a fresh, Cloud Native stack, using PaaS services wherever possible to create the *Thinnest Viable Platform.*[24] This painful but clarifying process forced a complete inventory of their digital assets. The results were stunning. "We found around 20 server systems where no one even knew what they were for anymore," Kerscher says. "We found test systems for applications that had been decommissioned years ago." This clutter wasn't migrated; it was simply cut away—a perfect example of

23 ***TF02 – Skunk Works Team:*** Small, autonomous team experiments rapidly, insulated from standard processes.

24 ***TF19 – Thinnest Viable Platform:*** Strictly prioritize MVP scope, deferring non-essential features.

applying the *Strangle Legacy*[25] and *Sunset Gracefully*[26] patterns.

Blueprint for leaders

1. **Reframe threats as mandates:** When facing an external shock—like a vendor closing or a new regulation—frame it internally, not as a problem to be managed, but as an unmissable opportunity to execute a change that was previously considered "too difficult".

2. **Mandate a "cleansing" with every migration:** Make it a non-negotiable policy that any large-scale migration must include a full audit and a "cleansing" phase. Build the *Business Case*[27] around the long-term value of eliminating technical debt and simplifying security.

3. **Choose strategic pain:** When presented with an easy path that repeats the past (lift-and-shift) and a hard path that builds the future (re-platform), have the courage to choose the hard path.

---

25 ***TF33 - Strangle Legacy:*** Systematically decommission legacy components, redirecting to new equivalents.

26 ***TF58 - Sunset Gracefully:*** Execute planned shutdown of obsolete systems, managing data.

27 ***TF09 - Business Case:*** Articulate rationale, benefits, costs and risks for initiatives.

Communicate[28] why short-term pain is a necessary investment for long-term gain.

Part 3: The Nachdruck pattern

The situation: The application of force

Nachdruck is not about motivation; it's about systematically removing the option of failure. It requires leaders to be persistent and forceful, making decisions that render it organizationally impossible to revert to old behaviors. It creates a vacuum that can only be filled by the new way of working, avoiding the trap of a *Perpetual Transition.*[29] This act of controlled demolition was the physical manifestation of Nachdruck. The philosophy is brutally effective. "The strategy only works when the old process is dead," Kerscher states. A fallback isn't a safety net. It's a guarantee of failure.

This pattern has two core components:

First, you must burn the boats. This was crystallized during a critical, late-night phone call. Just weeks before signing a multi-year outsourcing contract that would have cemented the old way of working for years, Kerscher called Hermann. "I called Benjamin and told him we shouldn't do it the same way, and he agreed fast. And then we changed

28 ***TF07 - Demo Your Ideas:*** Communicate progress engagingly to build understanding and support.

29 ***AP03 - Perpetual Transition:*** Endless churn of tools/priorities prevents stable new baseline.

our minds," he recalls. The call was not a debate; it was a pact to reverse course, reject the safe path and commit to the harder, cleansing reinstallation precisely because it would kill the old way for good.

Second, speed must be leveraged strategically. This was evident when it came time to migrate their massive SAP landscape. This was the crown jewel, the most complex part of their IT, which they had pragmatically decided to tackle only after building a solid cloud foundation. The internal plan was the usual, rather conservative 18 months from previous migrations. Hermann's team at Zoi challenged them, claiming it could be done in 12. By getting the board to agree to migrate even during their high season, a period normally considered sacred, they finished in one year, proving that most timelines are padded with institutional fear, not technical constraints. As Hermann notes, aggressive timelines starve institutional resistance.

Blueprint for leaders

1. **Execute a decommissioning plan:** For any new initiative, create a public, aggressive and irreversible decommissioning plan for the legacy system it replaces. Link executive bonuses and team success metrics to the decommissioning date, not just the new system's launch date.

2. **Set "unreasonable" timelines:** To bypass bureaucracy, define the desired end date and work backward. An aggressive timeline forces parallel work, eliminates unnecessary reviews and prevents resistance from organizing.

3. **Challenge your suppliers:** Actively reject vendor limitations. When a manufacturer insisted their system couldn't run in the cloud in 2018, Kärcher initially accepted it. A year later, they migrated it themselves flawlessly. Never let a legacy supplier dictate the limits of your future-state architecture.

Part 4: From project to competency

The situation: Building the new normal

The 2019 migration was not the end of the story; it was the beginning of a new corporate competency. It built a muscle for change, which the company immediately began to flex in successive waves.

- **Wave 2: Cultural transformation (2020–2022):** They migrated 16,000 employees to Google Workspace. This was a *Holistic Transformation*[30] that fundamentally altered daily digital tools. It was only possible because the technical groundwork had been laid. As Hermann explains: "Kärcher had learned how to use the public cloud. Mentally, everyone on every layer already understood cloud, already understood what SaaS means." When confronted with skepticism, the argument was a simple, powerful question: "If you could rebuild Kärcher from scratch on a green field, what would you use?" The reluctant answer: "I would

30 ***TF35 – Holistic Transformation:*** Address changes in teams, processes and culture alongside technology.

use G Suite," ended the debate. The impact was profound. "Everyone is working differently. We killed attachments. People work integrated, worldwide, in real time." The key lesson, according to Kerscher, was that technology is only half the battle. "The cultural change is everything."

- **Wave 3: Leadership and operational transformation (2023):** This new maturity was best illustrated by their new factory in Vietnam. Annoyed that a new factory in the US had recently been built the "old way", Hermann proactively approached CEO Hartmut Jenner to ensure the Vietnam plant would be Cloud Native. The CEO's response was simply: "What else?" For Hermann, this was the "perfect moment". "This man with an engineering management background, 60 years old, manufacturing ... for him, it was absolutely clear," he says. The factory, a fully Cloud Native production site with no local servers, was built from greenfield to the first product rolling off the line in just 11 months, a feat impossible with a traditional approach. It saved an initial €200,000 on hardware alone and created a global template, a new *Reference Architecture.*[31]
- **Wave 4: Strategic transformation (2024):** Kärcher's newfound agility was tested when, just two weeks after losing a three-digit million sum in revenue overnight due to sanctions on Russia, the leadership team pitched an unbudgeted, multi-

31 ***TF27 – Reference Architecture:*** Define documented, proven architectural patterns for consistency.

million-dollar "AI for everyone" initiative. While other departments faced cuts, Kerscher recalls asking the CFO: "If it's really a good idea to now come to the Board and ask for some more millions." They presented a simple slide with two waves: the first showed how the cloud had changed the company, the second showed the opportunity to do it all again with AI. "They listened to us for 15 minutes, super silent," Hermann recalls. "Then they looked at each other and the first one said: 'I think we have to do that.'" By March 2025, the bet was already paying off. The overall Gemini utilization rate had reached 63%, with employees at the headquarters hitting 74%, and employees prompting an average of six days per month. This progress is tracked via monthly reports to the Board, a clear application of *Data-Driven Decision Making.*[32]

Blueprint for leaders

1. **Sequence your waves:** Use a successful technical transformation (like the cloud migration) to earn the credibility to launch a more difficult cultural one (like the Google Workspace rollout).[33]

2. **Productize your success:** Don't treat a successful project as a one-off. Immediately turn it into

32 ***TF37 – Data-Driven Decision Making:*** Foster culture of decisions informed by data and analysis.

33 ***TF35 – Holistic Transformation:*** Address changes in teams, processes and culture alongside technology.

a "template" or "blueprint" for the rest of the organization, as Kärcher did with the Vietnam factory.[34] This scales the value of the initial investment.

3. Leverage momentum for the next big bet: When pitching the next wave (like AI), frame it as the logical continuation of the journey. Use past successes as proof that your team can deliver, transforming the conversation from "Can we do this?" to "How quickly can we do this?"

Conclusion: The mandate for the future

Kärcher did not just modernize its IT. It built a new engine for transformation, ensuring the company avoids *Post-Transformation Stagnation.*[35] The company that once struggled with e-commerce can now build a Cloud Native factory in 11 months and deploy generative AI as a strategic response to a market downturn. Without this journey, Kerscher states, the company's massive growth "would never ever have been possible".

Looking back, both leaders offer one key piece of advice for others: "Do it faster." They believe the biggest limitations are often self-imposed, based on outdated thinking and

34 ***TF27 - Reference Architecture:*** Define documented, proven architectural patterns for consistency.

35 ***AP31 - Post-Transformation Stagnation:*** Halting continuous improvement erodes transformation benefits over time.

a reluctance to cut ties with old suppliers and processes. The fact that "everyone, from the top floor to the factory floor, now understands that our future is in the cloud is our single greatest asset from this journey."

The lesson is clear and brutal. The future doesn't belong to organizations that gradually adapt. It belongs to those that develop the discipline and courage to deliberately and forcefully abandon the past.

Case study: Ortec Finance's pattern-driven transformation

By Joris Cramwinckel and Milan Seijbel

For many established enterprises, the journey from a traditional, proficient operational state to a dynamic, Cloud Native model is fraught with peril. It is a path that demands more than new tools; it requires a fundamental shift in architecture, process and culture. Ortec Finance, a leading global provider of technology and solutions for risk and return management and investment decision-making, stands as a compelling example of an organization that not only were successfully riding this wave but did so by consciously applying a pattern-based strategy, making their story a powerful illustration of the principles outlined in this book.

What makes their journey particularly insightful is that it was guided by the precursor to this work, the 2019 book *Cloud Native Transformation*. Their experience provides a real-world validation of a pattern-based approach and offers a bridge from the lessons of the Cloud Native wave to the challenges of the AI Native future now on the horizon.

As you'll see, Ortec Finance moved through the steps of transformation we outlined in Part II, using all six modes of operation in the process to deliver a highly successful Cloud Native transformation.

The "why": recognizing the need for a new wave

Founded in the early 1980s by econometricians from Erasmus University in Rotterdam, Ortec Finance has a long history of using mathematical models to help the financial sector make better investment decisions. By 2019, they were not a stagnant, Waterfall-based organization. They had already undergone a significant reorganization to create smaller, more autonomous teams that combined business and software engineering. This enabled a more focused, end-to-end way of working. They had even implemented "Chapters"—groups inspired by the Spotify model—to provide technical leadership and ensure quality across the company, driven by knowledge rather than pure hierarchy.

Despite these forward-thinking steps, significant friction remained. The company's strategic "big hairy audacious goal" is to become the global standard and double every five years, and it was clear their current operational model had constraints. The primary bottleneck was a classic one: the operations department was still a separate, centralized back office. Development teams had a "build" responsibility, but not a "run" responsibility. They would throw completed software "over the fence" to an Ops team that was hesitant to adopt new technologies, as they had to service an ever-increasing variety of stacks without having been part of the development process. This left the Ops engineers in a position of high responsibility but low influence, a recipe for burnout and a drag on innovation. The strategic drivers for change were clear: improved growth enablement, faster delivery and holistic quality assurance.

Steps 0 and 1: From Pioneering to a deliberate decision

Ortec Finance's journey into the new wave didn't begin with a sudden mandate but with a dedicated **Pioneering mode (Step 0)**. As early as 2015, the company began formally investing in technology research beyond its core econometrics, creating a labs function to explore new paradigms. This team, insulated from the pressures of the main "factory", experimented with containerization and new technology stacks, recognizing their potential to increase engineering productivity.

This foundational work culminated in the outlining of a comprehensive Enterprise Tech Strategy (ETS). This strategy, developed jointly, defined clear objectives and the actionable steps required to achieve them, ensuring alignment across the CTO's office, from labs to operations, on the necessity and direction of the impending transformation. This strategic framework was then formalized, providing a clear roadmap before specific Cloud Native elements were piloted in practice.

A key pioneering effort is a greenfield project to build a web portal for monitoring the balance sheet risks of institutional investors. This project served as a perfect example of the *Research Through Action (TF16)* pattern and the first *Proof of Concept – PoC (TF06)*. While the project was ultimately not a commercial success, it was a vital technical and organizational success. It provided a safe-to-fail environment that proved the value of the new technology stack and uncovered real-world challenges without disrupting the core business.

This groundwork laid the foundation for a formal **Decision to Transform (Step 1)**. A crucial enabler was an organizational change that brought the previously separate operations department under the CTO, Milan, creating a unified technology umbrella. Around this time, Joris, then in an R&D role, discovered the *Cloud Native Transformation* book and promoted it within the CTO's office, becoming the initiative's *Transformation Champion (TF12)*.

The book and its patterns resonated deeply. As Milan recalled: "Your book came by, and then we saw that Cloud Native ticks … at least half of the boxes that we wanted to achieve with our Enterprise Tech Strategy (ETS)." The leadership team used the book's pattern cards to chronologically map out their transformation, creating a clear *Business Case (TF09)* and establishing a guiding *Vision First (TF14)*. With Milan ensuring *Executive Commitment (TF11)*, the company was ready to move from theory to practice.

Steps 2, 3 and 4: Riding the wave – Bootstrapping, Scaling and Optimizing

With the decision made, Ortec Finance entered the **Bootstrapping & Bridge-Building mode (Step 2)**. A dedicated, cross-functional *Core Team (TF13)* was formed to build the MVP: their internal cloud platform, dubbed "The Orca Platform" (ORtec finance Cloud Application). As the Orca platform was being built, the team began internal advocacy efforts to promote it and generate excitement and anticipation for the improved way of working.

As they prepared to move into **Scaling and Retiring modes (Step 3)**, they adopted a strategy of *Gradual Onboarding (TF32)*. Instead of a "big bang" migration, they developed a systematic process to bring teams on to the Orca platform. A cornerstone of this was the "ORCA Academy", an internal curriculum that served as a *Dev Starter Pack (TF26)*, teaching engineers everything from Kubernetes to GitOps principles.

Their strategy wisely dictated that applications should be modernized before being moved to the new platform, avoiding a pure "lift and shift" approach. The final gate before any application went to production was a readiness assessment covering three areas: Is the platform ready? Is the application ready? And, most importantly, is the team ready? To help and guide teams with these challenges, we created a central onboarding team, formed around the *Transformation Champion*. We labeled it "CAT" (Cloud Acceleration Team).

To answer the last question, they implemented one of their most powerful and effective practices: **fire drills**.[36] These multi-day sessions involved intentionally breaking the system in a staging environment to simulate incidents. This was not a grading exercise, but a method to build comfort, expose blind spots and solidify procedures in a low-risk setting. The fire drills helped overcome one of the biggest cultural hurdles: the engineering teams' fear of 24/7 "run" responsibility. By experiencing the "run" responsibilities in a controlled way, teams gained the confidence and skills needed for the new operational model.

As they entered a broader **Scaling and Optimizing mode (Step 4)**, they formalized a *Platform Team (TF25)* to manage the Orca platform as a product, and the team became a direct report to the CTO. This central team owned the platform, allowing the product-focused engineering teams to concentrate on delivering business value. This structure prevented the *Unmanaged Shadow IT Proliferation (AP07)* pitfall, where multiple teams build their own competing platforms.

Step 5: A new maturity—the benefits of the Cloud Native shore

Today, Ortec Finance is operating in a state of **Optimizing and Innovating (Step 5)**. While the full transformation is planned for completion by 2027, the benefits are already profound.

---

36 https://openpracticelibrary.com/practice/fire-drills/

Product owners across the company confirm the success of the transformation, though their reasons differ. For one product, the elasticity of the cloud removed resource constraints that had capped their growth. For another, running costs were greatly reduced by optimizing infrastructure choices. For all products, the assured quality provided by the GitOps paradigm has been more powerful than initially expected. Joris noted, "We are about to release features now which weren't possible at all to think of," particularly in the AI domain where they now have access to on-demand GPUs and can innovate far more rapidly.

One of the most significant benefits, which they didn't fully anticipate, was c**ost transparency**. The old model of opaque, centralized Ops charging was replaced by a transparent, application-level, variable cost structure. This functionality is not typically offered by suppliers as a standard feature. Significant effort was required to aggregate and fine-tune individual component costs to achieve accuracy at the application and system levels. This empowered product owners, who could now directly see the financial impact of their architectural decisions. This shift forced them to engage with technology choices on a deeper level, moving conversations from "Is it a good idea?" to a more concrete discussion about cost and value. This is a real-world application of the *Measure What Matters (TF36)* pattern, leading to better *Data-Driven Decision Making (TF37)*.

Step 6: Looking to the next wave – AI Native on the horizon

True to the "Waves of Innovation" concept, Ortec Finance is not resting on its laurels. Having learned how to transform, they are already in **Pioneering mode (Step 6)** for the next wave: AI Native.

Their exploration of AI began in parallel with their Cloud Native research. They are already treating AI models as software artifacts, complete with model registries and MLOps lifecycles. They are building their own AI models, not just using off-the-shelf tools, and are creating interfaces that allow their sophisticated econometric models to be used to train other AI models in a machine-to-machine fashion.

They astutely recognize that the AI Native wave is less mature than Cloud Native was when they began their first journey. "With AI, I have truly no idea ... the possibilities are still wide, while the potential seems huge," Milan commented, highlighting the uncertainty that defines this new frontier. Their approach is strategic and pragmatic. They have divided their efforts into two streams: **AI to improve productivity** (e.g. office or software development automation) and **AI to enhance our solutions to clients**. This mirrors the balanced approach of a mature learning organization, investing enough to understand the new wave and prepare for it, without making a premature *Bleeding Edge Gamble (AP02)*.

Reflections and advice

Looking back, the team at Ortec Finance offers valuable advice. They emphasize the sheer effort of communication required to keep everyone onboard during a long transformation. They also acknowledge that they would have focused more on cost control and vendor management from the beginning.

Their journey demonstrates that a successful transformation is not a single project but the development of an organizational capability. By using patterns, starting with small, dedicated teams, securing executive buy-in and patiently navigating the cultural shifts, they have remade themselves. Ortec Finance is a company that has moved from one mature state to another. In doing so, it has acquired the skill to ride the waves of innovation, ready for whatever comes next.

Inspired by these real-world transformations? Scan the QR code to access the Waves of Innovation hub for more case studies, in-depth discussions on our podcast and the full interactive pattern library.

Mastering the Tides of Change–From Cloud Native Proficiency to the AI Native Horizon

Our journey together through this book has charted a significant course, navigating the evolution of IT from the structured predictability of Waterfall methodologies to the dynamic, transformative currents of the Cloud Native paradigm. We've seen that embracing Cloud Native was far more than a technological upgrade. It demanded a holistic transformation impacting architecture, operational processes, team structures and the very culture of organizations. Now, as many are mastering or sustaining this Cloud Native maturity, the next immense wave, AI Native, is already forming on the horizon and promising even more profound shifts.

Throughout these pages, we've emphasized that successfully riding these waves of innovation is not a matter of chance, but of structured, adaptable strategy. We introduced a six-step transformation journey, underpinned by six distinct modes of operation, as a reliable compass:

- **Step 0 (Pioneering mode):** Initiating exploration by creating research labs to identify and experiment with future technologies like Cloud Native or AI. This involves patterns like *Learn and Explore (TF01)* and establishing *Skunk Works Teams (TF02)*.
- **Step 1 (Decision mode):** Making the crucial, leadership-backed decision to embark on a Cloud Native (or any other major) transformation, supported by a compelling *Business Case (TF09)* and unwavering *Executive Commitment (TF11)*.
- **Step 2 (Bootstrapping & Bridge-Building mode):** *Forming a Core Team (TF13)* to construct the initial MVP (*Deliver the MVP (TF18)*) while simultaneously ensuring essential connections (*Bridge the Old World (TF22)*) are built back to existing legacy systems.
- **Step 3 (Scaling and Retiring modes):** Methodically onboarding more teams on to the new platform (*Gradual Onboarding (TF32)*) while systematically retiring parts of the old environment using patterns like *Strangle Legacy (TF33)*.
- **Step 4 (Scaling and Optimizing modes):** Expanding the new paradigm throughout the organization, focusing on standardization, creating robust IDPs (*Platform as a Product (TF24)*) and fine-tuning systems for efficiency (*Continuous Optimization (TF42)*).

- **Step 5 (Optimizing and Innovating modes):** Operating from a new state of maturity, embedding continuous improvement (*Continuous Optimization (TF42)*) and fostering rapid, incremental innovation (*Nurture Incremental Innovation (TF49)*).
- **Step 6 (Pioneering mode again):** With one transformation largely complete, re-engaging the Pioneering mode to actively scan for and explore the next disruptive wave, such as AI Native.

This cyclical journey highlights that transformation is not a one-time event but an ongoing organizational capability. It demands a holistic perspective, as captured in our Innovation Waves Maturity Matrix, recognizing that progress must be balanced across multiple dimensions—from culture and team structure to architecture and development processes.

Adopting a pattern language has been central to our discussion, providing a shared vocabulary to understand these complex shifts, implement proven solutions (transformation patterns and paradigm patterns) and consciously avoid the common pitfalls and anti-patterns detailed in Chapter 7. These mistakes—like treating disruptive change as incremental (*Incremental Facade (AP04)*), never truly finishing a transformation (*Perpetual Transition (AP03)*) or navigating by hype rather than a solid business case—serve as critical lessons as we approach new frontiers.

Sustaining the hard-won gains of a Cloud Native transformation, as explored in Chapter 8, requires persistent effort. It involves treating your IDP as an evolving product (*Platform as a Product (TF24)*), nurturing a culture of quality and continuous improvement (*Continuous Optimization (TF42)*), ensuring aligned and committed leadership (*Executive Commitment (TF11)*), applying strategic budgeting (*Finance Topologies (TF10)*) and even embracing sustainability as a proxy for operational efficiency.

Now, the AI Native wave beckons, promising a fundamental "Intelligence Revolution". As detailed in Chapter 9, this is not merely Cloud Native with added AI features. It suggests a paradigm where AI is the intrinsic core, driving *Model-Centric Architectures (AIN01)*, demanding sophisticated *Data Fabrics for AI (AIN02)*, enabling *Self-Evolving Systems (AIN25)* and potentially fostering complex *Agentic Architectures (AIN04)*. The very nature of development is poised to shift with the "time reversal", where AI's speed in execution elevates human focus to strategic intent, ethical guidance and validation. This will make skills like *Prompt Engineering (AIN13)* and *Human-AI Collaboration Design (AIN19)* paramount.

However, AI Native is still in its pioneering days, much like Cloud Native was around 2014. The technology is rapidly evolving (*AI Technological Immaturity (AP40)*), best practices are emergent and we face significant challenges related to:

- Data governance (*Data Governance Failure (AP41)*)
- Model explainability (*Explainability-by-Design (XAI) (AIN07)*)
- Security (*Adversarial Defense Mechanisms (AIN23)*)
- The AI skills gap

- Profound ethical considerations (*Ethical Misalignment & Amplified Bias (AP37)*)

These challenges must be proactively addressed using emerging patterns like *Bias Mitigation Pipelines (AIN22)* and *AI Trust Framework Integration (AIN21)*.

The crucial insight is that the structured, learning-focused transformation journey we've detailed for Cloud Native—from Pioneering through Scaling to sustained Innovation—is precisely the approach required for AI Native. There are no shortcuts. Organizations must begin now with active exploration and experimentation in Pioneering mode, building internal knowledge and iteratively validating potential use cases before contemplating broader adoption.

Imagine your organization as a vessel that has just learned to master the powerful, sometimes turbulent, Cloud Native currents. You've refitted your ship, retrained your crew and learned to navigate with new charts and instruments. But as you look to the horizon, an entirely new kind of current is forming—the AI Native swell. It is driven by different forces, demands different skills and perhaps even a different kind of vessel. Do you attempt to sail these new waters with your existing Cloud Native rigging, hoping for the best? Or do you, having learned the paramount importance of adaptation, once again send out your most skilled pioneers to understand these new currents, to experiment with new designs and to prepare the entire fleet for what's to come?

The history of technology, and indeed the history of successful enterprise, is a testament to the power of adaptation. The frameworks, patterns and step-by-step guidance offered in this book are designed to equip you not merely for a single transformation, but for the ongoing process of innovation that defines our modern era.

The ultimate competitive advantage lies not in mastering one specific wave, but in building an organization that excels at navigating all of them. This is an organization that embraces continuous learning, views transformation as a core competency and meets each new technological frontier with foresight, courage and a well-honed ability to change. The ability to transform is the most critical, enduring capability, ensuring that your organization can not only ride the current wave but is also prepared to catch, and perhaps even shape, the next.

Continue your transformation journey with us. Scan the QR code to access the Waves of Innovation hub, where you'll find the complete patterns library, the AI Native Assessment, our newsletter and the opportunity to contact us with your questions.

About the Authors

Pini Reznik

Pini Reznik is the CEO and co-founder of re:cinq, where he helps organizations build dependable, AI-ready cloud platforms and the operating models to run them. A former software engineer, he co-founded a Cloud Native consultancy in 2014 and has since led transformation programs across industries—from platform engineering and SRE practices to *Team Topologies* and change management. Pini co-authored the O'Reilly book, *Cloud Native Transformation: Practical Patterns for Innovation*, and has been documenting engineering and organizational design patterns since 2018. Over the last decade he has guided dozens of companies through the shift to Cloud Native, accelerating software delivery while reducing operational risk and preparing teams for the AI Native era.

Michael Müller

Few leaders possess the first-hand experience of navigating a complete technological paradigm shift from inception to maturity. For more than 20 years, Michael Müller has built a career on exactly that, operating at the forefront of the cloud revolution. His senior leadership roles were defined by steering organizations through the complexities of technology transitions, giving him a deep understanding of the foundational logic that underpins successful transformation.

As a recognized authority on large-scale technological change, his focus has always been on not just driving technical progress, but ensuring its strategic alignment and long-term business impact. *Waves of Innovation* is the culmination of this experience, offering executives a strategic framework built on a rare understanding of how to lead when the ground is shifting beneath your feet.

Appendix 1

A Glimpse into the AI Native Future

This appendix peers into the future, exploring how AI Native—a natural evolution of Cloud Native—is beginning to reshape IT, software development and other disciplines. Just as the full scope of today's Cloud Native ecosystem was difficult to predict in 2014–2015, the AI Native landscape, while becoming clearer, still holds significant uncertainties (join our Waves of Innovation newsletter to navigate this evolving landscape with us: https://re-cinq.com/newsletter). What follows is not presented as definitive truth, but as a reasoned prediction. It is born from a synthesis of current research, emerging trends and expert analysis, including insights from leading LLMs and generative AI of the 2024–2025 era.

It is important to acknowledge that current AI models, while exceptionally powerful and increasingly capable of sophisticated reasoning and generation, primarily function as tools that augment human intellect rather than replacing true, original human ideation. The creation of this text, therefore, has been a collaborative endeavor: human-driven ideas were structured, expanded and refined with the assistance of AI, which processed and synthesized vast amounts of information from the provided research. This process itself mirrors the AI Native methodology discussed herein—a seamless human-AI partnership where humans guide and AI executes and elaborates. This collaborative approach validates the AI Native vision, reflecting how humans and AI can work together to envision and build the future.

1. The dawn of the AI Native era: a human-AI collaborative vision

The emergence of AI Native signifies a pivotal moment, promising to redefine technology and human interaction with digital systems.

Defining AI Native: beyond tools to intrinsic intelligence

AI Native is a paradigm where artificial intelligence forms the intrinsic, intelligent core of systems, software and organizational workflows. Capabilities like learning, adaptation and autonomous decision-making are woven into their fabric from inception. This evolution marks a significant departure from previous models where AI was merely an add-on feature.

The transition can be likened to an "Intelligence Revolution", augmenting human cognitive power much as the Industrial Revolution augmented physical muscle power. Further convergence with advanced robotics could usher in a "Cyber-Physical Revolution", enabling intelligent machines to act autonomously in the physical world.

Understanding AI Native as a fundamental paradigm shift, comparable to the move from Waterfall to Cloud Native, is crucial for organizations. Superficial approaches, treating AI as a simple upgrade, will likely falter, mirroring past Cloud Native transformation underestimations. The change is profound, affecting core system architecture and organizational operational DNA.

The symbiotic partnership: human and AI responsibilities

The AI Native era is characterized by a symbiotic human-AI partnership, each leveraging unique strengths. This necessitates an evolved delineation of responsibilities.

Human responsibilities:

Human roles shift towards strategic guidance, ethical oversight and critical validation:

- **Setting intent:** Defining high-level goals and strategic outlines for AI systems, often via sophisticated prompt engineering, positioning humans as "AI orchestrators" or "AI systems strategists".
- **Ethical governance and value alignment:** Ensuring AI outputs align with human values, ethical

principles (fairness, transparency, sustainability) and societal norms through robust governance frameworks.

- **Validation and verification:** Critically assessing AI-generated outputs for performance, accuracy, safety and business alignment.
- **Managing the human-AI interface:** Designing and refining interaction models and collaborative workflows for effective human-AI usability.
- **Contextual understanding and critical thinking:** Providing nuanced understanding, common-sense reasoning, creative problem-solving and domain expertise that AI currently lacks.

This elevation to strategic and ethical stewardship means human value shifts from execution to guidance, necessitating societal and organizational focus on developing skills in advanced prompt engineering, ethical reasoning and critical validation.

AI responsibilities:

AI systems handle technical execution, leveraging data processing, pattern recognition and automation:

- **Task execution:** Designing, coding, testing, deploying and evolving software based on human-defined intent.
- **Data processing and pattern recognition:** Analyzing vast datasets to learn patterns, generate insights and inform automated decisions.
- **Adaptation and self-learning:** Continuously improving performance and adapting behavior

based on new data and feedback, potentially leading to self-evolving systems.
- **Monitoring and autonomous operations:** Tracking system performance, identifying anomalies and potentially managing or sunsetting systems autonomously under human oversight.

Trust is foundational for this partnership. AI must be designed for trustworthiness (transparency, explainability, reliability, security), while humans must develop confidence in AI capabilities. Failure to cultivate this trust will impede AI task delegation and slow AI Native adoption. Investment in "responsible AI" is a practical necessity for realizing the AI Native vision.

2. Projected technological advancements: a pragmatic horizon scan (mid–2025 onwards)

The trajectory of AI Native development will be shaped by technological advancements over the coming years. A pragmatic outlook, balancing optimistic predictions with an awareness of limitations, is essential.

A "skepticism/reality check" for each forecast is a reminder that widespread, impactful adoption often follows a more measured timeline than initial excitement suggests. This hype-versus-reality pattern helps organizations avoid the bleeding edge gamble.

AI capability progression is a web of interconnected developments. Advances in foundational models drive needs for energy-efficient hardware and sophisticated governance. Recognizing these interdependencies is vital; bottlenecks in one area can temper progress. A holistic view of the AI stack (data, compute, MLOps) is necessary for realistic planning.

Terminology like "AGI components" will remain fluid. Organizations should focus on tangible value rather than ill-defined AGI goals to avoid "AI winter" disillusionment.

The AI landscape is maturing into a complex, specialized ecosystem, with specialized hardware (neuromorphic chips, quantum accelerators), databases (vector databases) and roles (prompt engineers, AI ethicists). Achieving "AI Nativity" requires navigating this diverse environment and avoiding tool sprawl.

The near horizon (12–18 months—by mid–2026): incremental enhancements and early adoption

- **More capable and multi-modal LLMs:**
  - *Prediction:* LLMs will show improved reasoning, longer context window and integrated multi-modal capabilities (text, image, audio, basic video), allowing nuanced oversight and richer content generation.
  - *Skepticism/reality check:* Gains in true understanding may be incremental. Bias, energy consumption and "hallucinations" will likely persist, with hype potentially outpacing real-world impact in complex domains.

- **Edge AI proliferation:**
  - *Prediction:* Sophisticated AI models will run efficiently on edge devices (IoT, automotive) for faster, privacy-preserving local processing.
  - *Skepticism/reality check:* Hardware power/energy constraints may limit advanced models on edge devices. Privacy rules and model management complexity could slow adoption.

- **AI-driven testing and QA tools:**
  - *Prediction:* Enhanced AI tools for automated testing, code validation and security vulnerability detection will reduce manual QA effort by an estimated 25–30%.
  - *Skepticism/reality check:* False positives/ negatives and lack of nuance for complex/ethical cases will limit full reliability. Human oversight remains critical.

- **Sophisticated ethics and explainability dashboards:**
  - *Prediction:* Advanced tools will monitor AI fairness and bias, providing clearer explanations for AI decisions in real time.
  - *Skepticism/reality check:* Metrics can oversimplify ethics. Deep explainability for complex models remains challenging, therefore human judgment is paramount.

- **Early AI agents for specific tasks:**
  - *Prediction:* AI agents will automate well-defined, narrow tasks in IT operations, SDLC (e.g. bug

triage) and business processes (e.g. report generation).
    - *Skepticism/reality check:* Limited autonomy scope. Integration challenges. Reliability concerns for high-accuracy/contextual tasks.

The mid-term outlook (three years—by mid–2028): maturing capabilities and broader integration

- **Emergence of foundational models for conceptual reasoning (proto-AGI (artificial general intelligence) building blocks):**
    - *Prediction:* Advanced AI models will show stronger conceptual reasoning, cross-domain knowledge synthesis and robust multilingual support.
    - *Skepticism/reality check:* True maturity and reliable application remain unproven. Adoption slowed by high costs, integration complexity, data needs and controllability/alignment concerns.

- **Early commercial neuromorphic chips:**
    - *Prediction:* Lab prototypes will transition to early commercial use in niche applications, offering 15–20% energy reduction for AI inference.
    - *Skepticism/reality check:* Scalability issues, high production costs and specialized software ecosystems may delay widespread use.

- **More autonomous data pipelines:**
  - *Prediction:* Data pipelines will self-clean, self-optimize and self-govern, reducing manual curation by 35–40%.
  - *Skepticism/reality check:* Automated cleaning errors (bias amplification, outlier removal) will require robust human checks and are not fully reliable for critical data without oversight.

- **More intuitive voice and multi-modal prompt systems:**
  - *Prediction:* Voice and multi-modal prompts (sketch-to-code, voice-to-UI) will become more effective in dev tools and business apps.
  - *Skepticism/reality check:* Misinterpretation of nuanced/ambiguous/technical prompts and accent/language biases will limit effectiveness for complex tasks.

- **Federated learning for enhanced privacy:**
  - *Prediction:* Decentralized AI training will see broader adoption for medium-scale apps where data privacy/sovereignty is critical.
  - *Skepticism/reality check:* Bandwidth limits, complex coordination and model performance consistency across datasets may hinder scaling.

- **AI-powered co-pilots for complex problem-solving:**
  - *Prediction:* AI assistants will offer meaningful collaboration on strategy, design and complex analysis, offering insights and drafting solutions.
  - *Skepticism/reality check:* True collaborative intelligence is nascent. Outputs will require

significant human validation, critical thinking and contextual refinement.

The five-year vista (by mid-2030): towards more autonomous and integrated AI

- **Advanced foundational models/early AGI components:**
  - *Prediction:* Models will achieve strides in long-context reasoning, abstract thinking and few-shot learning, cutting training data needs by 25–30% for certain tasks.
  - *Skepticism/reality check:* May still be overhyped as "human-like"; likely to struggle with common sense, novel situations and nuanced ethics without human guidance.

- **Niche quantum acceleration for AI:**
  - *Prediction:* Early quantum-classical hybrids may speed specific AI tasks (optimization, discovery) by 15–20% in specialized settings.
  - *Skepticism/reality check:* Hype may outstrip reality—costly, unstable, limited to specialized problems and research-confined.

- **Augmented interfaces as standard:**
  - *Prediction:* Gesture, voice, brain-computer interface (BCI) prototypes in 40–50% of pro software/creative tools; enabling sophisticated no-code/low-code.
  - *Skepticism/reality check:* Accessibility issues, high error rates in complex prompts and learning curves may slow mainstream adoption.

- **AI-driven predictive security:**
  - *Prediction:* AI will embed real-time threat prediction, detection and autonomous response in 60–70% of critical systems, reducing known vector breaches by 20–25%.
  - *Skepticism/reality check:* New adversarial attacks targeting AI will emerge. Human oversight and novel defense strategies remain key.

- **Significant strides in energy-efficient AI:**
  - *Prediction:* Neuromorphic chips will be more common. Model optimization will cut AI energy use by 30–35% in many production environments.
  - *Skepticism/reality check:* Overall savings may be partly offset by exponentially growing AI demand/scale. Regulation and innovation are needed for global impact.

- **Highly autonomous self-healing infrastructure:**
  - *Prediction:* AI will autonomously predict, prevent and fix 50–60% of system failures in advanced cloud/edge.
  - *Skepticism/reality check:* Over-reliance risks complex cascading failures. Human intervention needed for critical/novel issues.

- **Widely adopted ethical AI frameworks and auditing:**
  - *Prediction:* Standardized, adaptable frameworks for AI fairness, transparency, accountability in 30–40% of large enterprises (often mandated); AI-assisted auditing.

- *Skepticism/reality check:* Frameworks/regulations often lag AI complexity; enforcement varies and "ethics washing" is a concern.

- **Democratized AI development platforms:**
  - *Prediction:* Advanced AI-powered low-code/no-code platforms for non-specialists to build, deploy and manage sophisticated AI apps.
  - *Skepticism/reality check:* Governance, security, responsible use and managing unintended consequences of widespread AI creation by non-experts become major challenges.

The following table summarizes these technological advancements and their skeptical outlook.

3. Reimagining software creation: new paradigms for an AI-driven world

AI Native capabilities, especially the "time reversal" where AI accelerates execution, shifting human effort to planning and validation, necessitate rethinking software development. Traditional Agile methods, structured around managing human execution cycles, become less relevant if AI achieves in hours what took weeks, pushing towards continuous flow and AI-mediated feedback.

FlowNative: the continuous current of AI-led development

Disclaimer: FlowNative is a speculative vision of future software development, not current reality.

Appendix 1:
A Glimpse into the AI Native Future

FlowNative is conceptualized as an AI Native software development methodology, replacing frameworks like Scrum with a continuous, prompt-driven, AI-orchestrated flow. It uses micro-cycles (hours to days) for rapid, adaptive delivery, where AI handles execution (design, code, test, deploy, evolve) while humans guide via intent, oversight and ethics. Built on "Fluid Networks", FlowNative emphasizes a seamless, wave-like process aligned with AI's speed and adaptability, reflecting the "time reversal". Unlike Scrum's sprints or Kanban's boards, FlowNative is envisioned as a dynamic system where stages blend, driven by AI autonomy and human strategic input.

Core principles of FlowNative:

- **Continuous flow:** Replaces iterative sprints with a fluid, ongoing process; stages (ideation to decommission) flow without rigid boundaries.
- **Prompt-driven execution:** Humans set goals via prompts; AI executes, iterating in micro-cycles.
- **Human-AI symbiosis:** Humans guide (intent, ethics), AI builds (code, deploy).
- **Adaptability over structure:** Fluid Networks dynamically form micro-clusters (three to five people) per task, dissolving when done.
- **Ethics and sustainability by design:** Embeds fairness, transparency and resource efficiency in every stage.

Stages of FlowNative (AI-executed, human-guided):

1. **Ideation:** Humans define goals via prompts; AI suggests refinements.

2. **Design:** AI generates prototypes; humans refine UX.

3. **Develop:** AI codes solutions, optimizing for performance/explainability.

4. **Test:** AI runs simulations; humans validate edge cases.

5. **Deploy:** AI deploys with zero-downtime mechanisms.

6. **Evolve:** AI adapts the system live using user data; humans guide improvements.

7. **Monitor:** AI tracks metrics; humans adjust via prompts or loop back.

8. **Decommission:** AI sunsets systems, preserving data and reducing resources.

Micro-cycles and lightweight ceremonies:

FlowNative uses AI-driven micro-cycles (hours to days) instead of fixed sprints. Feedback is continuous. Ceremonies are minimized and AI-mediated:

- **Intent kickoff (daily, 15mins):** Humans set/refine prompts; AI suggests enhancements.
- **Oversight sync (ad hoc, 10–20mins):** Humans validate AI outputs via dashboards.
- **Ethics check (weekly, 30mins):** Micro-cluster audits fairness using AI tools.

- **Debrief pulse (weekly, 15mins):** Clusters reflect on flow; AI shares data.

FlowNative implies a radical transformation of project management, focusing on defining strategic "currents" for AI navigation.

Fluid Networks: dynamic teaming in the age of AI

Fluid Networks is a speculative AI-orchestrated organizational structure for AI Native development, replacing fixed teams with temporary, task-specific micro-clusters of three to five people. These form and dissolve based on real-time needs, guided by AI. They respond to the "time reversal" by emphasizing adaptability and lean staffing.

Core characteristics of Fluid Networks:

- **Dynamic clustering:** AI assigns individuals to micro-clusters per task, dissolving them on completion.
- **Role flexibility:** Participants switch roles based on AI's skill-matching, requiring generalist skills (prompting, judgment).
- **AI coordination:** AI uses data (project status, individual strengths) to form clusters and facilitate async collaboration.
- **Lean and scalable:** Aims for lean staffing (e.g. 10–20 humans guiding AI for outputs of 50+ Cloud Native teams).
- **Task-centric focus:** Structure is oriented around short-lived tasks, aligning with FlowNative's micro-cycles.

Structure, operation and roles within Fluid Networks:

AI forms clusters (e.g. product manager (PM) as intent setter, data curator, ethics guardian for ideation) lasting for the task, then reassigns members. Key roles:

- **Intent setter:** Defines goals via prompts.
- **Data curator:** Prepares/validates data for AI.
- **Oversight validator:** Critically reviews AI outputs.
- **Ethics guardian:** Ensures fairness/ethical compliance.
- **AI whisperer:** Provides deep-tech expertise for edge cases (10–20% of staff).

Enabling factors for Fluid Networks:

- **AI-driven assignment:** Real-time skill-to-task matching.
- **Augmented tools:** Dashboards, AI tutors, sandboxes supporting cluster work.
- **Cultural shift:** Embracing adaptability, fluidity—"steer, don't sweat".

Fluid Networks present a significant challenge to conventional structures, implying an adaptable workforce with generalist skills, requiring rethinking of HR and career models.

The evolving developer engagement model for autonomous software creation

This model, inspired by self-driving car autonomy levels, outlines stages based on developer engagement versus

AI system autonomy. It reflects increasing trust in AI capabilities dependent on robust governance, security and explainability.

Levels of developer engagement:

1. **Level 1: Developer in-the-loop/system assists:**

    - *Description:* Developer fully immersed, driving coding/design; AI assists with code completion, suggestions, basic testing.
    - *Developer role:* Actively codes, designs, debugs, makes all critical decisions.
    - *System role:* Provides suggestions, automates minor tasks, offers insights.

2. **Level 2: Developer on-the-loop/system generates:**

    - *Description:* Developer delegates significant code/component generation to AI based on specs/prompts.
    - *Developer role:* Specifies, reviews, guides, integrates, monitors, ready to intervene.
    - *System role:* Generates substantial code blocks or components.

3. **Level 3: Developer supervises/system creates:**

    - *Description:* Developer steps back from continuous monitoring for defined tasks; AI takes high-level requirements to create, test, deploy features/apps.

- *Developer role:* Sets objectives, defines constraints, reviews milestones, validates overall functionality, intervenes for novel problems or system limits.
- *System role:* Autonomously develops, tests, potentially deploys features/applications.

4. **Level 4: System owns/developer governs:**

- *Description:* For specific, well-defined software/ tasks, AI manages the entire lifecycle with minimal direct developer intervention in creation.
- *Developer role:* Governance, strategic direction, ethical boundaries, compliance, overseeing overall system performance and impact.
- *System role:* Independently manages full software lifecycle for defined tasks (maintenance, evolution) within human-set governance.

Quality and reliability emphasis: Levels 3 and 4 require AI to produce robust, secure, maintainable and verifiably correct software, including automated testing, adherence to standards, security best practices and clear articulation of when human expertise (fallback) is needed.

Appendix 1:
A Glimpse into the AI Native Future

Table 1: Developer-Engagement Model for autonomous software creation

Level of autonomy	Primary developer role	Primary system role	Key characteristics /examples	Implied human skills
1. Developer in-the-loop/ system assists	Active coder, designer, debugger	Intelligent assistant (suggestions, minor task automation)	AI co-pilots (e.g. GitHub Copilot), real-time documentation, basic test generation	Core programming, debugging, critical assessment of AI suggestions
2. Developer on-the-loop/ system generates	Specifier, reviewer, guide, integrator, monitor	Code/ component generator	AI generates functions/ modules/UI segments based on prompts/ specs (e.g. HULA framework)	Advanced prompt engineering, code review, system integration, architectural judgment
3. Developer supervises/ system creates	Objective setter, validator, interventionist (for exceptions)	Autonomous feature/application creator and tester	AI takes high-level requirements to create, test, deploy features/ apps	Strategic thinking, defining clear acceptance criteria, risk assessment, complex problem-solving for AI limitations
4. System owns/developer governs	Strategic director, governance setter, ethical overseer	Autonomous lifecycle manager (for defined tasks)	AI manages full lifecycle (maintenance, evolution) for standardized software types	AI ethics, policy development, risk management, strategic foresight, systems thinking

4. The shifting landscape of work and skills in the AI Native future

AI Native systems will fundamentally reshape work, evolving roles, creating new specializations and shifting valued workforce skills. The focus will be on task augmentation and role redefinition rather than simple job displacement.

Prompt engineering: the new lingua franca for human-AI interaction

Prompt engineering—crafting clear, effective instructions (prompts) to guide AI models—is critical in the AI Native era. It's evolving beyond text to multi-modal inputs and context-aware interactions, using advanced techniques like zero-shot, few-shot and chain-of-thought prompting. As AI handles more execution, human value shifts to providing clear direction. This means effective prompting is key. It's becoming a core competency across roles, a new "literacy" for the AI age, with growing market demand for skilled prompt engineers.

The transformation of non-IT roles: augmentation, adaptation and new opportunities

AI's impact extends beyond IT, reshaping roles across sectors through task augmentation and role redefinition:

- **Call centers:** AI chatbots handle routine queries. Human agents manage complex/empathetic interactions and AI coaching.

- **Healthcare:** AI assists diagnostics (image/data analysis). Clinicians focus on patient care, complex cases, ethics.
- **Education:** AI enables personalized learning. Teachers mentor, guide critical thinking and human skills.
- **Retail:** AI optimizes inventory, predicts demand, personalizes marketing. Staff enhance customer experience, strategic merchandising.
- **Creative industries:** Generative AI automates basic asset creation, supports ideation. Professionals focus on strategy, originality, refining outputs.

Generally, AI automates routine tasks, allowing humans to upscale to strategic thinking, creativity, ethical judgment and interpersonal interactions. The narrative shifts from "job displacement" to "task augmentation" and "job redefinition". While some automatable roles face displacement, many will see AI augment capabilities, underscoring the need for proactive workforce planning and reskilling in uniquely human skills.

Humanity's enduring role: strategy, creativity, ethics and oversight

Despite AI's advancements, humans retain crucial roles centered on functions AI cannot replicate: strategic direction, true originality, ethical judgment and ultimate oversight. Humans will:

- Define AI strategy and purpose.
- Establish ethical boundaries.

- Provide nuanced understanding and creative insights for novel problems.
- Oversee AI operations, validate outputs and intervene when AI falters.

The speculative "2% mental farmers" concept suggests a core of human experts feeding intent into autonomous AI systems. However, this human stewardship relies on governable, transparent and trustworthy AI. Without it, effective oversight is compromised, risking harmful outcomes and hindering a beneficial human-AI collaborative future.

5. Navigating the AI Native frontier: key risks and strategic mitigations

The AI Native journey, while promising, involves significant technical, ethical, operational and societal risks requiring proactive identification and mitigation. These risks are often interconnected—AI opacity (Risk 2) exacerbates ethical bias (Risk 3) and complicates accountability (Risk 10). Data quality issues (Risk 6) can fuel bias and overreliance (Risk 7). Mitigation must be holistic, integrated within a comprehensive AI governance framework.

The effectiveness of mitigations hinges on evolving human roles and capabilities, underscoring AI Native as a human-AI partnership, not full AI autonomy in critical functions. Upskilling and a culture of responsible AI stewardship are essential. Retaining deep technical literacy ("AI Whisperers") is vital for edge cases and complex debugging, countering a view of all human roles becoming mere "prompters".

Table 2: Key risks in AI Native adoption and multi-layered mitigation strategies

Risk category & examples	Description	Mitigation layers & examples
1. Loss of technical literacy	Humans may lose deep technical understanding as AI handles more execution tasks.	**Technical:** AI-generated summaries of its operations; AI tutors for on-demand explanations. **Procedural:** Regular "deep-dive" sessions on AI system internals for key personnel. **Cultural:** Value and reward continuous learning; maintain "AI Whisperer" roles with deep expertise.
2. AI opacity (black box)	Difficulty trusting, auditing or debugging AI due to opaque internal decision-making processes.	**Technical:** Implement explainable AI (XAI) techniques and tools (e.g. SHAP, LIME); favor open-source models where feasible for transparency. **Procedural:** Mandate AI systems to provide human-readable justifications for critical decisions; regular human checks and audits of AI outputs. **Cultural:** Foster critical thinking about AI outputs; retain tech-savvy staff for complex issue diagnosis.
3. Ethical bias in AI outputs	AI systems learning and perpetuating biases present in training data, leading to unfair or discriminatory outcomes.	**Technical:** Implement bias mitigation pipelines; use diverse and representative training data; employ fairness-aware ML algorithms; use large concept models for structured reasoning where appropriate. **Procedural:** Establish ethical AI review boards; conduct regular ethics audits; define clear ethical guidelines and data sourcing policies; allow human override for biased decisions. **Cultural:** Train teams on recognizing and mitigating bias; promote diversity within AI development teams.

Table 2: Key risks in AI Native adoption and multi-layered mitigation strategies *continued...*

Risk category & examples	Description	Mitigation layers & examples
4. Energy overuse & environmental impact	Significant energy consumption from training and operating large-scale AI models.	**Technical:** AI-driven sustainability optimization of workloads; adopt energy-efficient hardware (e.g. neuromorphic chips); optimize model architectures (pruning, quantization). **Procedural:** Implement policies for decommissioning idle AI systems and resources; track and report on AI energy consumption. **Cultural:** Promote awareness of AI's environmental footprint; advocate for industry-wide energy standards.
5. Cultural resistance to new work models	Teams and individuals may resist dynamic, role-shifting structures and AI-led coordination.	**Technical:** Use AI for intelligent task assignment and coordination to demonstrate efficiency. **Procedural:** Phased rollout of new work models; clear communication of benefits; provide support and coaching during transition. **Cultural:** Promote a mindset of guiding AI rather than direct execution; provide training on role fluidity and prompt engineering; celebrate early successes of new models.
6. Data quality & governance issues	Poor, biased or insecure data leading to flawed AI outputs and compromised systems.	**Technical:** AI-driven data cleaning, validation and curation tools; implement data fabric for AI and data-as-a-product principles; use synthetic data generation cautiously with validation. **Procedural:** Establish robust data governance frameworks; human data curation and validation loops; prioritize diverse and ethically sourced data. **Cultural:** Foster a data-aware culture where data quality is a shared responsibility.
7. Overreliance on AI/ automation complacency	Reduced human critical thinking, vigilance and intervention due to excessive trust in AI.	**Technical:** Design AI systems with clear indicators of confidence levels; implement fail-safe mechanisms for human intervention. **Procedural:** Mandate regular human-AI synchronization points for critical processes; conduct sandbox testing to understand AI behavior and limitations; require human validation of AI intent and critical outputs. **Cultural:** Encourage critical questioning of AI outputs; maintain skills for manual override and problem-solving.

Risk category & examples	Description	Mitigation layers & examples
8. AI-specific security vulnerabilities	AI systems introducing new attack vectors like prompt injection, model poisoning, adversarial attacks, data leakage.	**Technical:** Implement AI-driven threat detection; employ prompt sanitization and input validation; use adversarial training and defense mechanisms; secure the AI supply chain. **Procedural:** Conduct regular security audits specifically for AI systems; develop incident response plans for AI-related breaches. **Cultural:** Raise awareness of AI-specific security threats among all users and developers.
9. Scalability challenges (infrastructure & MLOps)	AI deployments overwhelming existing infrastructure or MLOps pipelines failing to scale with demand.	**Technical:** Design AI systems with scalability in mind from the outset; leverage AI for self-healing and auto-scaling infrastructure; conduct rigorous load testing. **Procedural:** Implement mature MLOps practices for managing the AI lifecycle at scale. **Cultural:** Human oversight of scalability metrics and proactive capacity planning.
10. Lack of accountability & diffused responsibility	Difficulty assigning responsibility when AI systems make flawed or harmful decisions.	**Technical:** Implement comprehensive AI audit trails logging decisions and data inputs; design systems with human ethical override capabilities. **Procedural:** Establish clear governance frameworks defining oversight roles and responsibilities for AI systems; align with legal and regulatory requirements for AI accountability. **Cultural:** Foster a culture where accountability for AI outcomes is clearly understood and accepted.
11. Ineffective prompt engineering/ resistance to prompt-driven workflows	Difficulty in crafting effective prompts leading to misaligned, suboptimal or incorrect AI outputs.	**Technical:** AI tools provide feedback on prompt clarity and effectiveness; develop libraries of structured prompt patterns. **Procedural:** Provide extensive training on effective prompt engineering techniques; establish best practices for prompt design and testing; create sandbox environments for prompt practice. **Cultural:** Encourage experimentation and learning in prompt engineering; share successful prompting strategies.
12. Job displacement & skill gaps	AI automating tasks leading to potential job displacement and creating demand for new skills that are in short supply.	**Technical:** AI-powered tools for personalized learning and upskilling. **Procedural:** Invest in comprehensive upskilling and reskilling programs focused on prompt engineering, AI oversight, data literacy and ethical AI; create new strategic roles focused on human-AI collaboration and AI governance. **Cultural:** Foster a "mental productivity" mindset where value is derived from guiding AI; promote diverse hiring practices to bring in new skills.

6. Conclusion: embracing the uncharted wave with foresight and adaptability

The journey into the AI Native future is a fundamental reordering of how systems are built, organizations operate and humans interact with technology. This appendix has aimed to glimpse this emerging paradigm, characterized by deep human-AI collaboration. From redefining software development with speculative methodologies like FlowNative and organizational structures like Fluid Networks, to profound shifts in technological capabilities and the nature of work, the AI Native era presents unprecedented opportunities and challenges.

Projected technological advancements—from more capable LLMs and edge AI soon, to potential AGI components and quantum-AI hybrids longer term—are compelling, yet must be viewed with pragmatic skepticism regarding timelines and societal impact. The human role transforms towards strategic intent, ethical governance, creative problem-solving and oversight, with skills like prompt engineering, data literacy and ethical reasoning becoming paramount. This vision relies on addressing AI's inherent risks—bias, opacity, security, misuse—through robust governance, ethical frameworks and a responsible culture.

The most vital organizational capability is cultivating continuous learning, proactive experimentation and profound adaptability. Lessons from Cloud Native—holistic change, avoiding superficial adoption, aligning technology with culture—are directly applicable.

AI Native is still forming. Organizations starting now with pioneering exploration, building internal knowledge and fostering an adaptive culture will be best positioned not just to react, but to shape this wave. The ability to transform, learned and relearned, remains the most critical capability for navigating the evolving tides of change. The future belongs to those who partner with AI to amplify humanity's best intentions.

Join the conversation as we explore the AI Native frontier. Scan the QR code to subscribe to our newsletter for the latest expert insights and trends. Let's follow the development of this new ecosystem together.

Appendix 2

Transformation and Paradigm Patterns Library

Introduction: a language for transformation

Patterns serve as a vital language to reduce "unknown unknowns" when navigating complex transformations. As architect Christopher Alexander highlighted, if we lack a word for something, we cannot consciously choose it. An architect's client may struggle to articulate needs for their future house beyond simple concepts like rooms or windows because they aren't aware of deeper architectural possibilities. Alexander proposed teaching clients this "language of what's possible" to enable collaborative planning, expand understanding and lead to better decisions. The challenge, of course, is bridging the gap between expert knowledge and client awareness without requiring years of study. Alexander's pattern language was his solution.

Similarly, this appendix aims to create a pattern language for AI Native and technology transformations. The goal is to foster a shared understanding of possibilities between experts and stakeholders (our "customers"), enabling better choices based on combined knowledge and experience. This process helps make the unknown knowable. While the ideas represented by patterns can still be complex and challenging to implement, each concept is explained in accessible human language, avoiding professional jargon. Patterns incorporate both accepted academic knowledge and the valuable experience of practitioners, functioning as general best practices rather than rigid, in-depth solutions. They can often be implemented in many different ways.

The development of these patterns builds on prior work, starting with patterns presented at the PLoP 2018 conference and later expanded into a full language for the *Cloud Native Transformation* book. Many of those original patterns remain relevant, while new ones reflect further experience in the field.

The structure of this library is divided into two main parts:

1. **Transformation patterns:** These are consistent principles applicable to the *process* of moving between any major technological wave.

2. **Paradigm patterns:** These capture the characteristic approaches and architectures specific to distinct innovation waves—Waterfall, Cloud Native and the emerging AI Native era.

We will only briefly touch upon Waterfall patterns, primarily to illustrate that even older paradigms had better and worse ways of operating. Cloud Native patterns, stemming from extensive experience, are detailed more thoroughly, with an emphasis on mature systems delivering maximum value. AI Native patterns are necessarily more speculative, reflecting the current state of industry understanding. These are initial sketches based on early trends and predictions. They will undoubtedly evolve as mature AI Native systems emerge and provide concrete lessons.

Finally, this appendix includes a list of common **pitfalls and anti-patterns**. Anti-patterns represent solutions that often seem like good ideas initially but consistently lead to negative outcomes in hindsight (like "magic pill" solutions for weight loss that ignore fundamentals). Pitfalls, conversely, are well-understood risks or challenges that organizations frequently stumble over despite knowing better (like knowing you need diet and exercise but choosing the snack and couch instead). Recognizing both is essential for navigating transformations successfully.

I. Transformation patterns

These patterns apply to the *process* of transformation itself, often providing relevant information regardless of the specific technological waves being navigated (e.g. moving from Waterfall to Cloud Native, or from Cloud

Native towards AI Native). They are organized by the typical phases or modes of operation observed during such shifts.

Phase: Research—Pioneering (Horizon 3 exploration)
This initial phase focuses on exploring emerging technologies, understanding their potential and assessing feasibility without disrupting current operations.

TF01 – Learn and Explore: When emerging technologies offer unknown value, premature investment is risky. This involves acquiring knowledge and assessing relevance with minimal initial outlay, enabling informed decisions on which innovations to pursue further.

Example: A team attends webinars and reads white papers on quantum computing to understand its potential impact on their industry.

TF02 – Skunk Works Team: When standard processes hinder rapid innovation and exploration of novel ideas, progress can stagnate. A small, autonomous team is insulated from bureaucracy to experiment quickly, fostering breakthrough concepts and accelerated learning.

Example: A dedicated "innovation lab" team rapidly prototypes a new AI service, bypassing usual project approval cycles for speed.

TF03 – Reduce Cost of Experimentation: High costs or perceived risks can deter vital experimentation with new technologies. Implementing accessible sandboxes, cloud resources and fostering psychological safety lowers barriers, encouraging more trials and learning.

Example: Cloud accounts with spending limits are provided to developers, allowing them to test new services without lengthy procurement.

TF04 – Sandbox Environment: Exploring new technologies directly in production or shared development environments is risky and disruptive. Providing safe, isolated spaces allows teams to prototype and experiment freely without impacting critical systems or ongoing work.

Example: Developers use a Kubernetes namespace with mock services to test a new microservice idea before integration.

TF05 – Test Hard Things First: Transformation projects can fail if core technical uncertainties aren't addressed early, leading to wasted effort. Prioritizing PoCs on the most critical and uncertain aspects quickly validates feasibility or identifies roadblocks.

Example: Before building a full data platform, the team first tests integrating a novel real-time analytics engine, its riskiest component.

TF06 – Proof of Concept – PoC: When the viability of a new technology or approach for a specific problem is uncertain, full-scale adoption is risky. Focused PoCs are executed to gain tangible evidence, quickly validating or refuting the concept's practical application.

Example: A team builds a small application using a new serverless platform to verify its performance and cost-effectiveness for their use case.

TF07 – Demo Your Ideas: Innovative ideas or early progress can lack visibility, hindering buy-in and feedback within the organization. Regularly and engagingly communicating progress and learnings through demos builds understanding, support and valuable input.

Example: The skunk works team presents a bi-weekly demo of their prototype to stakeholders, gathering feedback and building excitement.

TF08 – Ideas Shelf: Not all good ideas are immediately feasible or align with current priorities, risking their loss. Maintaining a backlog of deferred but promising ideas retains them as future options when timing or resources become favorable.

Example: A promising but currently unfundable AI project idea is documented and stored in an innovation backlog for later review.

TF09 – Business Case: Embarking on major transformation initiatives without clear justification leads to wasted resources and misaligned efforts. Developing a robust business case articulates the rationale, benefits, costs and risks, ensuring strategic alignment and informed commitment.

Example: A detailed document outlines the expected ROI, implementation costs and market benefits of migrating to a Cloud Native architecture.

TF10 – Finance Topologies: Applying a single funding model across all types of initiatives can stifle innovation or misallocate resources. Adopting differentiated funding models suits diverse needs like core operations, transformation projects and speculative innovation appropriately.

Example: Innovation projects get seed funding for PoCs, while platform enhancements follow a more traditional budget approval cycle.

Phase: Development—Bootstrapping & Bridge-Building (Horizon 2 initiation) *Once a decision to transform is made, this phase involves laying the initial foundation (the Minimum Viable Platform) and connecting it to existing legacy systems.*

TF11 – Executive Commitment: Major transformations often face internal resistance and require significant resource allocation, risking failure without strong leadership. Securing active, visible executive backing ensures priority, resources and crucial support to navigate organizational obstacles.

Example: The CEO publicly endorses the AI transformation initiative and allocates a dedicated budget and key personnel.

TF12 – Appoint Transformation Champion: Diffused responsibility for a major transformation can lead to a lack of direction and accountability. Designating a single, empowered leader to steer the transformation's execution provides clear ownership and decisive guidance.

Example: A senior director is named the Head of Digital Transformation, responsible for the overall success of the initiative.

TF13 – Form the Core Team: Kickstarting a transformation requires focused effort and diverse skills often unavailable in existing siloed structures. Establishing a dedicated, cross-functional team builds the initial platform (MVP) and establishes core new practices.

Example: Experts from engineering, product and operations form a dedicated team to build the company's first internal developer platform.

TF14 – Vision First: Without a clear understanding of the transformation's purpose, teams may make misaligned or suboptimal decisions. Clearly defining and communicating the strategic vision—the "why" and "what"—guides choices and unifies efforts across the organization.

Example: Leadership shares a compelling narrative of becoming an AI-first company, explaining the market drivers and desired future state.

TF15 – Cultivate Psychological Safety: In transformative efforts involving new and uncertain work, fear of failure can stifle experimentation and honesty. Fostering an environment where teams feel safe to try, admit mistakes and learn openly is crucial for progress.

Example: Team retrospectives emphasize learning from failures without blame, encouraging open discussion about what went wrong and why.

TF16 – Research Through Action: Purely theoretical planning for transformation often misses real-world complexities and incorrect assumptions. Using the act of building the MVP and necessary integrations uncovers practical challenges and validates assumptions through tangible experience.

Example: While building the initial cloud platform, the team discovers unforeseen security compliance issues that require immediate adjustments.

TF17 – Adaptability over Efficiency: During the initial bootstrapping phase of a transformation, requirements and understanding evolve rapidly, making premature optimization wasteful. Emphasizing designs that favor adaptability allows for easier changes, deferring heavy optimization until patterns stabilize.

Example: The initial platform uses loosely coupled services and simple integrations, prioritizing flexibility over raw performance for early iterations.

TF18 – Deliver the MVP: Trying to build a perfect, all-encompassing new platform from the start often leads to delays and solutions misaligned with user needs. Building and delivering the smallest possible product version providing real value enables crucial early feedback.

Example: The first version of the internal developer platform only offers CI/CD and basic Kubernetes, addressing the most pressing developer needs.

TF19 – Thinnest Viable Platform: Scope creep during initial platform development can delay value delivery and overcomplicate the first offering. Applying strict prioritization to the MVP scope, deferring non-essential features, ensures faster delivery of core functionality.

Example: The core platform team defers building an advanced monitoring dashboard, focusing instead on reliable automated deployments for the MVP.

TF20 – Delayed Automation: Attempting to automate rapidly evolving processes too early in a transformation can lead to wasted effort and brittle solutions. Automation is introduced iteratively, starting with stable tasks and delaying for processes still in flux and under refinement.

Example: Manual approval steps are kept for initial platform service provisioning, with automation planned once the workflow is proven stable.

TF21 – Best Tool for the Task: Rigid adherence to existing enterprise tool standards can slow down a specialized core team bootstrapping new capabilities. Allowing this team flexibility in selecting tools best suited for novel tasks accelerates initial progress and innovation.

Example: The platform core team chooses a new NoSQL database for a specific MVP feature, even if it's not yet an enterprise standard.

TF22 – Bridge the Old World: New platforms often need to coexist and interact with established legacy systems during a transformation, creating integration challenges. Designing explicit integration layers or "bridges" allows necessary communication and data flow between new and old systems.

Example: An API gateway is implemented to expose specific legacy system functionalities securely to new Cloud Native applications.

TF23 – Staged Funding: Committing large, upfront budgets to long, uncertain transformation initiatives carries high financial risk if assumptions prove wrong. Adopting funding released in tranches, tied to achieving specific, validated milestones, allows for course correction and risk mitigation.

Example: The project receives initial funding for PoC and MVP, with subsequent funding dependent on successful delivery and positive review.

Phase: Introduction—Scaling (initial rollout and platform growth) *With an MVP in place, the focus shifts to onboarding the first wave of teams, refining the platform based on early usage and preparing for broader adoption.*

TF24 – Platform as a Product: Treating an internal platform merely as a cost center can lead to poor developer experience and low adoption. Managing the internal platform (IDP) with a product mindset, actively seeking developer feedback, improves its value and usability.

Example: The platform team conducts user interviews with developers and maintains a public roadmap for the IDP's features.

TF25 – Establish Platform Team: Once an MVP platform proves valuable, its ongoing development, maintenance and support require dedicated ownership to avoid neglect. Formalizing a dedicated team ensures the IDP's roadmap, operations and evolution are proactively managed and supported.

Example: A permanent "platform engineering" team is created with dedicated engineers, a product manager and support staff for the IDP.

TF26 – Dev Starter Pack: New users adopting a platform face a learning curve that can slow down their productivity and transformation adoption. Developing comprehensive resources like templates, SDKs and tutorials accelerates onboarding and productivity for teams using the platform.

Example: The platform team provides "hello world" application templates and CI/CD pipeline examples for common programming languages.

TF27 – Reference Architecture: Inconsistent architectural approaches across teams using a new platform can lead to complexity, integration issues and reduced maintainability. Defining documented, proven architectural patterns promotes consistency, best practices and accelerates development for common scenarios.

Example: A guide details how to build event-driven microservices on the new platform, including recommended libraries and configurations.

TF28 – Internal Service Catalog: As platform capabilities and shared services grow, developers may struggle to discover and utilize them effectively. Creating a catalog of available platform services and shared components, with clear documentation, improves discoverability and promotes reuse.

Example: A searchable portal lists all available internal APIs, managed databases and messaging services with usage instructions.

TF29 – Build the Right Thing: Developing platform features without validating actual user needs can lead to wasted effort and a solution nobody wants. Implementing tight feedback loops with initial adopter teams ensures the platform evolves to meet validated, real-world requirements.

Example: The platform team holds weekly syncs with pilot application teams to gather feedback and prioritize upcoming features.

TF30 – Prepare for Scale: A platform successful with early adopters may falter under wider organizational load if not designed for scalability and reliability. Proactively enhancing platform architecture, performance and operational tooling prepares it for successful broader adoption.

Example: Before wider rollout, the platform team conducts load testing and implements more robust monitoring and alerting systems.

TF31 – Reverse Conway Maneuver: If existing team structures reflect an old architecture, they can inadvertently hinder the adoption of a new one. Consciously designing team structures and communication pathways to mirror and promote the desired target architecture facilitates the change.

Example: To foster microservices, the organization shifts from component-based teams (UI, backend, DB) to small, autonomous, product-focused teams.

Phase: Scaling—Scaling and Optimizing (wider rollout and efficiency focus) *This is the main rollout phase, bringing more teams on to the new platform while simultaneously focusing on standardizing, automating and retiring legacy components.*

TF32 – Gradual Onboarding: Attempting to migrate all teams to a new platform simultaneously can overwhelm support capacity and create widespread disruption. Rolling out the platform to remaining teams in manageable, planned cohorts ensures better support and smoother transitions.

Example: Application teams are scheduled to migrate to the new IDP in waves of five teams per quarter, with dedicated support.

TF33 – Strangle Legacy: Allowing legacy systems to persist indefinitely alongside new ones creates operational overheads and hinders full transformation benefits. Systematically decommissioning legacy components by redirecting traffic or functionality to new equivalents gradually retires the old.

Example: New user registrations are routed to the new identity service, while existing users are gradually migrated from the legacy system.

TF34 – Protect the Core: During a lengthy transformation, critical legacy systems that still support the business can become unstable if neglected. Maintaining essential maintenance, security and stability for these systems is vital until they are fully retired or replaced.

Example: A dedicated small team continues to apply security patches and fix critical bugs on the mainframe system during the cloud migration.

TF35 – Holistic Transformation: Focusing solely on technological changes during a transformation often leads to cultural resistance and process misalignments. Explicitly addressing and adapting team structures, operational processes and organizational culture alongside technology ensures a more complete and successful shift.

Example: Alongside new tools, the company invests in Agile coaching, DevOps training and workshops on collaborative practices.

TF36 – Measure What Matters: Without clear metrics, it's difficult to assess the progress, impact and success of a transformation initiative. Tracking key metrics for platform adoption, team performance (e.g. DevOps Research and Assessment (DORA)) and financial outcomes (FinOps) provides objective insights.

Example: Dashboards track deployment frequency, lead time for changes and cloud spend efficiency as indicators of transformation success.

TF37 – Data-Driven Decision Making: Decisions based on gut feelings or outdated assumptions can derail transformation efforts. Fostering a culture where choices regarding platform evolution, process changes and priorities are informed by collected data and objective analysis leads to better outcomes.

Example: Platform feature prioritization is based on usage data and feedback scores rather than solely on individual requests.

TF38 – Establish Team Communication APIs: As more teams adopt new ways of working, unclear interaction patterns between them can lead to friction and delays. Defining clear, standardized modes of interaction and collaboration between teams (referencing concepts like *Team Topologies*) improves flow.

Example: Stream-aligned teams request support from platform teams via a well-defined ticketing system and API for self-service.

TF39 – Automation Everywhere: Repetitive manual tasks across the software lifecycle consume valuable time and are prone to error, slowing down the transformation. Relentlessly pursuing automation for tasks like testing, deployment, infrastructure provisioning and operations frees up teams for higher-value work.

Example: Security compliance checks and infrastructure provisioning are fully automated within the CI/CD pipelines on the new platform.

TF40 – Lift and Shift at the End: Some stable legacy applications may be too costly or complex to rewrite with little benefit during a transformation. Migrating these with minimal changes (lift and shift) late in the process can be a pragmatic approach once the new platform is mature.

Example: An old, stable internal reporting tool is moved to a VM in the cloud with minor changes, freeing up on-premise hardware.

TF41 – Finish the Transformation: Open-ended transformation efforts can lead to fatigue and unclear objectives for the organization's "new normal". Defining clear criteria for completing the main disruptive phase helps pivot focus towards continuous improvement on the new foundation.

Example: The transformation is declared "complete" when 90% of applications are on the new platform and key DORA metrics are met.

Phase: Maturity—Innovating and Optimizing (Horizon 1 enhancement) *Once the transformation is largely complete, the organization operates within the new paradigm, focusing on continuous improvement, efficiency and ongoing innovation.*

TF42 – Continuous Optimization: Once a new platform is established, processes can still become stale or inefficient if not actively managed. Embedding a culture (e.g. Kaizen) of regularly reviewing, measuring and incrementally enhancing operations ensures ongoing improvement and efficiency.

Example: Teams hold monthly "improvement days" to identify and implement small enhancements to their workflows and tools.

TF43 – Efficiency over Adaptability: While early transformation prioritizes adaptability, mature systems running at scale face increasing pressure for cost and performance. Shifting strategic priority towards optimizing performance and cost-effectiveness becomes key for these established systems and platforms.

Example: The platform team now focuses on optimizing cloud resource utilization and streamlining core platform services for better performance.

TF44 – Maximize ROI: The ultimate goal of transformation is to deliver business value, which can be lost if not actively pursued post-rollout. Focusing efforts on fully leveraging the new platform's capabilities to drive business initiatives ensures anticipated benefits are realized.

Example: Sales teams use the new data analytics platform to identify new market opportunities, directly increasing revenue.

TF45 – Minimize Cognitive Load: As platforms grow, their complexity can overwhelm developers, reducing their productivity and focus on business logic. Enhancing the IDP to abstract underlying complexities and provide clear, opinionated "paved paths" simplifies the developer experience.

Example: The IDP offers a "one-click" service creation that handles all boilerplate setup, networking and initial CI/CD configuration.

TF46 – Avoid Reinventing the Wheel: Teams independently building similar solutions wastes effort and leads to inconsistencies across the organization. Encouraging and facilitating the reuse of existing platform capabilities, shared services and reference architectures promotes efficiency and standardization.

Example: A new application reuses the existing centralized authentication service instead of building its own user management features.

TF47 – Enable Self-Service: Reliance on a central platform team for common operational tasks creates bottlenecks and slows down application teams. Building robust self-service capabilities into the IDP for resource provisioning, configuration changes and deployments empowers developers.

Example: Developers can provision new databases or adjust scaling parameters for their services through a self-service portal without filing tickets.

TF48 – Cultivate Observability: In complex, distributed systems, understanding behavior and diagnosing issues without deep insight is difficult and time-consuming. Implementing comprehensive observability (logs, metrics, distributed traces) provides the necessary visibility for effective operations and troubleshooting.

Example: Application teams use a centralized platform to view correlated logs, metrics and traces for their services to debug issues quickly.

TF49 – Nurture Incremental Innovation: Large, infrequent releases carry high risk and delay value delivery in a mature, agile environment. Leveraging platform agility to enable rapid, frequent deployment of small, valuable changes fosters continuous innovation and responsiveness to market needs.

Example: Product teams release new features or A/B tests multiple times a week, enabled by the platform's CI/CD capabilities.

TF50 – Specialized Teams: As the new paradigm matures, generalist teams may lack the deep expertise needed for optimizing specific complex areas. Utilizing appropriate team structures (like *Team Topologies*) and allowing for increased specialization enhances efficiency and capability in key domains.

Example: A dedicated "database reliability engineering" team is formed to manage and optimize all data storage services on the platform.

TF51 – Minimize Surface of Innovation: If application teams spend too much time on underlying infrastructure concerns, their focus on business innovation is diluted. Encouraging teams to innovate primarily on top of the stable, abstracted IDP maximizes their delivery of unique business value.

Example: Product teams focus on building new user-facing features, relying entirely on the IDP for infrastructure, security and deployment.

TF52 – Reflective Breaks: Continuous high-paced work without pause can lead to burnout and missed opportunities for strategic learning and improvement. Instituting regular, structured opportunities for teams to pause, reflect on their work and plan improvements fosters sustainability.

Example: Once a quarter, teams dedicate a "reflection day" to review recent successes and failures, and update their working agreements.

TF53 – Foster Learning Organization: In a constantly evolving technological landscape, an organization's ability to learn and adapt is key to sustained success. Implementing mechanisms that encourage systemic knowledge sharing, experimentation and adaptation builds organizational resilience and agility.

Example: The company hosts regular internal tech talks, communities of practice and "fail fests" to share learnings widely.

TF54 – Dynamic Strategy: In rapidly changing environments, rigid long-term strategic plans quickly become outdated and irrelevant. Adopting a dynamic approach to strategy, with short-term objectives, regular environmental sensing and adaptive planning, allows for timely adjustments.

Example: The company reviews its technology strategy quarterly, adjusting priorities based on market shifts and internal progress assessments.

TF55 – Periodic Checkups: Over time, even well-designed systems and processes can degrade or become misaligned with current needs if not actively reviewed. Implementing structured "health checkups" for key systems, architectures and team processes helps identify and address issues proactively.

Example: An annual architectural review assesses if critical systems still meet non-functional requirements and align with business goals.

Phase: Decline—Retiring (managing end-of-life) *This phase deals with the planned decommissioning of systems or components that are being replaced or are no longer needed.*

TF56 – Minimal Legacy Change: Continuing to invest in significant development on legacy systems slated for retirement diverts resources from the transformation.

Freezing non-essential development on these systems, focusing only on critical fixes, preserves resources for new initiatives.

Example: Only critical security patches are applied to the old CRM system; all new feature requests are directed to its replacement.

TF57 – Free Up Resources: As legacy systems are decommissioned, the personnel, infrastructure and budget tied to them can be reallocated inefficiently if not planned. Proactively planning for and redeploying these resources from wound-down systems maximizes their utility for new priorities.

Example: Engineers previously supporting a legacy application are retrained and assigned to new product teams using the modern platform.

TF58 – Sunset Gracefully: Simply turning off obsolete systems without a plan can lead to data loss, broken dependencies and user dissatisfaction. Executing a planned process to shut down these systems, including data archiving, stakeholder communication and dependency removal, ensures a smooth transition.

Example: Users are given three months' notice before an old file-sharing service is decommissioned, with clear instructions for migrating data.

TF59 – Team Reduction/Reallocation: As systems are retired and roles become redundant, managing the human resource aspect sensitively and strategically is vital. This involves reallocating personnel to new roles where possible, or managing team reductions with clear communication and support.

Example: After a legacy system is fully retired, its small support team is integrated into larger platform or product teams.

II. Paradigm patterns

These patterns are characteristic of the dominant approaches, architectures and practices within specific technological eras or waves.

Waterfall/Monolithic patterns

Patterns characterizing the traditional, sequential approach optimized for predictability, often resulting in large, tightly-coupled systems.

WF01 – Comprehensive Upfront Design: When projects require clear, stable initial direction, ambiguity can derail implementation. This involves extensive upfront requirements and design phases to create detailed specifications, aiming for predictable execution based on a comprehensive blueprint.

Example: A year-long project to build an accounting system starts with a six-month requirements and detailed design phase before coding.

WF02 – Sequential Phase Execution: For projects needing structured progression and distinct stages, managing overall complexity is crucial. Work is divided into discrete, sequential phases like design then implementation, ensuring formal sign-offs control movement to the next stage.

Example: A construction project completes all architectural designs and gets approval before any groundbreaking or material procurement begins.

WF03 – Phase-Gate Quality Control: To maintain quality in phased projects, errors can propagate if unchecked. Formal reviews and quality checks act as gates after each major phase, ensuring standards are met before work proceeds to the next stage.

Example: After the coding phase, a software module undergoes a rigorous quality assurance review before it's approved for system integration.

WF04 – Centralized Planning & Coordination (PMO): In organizations with many projects needing consistent oversight, decentralized efforts can lead to chaos. A central PMO handles master planning, resource allocation and progress tracking, ensuring standardized execution and better control.

Example: A large corporation's PMO oversees all IT projects, assigning project managers and tracking budget adherence across departments.

WF05 – Comprehensive Documentation: For projects requiring clear knowledge transfer between phases, misunderstandings can derail progress. Thorough, formal documentation is mandated as the primary output of each phase, serving as the definitive guide for subsequent work.

Example: The design team produces a 500-page specification document handed over to the development team as their primary implementation guide.

WF06 – Late-Stage Integration & Testing: When components are developed in parallel isolation, integration issues can be numerous and complex. Components are integrated only near project completion, followed by formal system-wide testing, risking late discovery of critical defects.

Example: Multiple software modules developed by different teams over months are combined for the first time during a dedicated integration week.

WF07 – Big Bang Release: For systems where partial functionality is not desired at launch, deploying many changes at once is high-risk. The entire integrated system is released in one large deployment event, leading to a complete initial offering.

Example: A new version of an enterprise software is deployed to all users globally overnight, replacing the old version entirely.

WF08 – Vertical Scaling: When an application's load outgrows its current server resources, performance suffers. Capacity is increased by adding more power (CPU, RAM) to existing hardware, improving performance on the same machine but hitting eventual physical limits.

Example: To handle more users, a company upgrades its main web server with a faster processor and doubles its memory.

WF09 – Layered Architecture: In large monolithic applications where code organization is challenging, maintaining logical separation is key. Code is structured into distinct horizontal layers (e.g. UI, business logic, data access), improving separation of concerns within a single deployment unit.

Example: A desktop application's code is divided so user interface classes only call business logic classes, which then call data access classes.

WF10 – Centralized Version Control: When teams need a single, authoritative source for code, managing concurrent developer changes is difficult. A central SCM repository (e.g. SVN) stores all code versions, enabling coordinated development but requiring network access.

Example: All developers check out code from and commit changes to a single Subversion server hosted in the company's data center.

WF11 – Shared Database Integration: To simplify data sharing between application modules, direct component-to-component integration can be complex. Multiple modules directly access a single, shared database schema, enabling easy data exchange but creating tight coupling and change fragility.

Example: An e-commerce site's order module and inventory module both read from and write to the same products table in one database.

WF12 – Batch Processing: For systems with resource-intensive tasks not needing real-time results, running them on-demand impacts performance. These tasks are executed periodically in large batches, often during off-peak hours, minimizing user impact but introducing data latency.

Example: A bank processes all end-of-day transactions and generates nightly reports for millions of accounts between 1am and 5am.

WF13 – Manual Build & Deployment: When automated build/deployment is absent, release processes are often inconsistent and slow. This relies on documented manual steps for compiling, packaging and deploying applications, ensuring procedural control but risking human error and delays.

Example: An operations engineer follows a 50-step checklist to compile code, copy files to servers and update configuration settings manually.

WF14 – Config-as-Data Services: When applications need environment-specific settings without recompilation, hardcoded values create rigidity. Configuration is stored as structured data separate from the application binary, allowing runtime adjustments and flexibility across different deployment environments.

Example: Database connection strings and API keys are stored in an external properties file, loaded by the application at startup.

Agile/Cloud Native patterns

Patterns reflecting practices enabling rapid delivery, scalability, resilience and adaptability, leveraging cloud infrastructure and DevOps culture.

CN01 – Iterative Value Delivery: To quickly deliver value and adapt to market changes, this pattern structures work into small, frequent software deliveries using methods like Scrum or Kanban. It enables continuous learning and risk reduction through early user feedback and adaptation.

Example: A team delivers usable e-commerce features bi-weekly, adapting plans based on user feedback to ensure market relevance.

CN02 – Automated Validation Pipeline (CI/CD): To ensure frequent code changes integrate correctly without manual delays, this pattern implements automated CI/CD pipelines for building, testing and release preparation. This provides rapid feedback, improves quality and enables frequent, reliable software delivery.

Example: Developers commit code, triggering automated builds, tests and release preparations, enabling rapid, reliable updates to production.

CN03 – Microservices Architecture: To overcome monolithic limitations on agility and scaling, this architecture breaks systems into small, autonomous services aligned with business capabilities. This allows independent deployment, fostering team autonomy and improved fault isolation for complex applications.

Example: An e-commerce site uses separate services for catalog, orders and payments, each independently deployable and scalable.

CN04 – Containerization: To ensure applications run consistently across all environments and simplify dependencies, this pattern uses containers like Docker. It packages applications and their dependencies into isolated, portable units, ensuring reliability and efficient resource use for deployments.

Example: A web app and its libraries are Dockerized, running identically on developer laptops, test servers and cloud production.

CN05 – Dynamic Scheduling (Kubernetes): To automate the complex management of containerized applications at scale, platforms like Kubernetes provide dynamic scheduling. Using declarative configurations, they manage deployment, scaling and healing, ensuring high availability and efficient resource utilization for applications.

Example: Kubernetes automatically scales a retail app's containers during peak sales and handles instance failures without manual intervention.

CN06 – Immutable Infrastructure: To prevent configuration drift and ensure predictable deployments, this pattern treats infrastructure as immutable. Changes involve deploying new artifacts (images) and replacing existing instances entirely, leading to consistent and reliable systems with easier rollbacks.

Example: To update a server, a new image is deployed, replacing the old one, ensuring consistency and preventing configuration drift.

CN07 – Optimize for Flow (Team Topologies): To accelerate value delivery by minimizing handoffs and dependencies, this pattern structures teams using models like *Team Topologies*. It creates autonomous, stream-aligned teams with end-to-end responsibility, enabling a faster flow of work.

Example: Stream-aligned teams own a specific business domain end to end, reducing handoffs and accelerating feature delivery.

CN08 – Platform Engineering/IDP: To empower developers and reduce reliance on central ops for resources, platform engineering provides an IDP. This offers automated, self-service capabilities, increasing developer speed, autonomy and ensuring consistent tooling across teams.

Example: Developers use a self-service portal (IDP) to provision databases and CI/CD pipelines, speeding up their workflow.

CN09 – Observability: To understand and debug complex distributed systems, observability designs systems to emit detailed telemetry (logs, metrics, traces). This provides deep insights into application behavior and performance, enabling faster issue resolution and proactive system optimization.

Example: Teams use distributed traces, metrics and logs to quickly pinpoint and resolve issues in their complex microservices environment.

CN10 – Design for Failure: Since failures are inevitable in distributed systems, this pattern architects for resilience using techniques like timeouts, retries and circuit breakers. This strategy helps prevent cascading failures, ensures graceful degradation and maintains higher system availability.

Example: A service uses circuit breakers and retries when calling dependencies, preventing cascading failures and improving system stability.

CN11 – Infrastructure as Code (IaC): To manage infrastructure consistently and avoid manual errors or drift, IaC defines resources using declarative code (e.g. Terraform) stored in version control. This enables automated, repeatable provisioning and robust change management for cloud environments.

Example: Cloud resources are defined in Terraform scripts, versioned in Git, ensuring consistent and repeatable environment provisioning.

CN12 – Service Discovery: For services in dynamic environments with changing IPs to reliably find each other, this pattern uses a mechanism where services register and query by logical names. This decouples services, enabling resilient communication and supporting dynamic scaling.

Example: Microservices in Kubernetes find each other using internal DNS names, not hardcoded IPs, adapting to dynamic instance changes.

CN13 – API Gateway: To simplify external client access to multiple backend microservices, an API gateway provides a unified entry point. It routes requests and handles cross-cutting concerns like authentication and rate limiting, encapsulating internal system complexity effectively.

Example: A mobile app communicates via an API gateway, which routes to backend services and enforces security policies centrally.

CN14 – Sidecar: To augment applications with functionalities like logging or monitoring without code changes, the Sidecar pattern deploys an auxiliary container alongside the main one. This decouples infrastructure concerns, enhancing modularity and simplifying the primary application logic.

Example: A sidecar container in a Kubernetes pod handles log forwarding for the main application, keeping app code clean.

CN15 – Service Mesh: To manage inter-service communication complexities like security and traffic control across many microservices, a service mesh provides a dedicated infrastructure layer. Often using sidecar proxies, it offers consistent policy enforcement and observability without application code changes.

Example: An Istio service mesh provides mTLS encryption and traffic routing for all microservices automatically via sidecar proxies.

CN16 – Database per Service: To ensure microservices are loosely coupled and can scale independently, each service manages its own dedicated database, accessible only via its API. This allows for independent data model evolution and technology choices per service component.

Example: An order's microservice uses its own database, distinct from the customer microservice's database, ensuring data independence.

CN17 – Event-Driven Architecture: For responsive and scalable systems, event-driven architecture decouples services by having them communicate through asynchronous events via a message broker. This improves resilience and allows services to react independently to occurrences or state changes within the system.

Example: When an order is placed, an "OrderCreated" event triggers inventory and notification services asynchronously via a message queue.

CN18 – Immutable Infrastructure Rollouts: To ensure consistent and reliable deployments, this pattern rolls out changes by replacing entire immutable instances built from versioned artifacts. This eliminates configuration drift and simplifies updates and rollbacks in dynamic production environments for applications.

Example: A blue-green deployment strategy replaces the entire old environment with a new one built from updated immutable images.

CN19 – Feature Flags/Toggles: To safely deploy code and control feature exposure, feature flags decouple deployment from release using remotely controlled toggles. This enables gradual rollouts to users, A/B testing and quick disabling of features without redeploying code.

Example: A new checkout feature is deployed but hidden by a feature flag, enabling release to select users for testing.

CN20 – GitOps: For managing infrastructure and applications declaratively, GitOps uses Git as the single source of truth. Automated agents ensure the live environment consistently reflects this version-controlled desired state, enhancing auditability and simplifying operational rollbacks.

Example: Kubernetes manifests in Git define the desired state; an agent like ArgoCD automatically applies updates to the cluster.

CN21 – Blue-Green/Canary/Rolling Releases: To deploy new application versions safely while minimizing downtime and risk, these strategies (blue-green, canary, rolling) allow controlled traffic shifting or incremental updates. This facilitates testing in production and enables quicker recovery from deployment issues.

Example: A new app version is released via canary, initially to 5% of users, then gradually to all if stable.

CN22 – Circuit Breaker: To prevent cascading failures from unresponsive dependencies in distributed systems, the Circuit Breaker pattern temporarily halts requests to a failing service. After repeated failures, it "opens", allowing quick failure and preventing resource exhaustion on the caller side.

Example: If a payment service fails repeatedly, a circuit breaker trips, stopping calls to it and preventing system overload.

AI Native patterns (speculative)

Patterns extrapolating how systems might be built with AI capabilities as their fundamental core, based on current trends.

AIN01 – Model-Centric Architecture: When AI is integral to system function, traditional design often treats models as peripherals, leading to integration issues. This architecture makes the model central, dictating data flow and interfaces, ensuring cohesive, AI-first system behavior.

Example: A logistics optimizer where route decisions are generated by a model, and all upstream data (traffic, weather) and downstream actions (driver alerts, warehouse updates) revolve around this model.

AIN02 – Data Fabric for AI: For AI systems needing high-quality, accessible data, siloed or poorly managed data hinders performance. A data fabric unifies infrastructure, automating ingestion, curation and governance, ensuring reliable data for robust AI performance and insights.

Example: A healthcare AI platform that automatically labels and versions patient data pipelines for model training, with audit trails for compliance.

AIN03 – Event-Driven AI Orchestration: In dynamic environments requiring immediate AI responses, batch processing creates unacceptable delays. Triggering AI actions via asynchronous events enables real-time responsiveness and decouples components for agile, adaptable AI systems that react instantly.

Example: A fraud detection system that reacts instantly to transaction events, scoring risk in real time.

AIN04 – Agentic Architecture: For complex AI tasks requiring diverse capabilities, monolithic models often lack flexibility. This architecture uses autonomous, goal-driven agents for perception, reasoning and action, enabling dynamic task delegation and specialized, collaborative intelligence.

Example: A software development agent that hires a testing agent to validate code before deployment.

AIN05 – Specialized Compute Orchestration: When AI workloads have diverse computational needs, general-purpose compute is often inefficient. Orchestrating specialized accelerators (e.g. GPUs, TPUs) for specific tasks optimizes hardware use, improving performance and cost-efficiency for demanding AI.

Example: A self-driving car that runs lightweight vision models on edge TPUs for real-time obstacle detection, while uploading data to the cloud for fleet-wide model retraining.

AIN06 – Vector-First Knowledge Management: Handling unstructured data for AI meaning is hard with relational databases. Storing and querying data as vector embeddings in specialized databases enables efficient semantic search and similarity matching, unlocking richer insights from complex data.

Example: A customer support chatbot that retrieves relevant knowledge base articles by comparing user queries to vector embeddings.

AIN07 – Explainability-by-Design (XAI): When AI decision-making lacks transparency, trust and adoption suffer. Embedding interpretability tools (e.g. SHAP, LIME) from the outset clarifies decision logic, fostering trust and enabling actionable insights from AI models.

Example: A loan approval model that highlights key factors (e.g. income, credit history) influencing a rejection decision.

AIN08 – Hybrid Edge-Cloud AI: For AI applications needing both local responsiveness and cloud power, a single compute location is often suboptimal. Distributing AI tasks between edge devices and the cloud balances latency, cost and privacy effectively for diverse scenarios.

Example: A manufacturing robot performs real-time quality checks using an onboard edge AI, while sending aggregated data to the cloud for predictive maintenance modeling.

AIN09 – Retrieval-Augmented Generation (RAG): When generative AI models produce outdated or unverified information, RAG enhances them by retrieving current, external knowledge before generation. This grounds outputs in facts, yielding more accurate and contextually relevant AI responses.

Example: A legal research AI that answers case law questions by retrieving recent rulings from a vector database and then synthesizing an answer.

AIN10 – Intent-Driven Development (IDD): When traditional detailed coding slows AI system creation, developers define high-level declarative intents for system behavior. AI tools then translate these goals into code, accelerating development and focusing effort on achieving desired outcomes.

Example: A developer sketches a UI in natural language and an AI generates the frontend code and backend APIs.

AIN11 – AI Tooling for SDLC Automation: In software development where repetitive tasks slow progress and introduce errors, AI-powered tools automate SDLC stages like code generation, testing and bug detection. This boosts developer productivity and improves overall software quality efficiently.

Example: Using an AI tool to automatically re-factor legacy code for better performance and maintainability.

AIN12 – MLOps Lifecycle Management: Managing the complex ML lifecycle reliably and efficiently is challenging with ad hoc processes. Applying DevOps principles (automation, CI/CD, monitoring) to ML workflows ensures reproducible, robust and scalable model management from data to deployment.

Example: A financial institution automates retraining credit risk models monthly using fresh transaction data, with full versioning and rollback capabilities.

AIN13 – Prompt Engineering: For generative AI, achieving precise, desired outputs is often difficult due to model ambiguity. Skillfully crafting, testing and refining input prompts effectively guides AI behavior, ensuring outputs align with specific needs for accuracy and tone.

Example: Iteratively designing prompts for an LLM to generate marketing copy in a specific tone and style, including negative constraints and few-shot examples.

AIN14 – Human-in-the-Loop Validation: In high-stakes AI applications where errors are costly or unacceptable, relying solely on AI can be risky. Integrating human expert review for critical outputs ensures reliability, safety and alignment before final action or deployment.

Example: A radiology AI flags ambiguous scans for a doctor's review before issuing a diagnosis.

AIN15 – AI-Driven Prototyping: When traditional prototyping is slow and resource-intensive, delaying feedback, AI tools can be used to accelerate the process. Leveraging AI to generate mockups, code or synthetic data rapidly creates interactive prototypes, speeding up ideation and user validation.

Example: Using an AI tool to generate multiple UI design variations for a new mobile app feature based on a textual description.

AIN16 – AI-Generated Test Case Development: Ensuring comprehensive test coverage for complex software is challenging and time-consuming. AI techniques automatically generate diverse test cases for software and models, improving coverage, finding edge cases and boosting QA efficiency significantly.

Example: An AI analyzes code changes and generates specific test cases that target the affected logic and potential regression areas.

AIN17 – Agile AI Teams: Traditional project methods struggle with AI's inherent experimental and data-dependent nature. Cross-functional teams adapt Agile methodologies for AI projects, fostering flexibility, rapid feedback and continuous improvement throughout the AI development lifecycle.

Example: An AI product team using two-week sprints to iterate on model improvements, new feature integrations and user feedback incorporation.

AIN18 – Ethical AI Review Integration: Ensuring AI systems are developed and used responsibly is critical, yet often overlooked without formal structures. Integrating formal ethical reviews against defined principles by dedicated bodies ensures fairness, transparency and accountability throughout the AI lifecycle.

Example: A company's AI Ethics Board reviews a new AI-powered recruitment tool to assess potential biases and ensure compliance with fairness guidelines before it's deployed.

AIN19 – Human-AI Collaboration Design: For tasks where human and AI capabilities are complementary, seamless interaction is key but often missing. Intentionally designing workflows, interfaces and safety protocols for human-AI teams enables productive, safe and synergistic collaboration.

Example: A warehouse robot that alerts human workers before moving heavy objects, ensuring safe collaboration, and that uses clear visual cues to indicate its intended path.

AIN20 – Data-as-a-Product (DaaP): When inconsistent or poorly managed data hinders multiple AI initiatives across an organization, treating data as a commodity fails. Managing key datasets as products with service level agreements (SLAs) and clear APIs ensures they are discoverable, reliable and reusable assets.

Example: A retail company's "customer behavior dataset" is offered with versioned APIs, comprehensive documentation and defined quality metrics for marketing and analytics teams.

AIN21 – AI Trust Framework Integration: Building trustworthy AI systems requires clear guidance, often lacking consistent internal standards for all aspects of AI. Adopting external frameworks (e.g. NIST AI RMF) for development and governance embeds principles like fairness and transparency, ensuring compliance and user trust.

Example: A government AI project that aligns its development process with the EU AI Act's high-risk system guidelines, including conformity assessments and documentation.

AIN22 – Bias Mitigation Pipelines: When AI models perpetuate or amplify societal biases present in data, it causes harmful outcomes. Implementing pipeline stages to detect, measure and reduce statistical biases using specific techniques promotes fairer outcomes and more responsible AI systems.

Example: A hiring AI audits its own decisions for gender/racial bias using predefined fairness metrics and automatically adjusts its scoring algorithms or data sampling if biases exceed acceptable thresholds.

AIN23 – Adversarial Defense Mechanisms: AI systems vulnerable to manipulative attacks can yield incorrect or harmful results, eroding trust. Incorporating defenses like input sanitization or adversarial training makes models robust against such attacks, ensuring reliability and security in operation.

Example: A facial recognition system that detects and rejects images with adversarial perturbations designed to fool the model.

AIN24 – Agentic DevOps Teams: Developing and managing complex multi-agent AI systems presents unique operational and integration challenges. Forming specialized DevOps teams with AI/ML roles using agile workflows effectively addresses agentic architecture complexities and supports their evolving lifecycle.

Example: A team building a supply chain AI composed of multiple interacting agents includes specialists for data pipelines feeding the agents, MLOps for agent deployment and monitoring and prompt engineers for configuring conversational agents within the system.

AIN25 – Self-Evolving Systems: For sustained improvement and adaptation in dynamic environments, static systems become outdated. Designing systems that continuously learn from new data and user feedback, adapting their behavior and capabilities over time, ensures ongoing relevance and effectiveness.

Example: A recommendation engine that refines its algorithms and suggestions based on real-time user interactions and evolving preferences.

III. Pitfalls and anti-patterns

Recognizing potential dangers (pitfalls) and commonly flawed responses (anti-patterns) is crucial for successful transformation. Pitfalls are inherent risks to anticipate, while anti-patterns are tempting but ultimately counter-productive solutions.

Transformation pitfalls and anti-patterns

Common failure modes related to the transformation process itself.

AP01 – Strategic Inertia: When transformative waves emerge, organizations may delay adoption due to inaction. This strategic inertia means reacting only under extreme competitive pressure, often leading to desperate, costly and ultimately insufficient responses.

Example: A retail giant ignores e-commerce for years, then scrambles as online competitors dominate, facing massive catch-up costs.

AP02 – Bleeding Edge Gamble: When new paradigms emerge, the allure of being first can be strong. Committing heavily before technology, skills and ecosystems mature is a gamble, risking significant investment in unproven or unstable solutions.

Example: A company invests millions in a novel AI hardware platform that quickly becomes obsolete before delivering any value.

AP03 – Perpetual Transition: During transformation efforts, a lack of clear end-goals can lead to indecisiveness. This results in endless churn of tools and priorities, preventing a stable new baseline and causing organizational fatigue and wasted resources.

Example: A company constantly switches cloud platforms and Agile frameworks, never stabilizing its new development environment or processes.

AP04 – Incremental Facade: When facing disruptive change, organizations may misjudge its depth. Treating fundamental shifts (culture, process, tech) as mere tool upgrades leads to superficial adoption, failing to address core transformation needs.

Example: A company adopts microservices by just containerizing monoliths, without changing team structures or DevOps practices, gaining little benefit.

AP05 – Cargo Cult Adoption: Observing successful transformations, organizations may focus on superficial elements. Imitating visible practices (e.g. specific tools, stand-ups) without adopting underlying principles or mindset shifts yields no real improvement or understanding.

Example: A team holds daily stand-up meetings but doesn't use them to coordinate work or solve impediments effectively.

AP06 – Illusion of Control: In inherently uncertain transformation processes, applying rigid, long-range planning common in stable environments creates false confidence. This over-planning often leads to brittle plans that quickly become irrelevant, hindering adaptation.

Example: A five-year detailed project plan for AI adoption is created, becoming obsolete within months due to rapid AI advancements.

AP07 – Unmanaged Shadow IT Proliferation: When central IT is slow or restrictive, business units may independently procure solutions. Allowing numerous "shadow IT" systems to scale without governance leads to integration chaos, security risks and duplicated costs.

Example: Multiple departments independently purchase different SaaS CRM tools, leading to data silos and integration nightmares for the company.

AP08 – Neglecting the Legacy Anchor: During transformation to new systems, existing legacy infrastructure can be overlooked. Failing to plan for managing and eventually decommissioning these legacy systems results in ongoing costs, complexity and security risks.

Example: A company migrates to a new ERP but leaves the old one running "just in case", incurring double licensing costs.

AP09 – Grand Canyon Jump: Faced with large-scale transformation, organizations might attempt to change everything at once. Attempting a "big bang" migration without vital MVP, learning and bridging phases usually leads to overwhelming complexity and failure.

Example: A company tries to move all its hundreds of applications to the cloud simultaneously over a single weekend, resulting in chaos.

AP10 – Tower of Babel: When transformation is needed, different organizational units might act independently without a shared strategy. This uncoordinated pursuit with disparate technologies and methods leads to internal fragmentation, wasted effort and incompatible solutions.

Example: Marketing, sales and engineering independently build their own AI chatbots using different vendors and data sources.

AP11 – Premature Scaling: After initial transformation successes, there's a rush to expand, but the new platform or processes might not be ready. Attempting widespread adoption before stability and adequate support are in place leads to widespread issues and erodes confidence.

Example: A new internal developer platform is rolled out company-wide after a small pilot, overwhelming the unprepared support team.

AP12 – Budget Blunder: Transformation initiatives are inherently uncertain, yet organizations often use financial controls for stable operations. Applying rigid budgeting or incentives unsuited for long-term, emergent change can stifle innovation and risk-taking.

Example: Teams are penalized for "failed" innovation experiments, discouraging exploration vital for AI adoption and long-term learning.

AP13 – Ignoring the Human Element: Transformations require new skills and mindsets, which can be overlooked amidst technological change. Underestimating or failing to address workforce upskilling, cultural resistance and mindset shifts critically undermines adoption and success.

Example: A company rolls out new AI tools without training employees, leading to low adoption and fear of job displacement.

AP14 – Lack of Clear Vision: Without a compelling reason for change, transformation efforts lack direction and stakeholder buy-in. Failing to establish or communicate a coherent vision—the purpose, target state and benefits—leads to confusion and resistance.

Example: Teams are asked to adopt cloud services without understanding how it aligns with the company's overall business strategy.

AP55 – Transformation Fatigue: When organizations undergo relentless or poorly managed change initiatives, they develop collective exhaustion. This "transformation fatigue" breeds widespread resistance and cynicism, crippling their ability to engage with new, even vital, transformations, and ultimately leading to strategic stagnation.

Example: An enterprise, after three back-to-back (and only partially successful) major re-platforming efforts over five years, fails to garner any internal enthusiasm or allocate sufficient resources for adopting essential AI-driven analytics, allowing more agile competitors to quickly seize emerging market opportunities.

Waterfall/Monolithic pitfalls and anti-patterns

Inherent limitations or common negative outcomes associated with the traditional Waterfall paradigm.

AP15 – Resistance to Change: In traditional Waterfall projects, requirements are fixed early, making adjustments difficult. The sequential structure means incorporating late-cycle changes is extremely costly and disruptive, often leading to outdated or misaligned products.

Example: A critical market shift occurs mid-project, but the Waterfall plan cannot accommodate the necessary scope changes without massive delays.

AP16 – Integration Hell: In Waterfall, components developed in isolation by different teams often hide compatibility issues. Integrating these only near project completion frequently leads to major unforeseen problems, extensive rework and significant delays.

Example: After months of separate development, two modules fail to connect due to mismatched interfaces, delaying product launch significantly.

AP17 – Delayed Feedback Loops: In the Waterfall model, users and stakeholders typically see functional software very late in the process. This delay means critical feedback on usability and requirements is received when changes are most expensive to implement.

Example: Users first see the complete software product months into development, only to find it doesn't meet their actual needs.

AP18 – Vertical Scalability Bottleneck: Monolithic applications often rely on increasing resources (CPU, RAM) of single servers for more capacity. This scale-up approach eventually hits hardware limits, becoming a costly bottleneck for handling increased load.

Example: A monolithic e-commerce site crashes during peak sales as its single, maxed-out server cannot handle the traffic.

AP19 – Siloed Handoffs: When specialized teams work sequentially in Waterfall, communication often relies solely on extensive documentation. This leads to misunderstandings, loss of context and delays as information is formally passed between isolated phase-specific teams.

Example: The development team misinterprets a thick requirements document from analysts, building features that don't match business intent.

AP20 – Misalignment with Dynamic Markets: The slow, rigid nature of Waterfall development makes it hard to adapt to evolving business needs. This inherent inflexibility hinders an organization's ability to respond effectively and timely to rapid market changes.

Example: A product developed over 18 months using Waterfall is outdated upon release due to new competitor offerings launched much faster.

Agile/Cloud Native pitfalls and anti-patterns

Common challenges or failure modes within Agile/Cloud Native environments.

AP21 – Unmanaged Technical Debt: In fast-paced development, pressure for features can sideline quality. Consistently neglecting code quality, re-factoring and testing for speed accumulates "debt", making future changes slow and costly while making the system brittle.

Example: A startup rushes features to market, ignoring bugs and poor code, leading to frequent outages and slow new development.

AP22 – Tool Sprawl/Ecosystem Complexity: The vast Cloud Native ecosystem offers many tools, but unmanaged adoption creates issues. Ad hoc adoption of numerous overlapping or poorly integrated tools without a coherent platform strategy leads to complexity and inefficiency.

Example: Different teams use three different CI/CD tools and four monitoring solutions, creating integration headaches and skill silos.

AP23 – Distributed Systems Complexity Challenge: While offering scalability, distributed Cloud-Native architectures introduce new operational hurdles. Managing interactions, state, failures and observability across many independent services is inherently complex and requires specialized skills.

Example: Debugging a performance issue involves tracing requests across ten microservices, proving difficult with inadequate distributed tracing tools.

AP24 – Uncontrolled Cloud Costs: The ease of provisioning cloud resources can lead to significant financial waste if not managed. Failing to implement cost visibility, governance (FinOps) and optimization results in excessive cloud spending from idle or overprovisioned resources.

Example: Developers leave large test environments running 24/7 in the cloud, leading to a surprisingly high monthly bill.

AP25 – Platform as Bottleneck: An IDP should accelerate teams, but poor design can hinder them. If the IDP is overly restrictive, slow to respond or lacks self-service, it becomes a bottleneck, frustrating developers.

Example: Developers wait days for the platform team to provision a simple database, slowing down feature delivery significantly.

AP26 – Nanoservice Proliferation: While microservices aim for focused components, extreme granularity backfires. Decomposing services into overly fine units creates an explosion of artifacts and dependencies, increasing operational complexity and reducing overall system comprehensibility.

Example: A simple user profile is managed by 20 tiny services, making deployments and debugging incredibly complex and fragile.

AP27 – Cloud Native/Distributed Monolith: Moving to the cloud without re-architecting can offer limited benefits. Migrating a legacy monolith directly into containers or VMs ("lift and shift") without adopting Cloud Native principles results in high costs and poor scalability.

Example: A large, stateful legacy application is deployed in a single container, failing to scale out or utilize cloud elasticity.

AP28 – Security Blind Spots: Traditional security practices may not cover dynamic, distributed Cloud Native environments adequately. Failing to adapt security to ephemeral resources, microservices and new attack surfaces creates significant vulnerabilities and compliance risks.

Example: A misconfigured cloud storage bucket with sensitive data is left publicly accessible due to a lack of cloud-specific security checks.

AP29 – Cloud Native Skills Gap: Effectively leveraging Cloud Native paradigms requires specialized knowledge which is often underestimated. Failing to invest in upskilling or hiring for cloud architecture, DevOps and container orchestration skills hinders successful adoption.

Example: A company struggles to operate its Kubernetes platform reliably due to a lack of experienced SREs and Kubernetes administrators.

AP30 – Blind Leap: When new paradigms emerge, failing to conduct adequate research before adoption is a significant risk. This "blind leap" involves committing to technologies or approaches without understanding their fit or implications, leading to ill-suited choices and wasted effort.

Example: A company adopts a specific Cloud Native platform based on hype, without researching if it matches their actual use cases or skills.

AP31 – Post-Transformation Stagnation: After a major transformation, organizations might prematurely declare "victory" and halt continuous improvement efforts. This complacency allows technical debt to accumulate and processes to degrade, eroding the transformation's benefits over time.

Example: After a successful cloud migration, a company stops optimizing cloud costs or re-factoring services, leading to creeping inefficiencies.

AP32 – Accidental Transformation: When significant technological shifts occur without strategic direction or clear objectives, the organization undergoes an "accidental transformation". This unplanned approach typically results in chaotic adoption, wasted resources and failure to achieve coherent business benefits.

Example: Various teams adopt different AI Native tools independently, leading to a fragmented and unsupported AI Native landscape within the company.

AP33 – Conway Conundrum: When adopting new software architectures, failing to consider the direct link (Conway's Law) between system design and team communication structures is a critical oversight. This "Conway conundrum" leads to misaligned teams struggling to work effectively with the new architecture.

Example: A company introduces microservices but keeps its large, siloed development teams, leading to coordination bottlenecks and slow delivery.

AP34 – Shiny Object Syndrome: In rapidly evolving tech landscapes, organizations may constantly chase the newest tools or fads without assessing their strategic fit. This "shiny object syndrome" leads to frequent disruptions, wasted investment and a lack of focus on proven solutions.

Example: A development team switches its primary programming language every year to the "latest thing", hindering deep expertise and project continuity.

AP35 – Culture Clash: Attempting to implement new methodologies (like Cloud Native or Agile) within a deeply entrenched, incompatible organizational culture (e.g. rigid hierarchy) causes friction. This "culture clash" often results in superficial adoption and active resistance, undermining the intended benefits.

Example: An Agile framework is mandated in a command-and-control environment, leading to teams just relabeling old Waterfall meetings as "sprints".

AP36 – Environmental Impact Neglect: While focusing on technological advancement or cost, the environmental footprint of IT operations can be overlooked. Neglecting sustainability, such as inefficient cloud resource usage, leads to unnecessary energy consumption and a higher carbon impact.

Example: Teams continuously run large, underutilized cloud servers for development and testing, significantly increasing the company's energy consumption.

AI Native pitfalls and anti-patterns (speculative)

Potential risks associated with the emerging AI Native paradigm.

AP37 – Ethical Misalignment & Amplified Bias: AI systems learn from data, which can contain societal biases, and their scale can amplify harm. Failure to embed ethical reviews and bias mitigation into AI design, training and operation from the start risks unfair or discriminatory outcomes.

Example: An AI hiring tool trained on biased historical data disproportionately rejects qualified candidates from underrepresented groups, perpetuating inequality.

AP38 – "Black Box" Challenge: Many advanced AI models make decisions through complex internal processes that are hard to interpret. This "black box" nature makes it difficult to understand, explain or debug AI reasoning, hindering trust and accountability.

Example: A medical AI diagnoses a rare condition, but doctors cannot understand its reasoning, making it hard to trust the output.

AP39 – Abdication of Oversight: As AI automates more tasks, humans may become overly reliant and less vigilant. Insufficient human oversight or intervention due to over-trust in AI, coupled with skill atrophy, can lead to undetected errors or system misuse.

Example: Content moderators overly rely on an AI to flag harmful content, leading to reduced human review and missed critical items.

AP40 – AI Technological Immaturity: The AI field is rapidly evolving and not all tools or techniques are production-ready. Adopting specific AI platforms or algorithms before they are robust, secure, scalable or well-supported can lead to unreliable or unsustainable solutions.

Example: A company builds a core product feature using a beta-stage AI library that is later abandoned by its creators.

AP41 – Data Governance Failure: AI systems are heavily dependent on vast amounts of high-quality data. Inadequate management of data quality, lineage, security, privacy and ethical sourcing critically undermines AI model performance, reliability and trustworthiness.

Example: An AI model trained on poorly labeled and unverified internet data produces inaccurate and misleading financial predictions.

AP42 – Naive Prompt Engineering: Interacting effectively with powerful generative AI like LLMs requires skill in crafting prompts. Assuming minimal effort is needed for good results leads to poorly designed prompts that yield suboptimal, incorrect or even unsafe AI outputs.

Example: A user asks an LLM a vague one-line question about a complex topic and receives a superficial, unhelpful answer.

AP43 – AI for Cost Reduction Only: Viewing AI solely as a means to automate jobs and cut operational expenses misses its broader strategic potential. Focusing only on headcount reduction overlooks opportunities for AI to enhance human capabilities, improve quality or create new value streams.

Example: A company implements AI chatbots solely to replace customer service agents, leading to poor customer experiences and missed innovation.

AP44 – Monolithic Model Syndrome: In complex AI systems, attempting to solve all problems with one giant model is appealing but flawed. This results in unwieldy, inflexible AI that is hard to train, maintain and scale effectively for diverse tasks.

Example: An AI attempts to handle customer service, fraud detection and marketing personalization with a single, enormous neural network.

AP45 – Data Silo Dependency: AI needs quality data, but reliance on fragmented, uncurated data silos creates significant issues. This starves models of comprehensive information, hindering performance and robust governance needed for effective AI systems.

Example: Marketing AI uses only sales data, ignoring customer service data in another silo, leading to incomplete customer views.

AP46 – Batch-First AI: When AI could offer immediate insights, defaulting to scheduled batch processing introduces unnecessary delays. This latency reduces AI responsiveness, making it unable to act on timely events or fresh data critical for decision-making.

Example: A fraud detection system updates risk scores nightly via batch jobs, missing real-time fraudulent transaction opportunities.

AP47 – Hardware Agnosticism: AI workloads have intensive compute needs, but ignoring specialized hardware leads to inefficiency. Using only general-purpose compute results in slower models, higher latency and increased operational costs for demanding AI applications.

Example: Training an LLM on CPUs instead of GPUs, resulting in excessively long training times and high costs.

AP48 – Vector Overload: When choosing AI data stores, misapplying vector databases to primarily structured data is inefficient. This adds complexity and can underperform relational databases for tasks they handle best, misusing specialized technology.

Example: Storing transactional order data with exact SKUs and prices in a vector database instead of an SQL database.

AP49 – Prompt-Only Development: When building with LLMs, assuming prompts alone can solve complex tasks oversimplifies system needs. This leads to brittle solutions lacking robust architecture, workflow integration and true problem-solving capability for business processes.

Example: Trying to build an entire CRM system solely by sending prompts to a generic LLM.

AP50 – MLOps Theater: When maturing ML operations, focusing only on tools without process, change is superficial. This MLOps "theater" creates a facade of automation while deep lifecycle issues remain unaddressed, hindering true ML agility and model reliability.

Example: A company buys an expensive MLOps platform but continues with manual model deployment and ad hoc monitoring practices.

AP51 – Trust Framework Window-Dressing: With calls for responsible AI, superficially adopting ethics frameworks for PR is a common misstep. This "window-dressing" fails to embed principles operationally, risking unethical outcomes and eroding genuine public trust.

Example: A company publishes an AI ethics statement but lacks internal processes to review models for fairness or transparency.

AP52 – Data Hoarding: Believing more data is always better for AI, organizations may collect excessively without clear purpose. This data hoarding leads to poor quality inputs, compliance risks (e.g. GDPR) and increased noise, hampering effective AI.

Example: A company collects every possible user click and mouse movement, overwhelming storage without a plan for its use.

AP53 – Agentic Chaos: When deploying multiple AI agents, lack of coordination can lead to disarray and unpredictable outcomes. This "agentic chaos" results in conflicting actions and unstable system behavior, undermining overall goals and reliability.

Example: Two AI agents managing inventory independently place conflicting orders, leading to overstocking and simultaneous shortages.

AP54 – Human-Last Collaboration: When integrating AI with human tasks, marginalizing human roles is a common design flaw. This "human-last" approach underutilizes expertise and demotivates staff, missing synergistic collaboration benefits and critical oversight.

Example: An AI system makes all underwriting decisions, leaving human underwriters to only review AI rejections with limited context.

Bring these patterns to life. Scan the QR code to explore the complete, interactive online patterns library and order a physical set of our pattern cards for a collaborative workshop with your team.

Glossary

Accountability: The principle that teams or individuals are responsible for their outcomes, crucial for ensuring follow-through during transformations and for managing systems effectively in mature operational states.

Agile: A set of principles and practices for software development emphasizing iterative cycles, cross-functional collaboration, customer feedback and adaptability, representing a significant shift from rigid Waterfall methods.

Agile Manifesto: The foundational document outlining the core values and principles of Agile software development, emphasizing individuals and interactions over processes and tools.

AI engineering: The discipline concerned with building, deploying and managing AI systems reliably and at scale, encompassing aspects like MLOps and data governance.

AI Native: A paradigm where applications and organizational structures are designed with AI at their core from inception, enabling continuous learning, adaptation and potentially autonomous operation, representing the anticipated next major wave of technological innovation.

AIOps: The application of AI and machine learning to automate and enhance IT operations, including monitoring, anomaly detection and performance management. It's particularly relevant in complex Cloud Native environments.

Autonomy: The degree of freedom given to teams (especially pioneering or stream-aligned teams) to make decisions, select tools and manage their own processes. Autonomy is essential for fostering innovation and agility.

Bureaucracy: Organizational structures characterized by rigid processes, multiple layers of approval and resistance to change, often hindering innovation and the adoption of more agile methodologies.

Cargo cult: The anti-pattern of adopting the superficial practices or tools of a successful methodology (like Cloud Native) without understanding or implementing the underlying principles and cultural shifts required for success.

Centralized control, distributed execution: An architectural principle, notably demonstrated by systems like Kubernetes, where a central control plane manages coordination and state, while workloads run in a distributed, peer-to-peer manner across nodes.

Cloud: Computing environments (public or private) where resources like servers, storage and networks are abstracted and available on-demand via programmatic interfaces, enabling key Cloud Native characteristics.

Cloud Native: An approach to building and running applications that fully leverages cloud computing principles, typically involving containers, microservices, dynamic orchestration and DevOps practices. It is aimed at achieving speed, scalability and resilience.

Cloud Native Computing Foundation (CNCF): An open-source foundation that hosts critical Cloud Native projects like Kubernetes, promoting collaboration and standardization within the ecosystem.

Cloud Native transformation: The complex, often multi-year, organizational shift required to adopt Cloud Native technologies, processes, team structures and culture effectively.

Cognitive load: The mental effort required by development teams to understand, manage and operate their systems. A key goal of platform engineering is to reduce this load through automation and abstraction.

Containers (Docker): Lightweight, portable units that package an application and its dependencies, enabling consistent deployment across different environments and forming a cornerstone of Cloud Native architecture.

Continuous delivery/Continuous integration (CI/CD): Practices and automated pipelines ensuring that code changes are frequently integrated, tested and kept in a release-ready state, enabling rapid and reliable deployments.

Continuous improvement: An ongoing organizational effort to refine processes, optimize systems and enhance quality, crucial for maintaining efficiency and avoiding stagnation after a major transformation.

Conway's Law: The principle stating that organizations design systems that mirror their own communication structures, highlighting the necessity of aligning team structures with desired architectures (e.g. microservices).

Culture (feature obsession, rules obsession, quality obsession): The dominant mindset and habits within an organization. Identified extremes include prioritizing new features above all else, rigidly adhering to rules and processes or fostering a deep commitment to quality and continuous improvement.

DevOps: A cultural and operational philosophy emphasizing collaboration, communication and integration between software development (Dev) and IT operations (Ops), crucial for enabling CI/CD and Cloud Native practices.

Disruptive innovation: Innovations that create new markets or value networks, eventually displacing established market leaders and technologies (as described by Clayton Christensen).

Edge computing: A distributed computing paradigm bringing computation and data storage closer to the sources of data, potentially interacting with AI Native systems for localized processing.

Empowerment: Granting teams the authority, resources and trust needed to make decisions and act autonomously. This is seen as more effective for driving cultural change than top-down mandates.

Experimentation: The practice of testing new ideas, technologies or processes, often through PoCs or in sandbox environments. This is crucial for learning and driving innovation, especially in Pioneering mode.

Feedback loops: Mechanisms for gathering information about system performance or user response and using it to inform subsequent development or operational adjustments. Feedback loops are essential for iterative improvement.

Finance topologies: An analogy extending *Team Topologies*, suggesting that budgeting structures and financial models should align with different operational needs (e.g. stable operations v uncertain transformation v lab-based innovation).

FinOps: A framework integrating financial accountability into cloud operations, enabling teams to understand and manage cloud spending effectively through monitoring and optimization.

FlowNative: A proposed software development methodology for the AI Native paradigm, emphasizing continuous, prompt-driven, AI-orchestrated flow with micro-cycles, replacing traditional frameworks like Scrum.

Fluid networks: A proposed dynamic, AI-orchestrated organizational structure for AI Native development, replacing fixed teams with temporary, task-specific micro-clusters guided by AI.

Generative AI (GenAI): A category of AI capable of creating new content (text, images, code), seen as a key driver of the potential AI Native wave.

Growth mindset: The belief that abilities can be developed through dedication and hard work, fostering a culture of learning, resilience and continuous improvement essential for navigating change.

Hierarchy: Traditional organizational structures with clear levels of authority and reporting lines, often contrasted with the flatter, more collaborative structures favored by Agile and DevOps.

Horizon 1/Horizon 2/Horizon 3: A strategic framework (Three Horizons) categorizing innovation initiatives based on time horizon and distance from the core business: Horizon 1 (optimize core), Horizon 2 (emerging opportunities/transformation), Horizon 3 (future possibilities/incubation).

Horizontal scaling: Increasing system capacity by adding more instances (e.g. servers, containers) rather than increasing the resources of a single instance (vertical scaling). This is a key benefit of Cloud Native architectures.

Immutable infrastructure: An approach where infrastructure components (servers, containers) are never modified after deployment. Updates are made by replacing old instances with new ones built from a common image.

Incremental innovation: Small, continuous improvements made to existing products or processes, typically managed within Horizon 1 (sustaining innovation).

Infrastructure as code: Managing and provisioning infrastructure (networks, servers, etc.) through machine-readable definition files (code), rather than manual configuration, enabling automation and repeatability.

Innovator's Dilemma: The concept (by Clayton Christensen) explaining why successful companies often struggle to adopt disruptive innovations, as they are focused on sustaining their existing, profitable business models.

Internal development platform (IDP): A platform built by an organization to provide developers with self-service tools and automated workflows for building, deploying and operating software, reducing cognitive load and increasing speed.

Iterative development: A software development approach involving repeated cycles (iterations) of development and testing, allowing for incremental progress and adaptation based on feedback.

Jevons Paradox: The observation that as technological improvements increase the efficiency of resource use, the rate of consumption of that resource often increases rather than decreases.

Kanban: An Agile methodology focused on visualizing workflow, limiting work in progress and managing flow to improve efficiency. It's often used as an alternative or complement to Scrum.

Kubernetes: An open-source container orchestration platform, widely adopted for automating the deployment, scaling and management of containerized applications. It's a central component of many Cloud Native stacks.

Large concept models (LCMs): A proposed type of AI model focused on conceptual reasoning, potentially offering advantages in areas like multilingual support and handling long-context information.

Large language models (LLMs): AI models trained on vast amounts of text data, capable of understanding and generating human-like language. Technologies like ChatGPT are prominent examples driving the GenAI trend.

Leadership (organizational v technical): Distinguishes between leaders focused on overarching strategy, vision and business alignment (organizational) and those focused on architecture, technology choices and engineering execution (technical). Alignment between both is crucial for transformation.

Lean startup: A methodology for developing businesses and products based on principles of validated learning, iterative development and minimizing waste.

Loosely coupled systems: Systems where components have minimal dependencies on each other, allowing them to be developed, deployed and scaled independently. This is a key characteristic of microservices architectures.

Machine learning (ML): A subset of AI where systems learn patterns from data without being explicitly programmed. ML is used for tasks like prediction, classification and anomaly detection.

Microservices: An architectural style structuring an application as a collection of small, independent and loosely coupled services, enabling faster development cycles and scalability in Cloud Native environments.

Minimum viable product (MVP): The simplest version of a product (or, in this context, a transformation platform) that can be released to gather feedback and validate assumptions, allowing for iterative refinement.

MLOps: Practices combining ML, DevOps and data engineering to manage the ML lifecycle efficiently and reliably, similar to how DevOps streamlines software delivery.

Monolith/Monolithic architecture: A traditional software architecture where an application is built as a single, tightly coupled unit, often contrasted with the distributed nature of microservices.

Movement (v mandate): The idea that significant cultural change is more effectively achieved by fostering a bottom-up social movement within the organization, rather than relying solely on top-down directives or mandates.

Observability: The ability to infer the internal state of a system from its external outputs (logs, metrics, traces), crucial for understanding and troubleshooting complex distributed systems like Cloud Native applications.

Orchestration: The automated configuration, coordination and management of complex computer systems and services, exemplified by container orchestrators like Kubernetes.

Ownership: Clearly defined responsibility for a service, component or process. Ownership is essential for accountability and effective management, particularly in distributed systems.

Paved path: Standardized, well-documented and easy-to-follow workflows provided by an IDP for common development tasks, simplifying processes and ensuring consistency.

Pets v cattle: An analogy describing the shift in infrastructure management from treating servers as unique, indispensable "pets" requiring individual care, to treating them as identical, disposable "cattle" that can be easily replaced.

Platform engineering: The discipline of designing, building and maintaining internal platforms (like IDPs) that enable application teams to deliver software more quickly and reliably.

Product Lifecycle (stages): The progression of a product through distinct phases: research, development, introduction, growth, maturity and decline. This is used as a framework for understanding technological evolution.

Proof of concept (PoC): A small-scale experiment or prototype designed to test the feasibility or demonstrate the potential value of a new idea or technology.

Prompt engineering: The skill of crafting effective instructions (prompts) to guide generative AI models in producing desired outputs (code, text, images). This is seen as a potentially crucial skill in the AI Native era.

Psychological safety: An environment where individuals feel safe to take risks, speak up, ask questions and admit mistakes without fear of negative consequences. This is considered vital for learning and innovation.

Research lab: A dedicated team or unit within an organization focused on exploring emerging technologies and long-term possibilities (Pioneering mode), often operating with autonomy outside standard hierarchies.

Resilience: The ability of a system or organization to withstand failures or disruptions and recover quickly. Resilience is a key goal of Cloud Native architectures and DevOps practices.

Sandbox environment: An isolated testing environment where developers can experiment with code or new technologies without affecting production systems.

Scalability: The ability of a system to handle increasing load or demand, often achieved through horizontal scaling in Cloud Native architectures.

Scrum: A popular Agile framework using fixed-length iterations (sprints), specific roles (Scrum master, product owner, development team) and defined ceremonies to manage product development.

Serverless: A cloud computing execution model where the cloud provider dynamically manages the allocation and provisioning of servers, allowing developers to run code without managing infrastructure.

Shadow IT: IT systems, software or services used within an organization without explicit approval or oversight from the central IT department, often arising when official processes are too slow or restrictive.

Silos: Organizational divisions or teams that operate independently and resist sharing information or collaborating with others, often hindering cross-functional initiatives like DevOps or transformation efforts.

Site reliability engineering (SRE): A discipline, originating at Google, that applies software engineering principles to infrastructure and operations problems, focusing on reliability, automation and reducing toil.

Staged funding: An investment approach, common in venture capital and recommended for transformations, where funding is released in tranches based on achieving specific milestones, allowing for course correction and reducing risk.

Stakeholder buy-in: Gaining the support and agreement of key individuals or groups affected by a change or initiative. This is crucial for securing resources and ensuring successful adoption.

Sustainability: In the context of IT, refers to minimizing the environmental impact (e.g. carbon footprint, energy usage) of operations. It's also used as a proxy for operational efficiency, as reducing waste often cuts both costs and environmental impact.

Sustaining innovation: Improvements to existing products or services for existing customers, typically managed within Horizon 1 and contrasted with disruptive innovation.

Team Topologies: A framework (by Skelton and Pais) for organizing business and technology teams for fast flow, defining types like stream-aligned, platform, enabling and complicated-subsystem teams and their interactions.

Technical debt: The implied cost of rework caused by choosing an easy (limited) solution now instead of using a better approach that would take longer. It accumulates over time if not managed, hindering future development.

Three Horizons framework: A strategic model categorizing innovation efforts into three time horizons based on their potential impact and uncertainty. It can be used for balancing short-term execution with long-term exploration.

Toil: Manual, repetitive, automatable operational tasks that lack enduring value and scale linearly with service growth. Reducing toil is a key focus of SRE.

Transformation Champion: A leader, often with executive backing, responsible for driving and orchestrating a major organizational transformation, bridging technical vision and organizational change.

Transformational change: Deep, systemic shifts in how an organization operates, often driven by major technological leaps and requiring changes to structure, processes, culture and potentially business models.

Transparency: Operating in an open manner where actions, decisions, data and processes are visible and understandable to relevant stakeholders. This fosters trust and collaboration.

Waste (operational): Inefficient use of resources (time, money, compute power, human effort) in operational processes. Identifying and eliminating waste is key to optimization and sustainability.

Waterfall: A traditional, sequential software development methodology characterized by distinct phases (requirements, design, implementation, testing, maintenance) and limited flexibility once a phase is complete.

Waves of Innovation: Major cycles of technological and cultural change (like Waterfall, Cloud Native, AI Native) that disrupt existing paradigms and eventually become the dominant mode of operation.

Zone to Win: A framework by Geoffrey Moore for managing innovation portfolios within established companies by dividing activities into four zones (Performance, Productivity, Incubation, Transformation) with distinct management approaches.

Recommended Reading List

- **Continuous Integration** (Martin Fowler, c. 2000/2006—online article): Seminal article on frequently merging code and automated testing. Relevant for understanding foundational practices enabling Cloud Native agility. *(Note: Publisher not applicable; see https://martinfowler.com/articles/continuousIntegration.html)*
- **Decentralization in Practice (paper by Google):** Discusses leveraging decentralization for innovation and agility in large organizations. Relevant to scaling and structuring Cloud Native/AI Native systems.
- **The Goal: A Process of Ongoing Improvement** (Eliyahu M. Goldratt and Jeff Cox, 1984, North River Press): Introduces Theory of Constraints via a business novel, focusing on bottleneck

management. Relevant for optimizing workflows during transformation and mature operations.

- **Zone to Win: Organizing to Compete in an Age of Disruption** (Geoffrey A. Moore, 2015, Diversion Books): Strategic framework for managing disruptive innovation alongside core business operations. Directly relevant to navigating the Cloud Native/AI Native waves.
- **The Culture Code: The Secrets of Highly Successful Groups** (Daniel Coyle, 2018, Bantam): Reveals elements like trust and vulnerability driving high-performing group cultures. Relevant to the critical cultural shifts needed for transformation success.
- **Building Microservices** (Sam Newman, 2015, O'Reilly Media): Practical guide to designing, deploying and managing microservices architectures. Directly relevant to implementing core Cloud Native technical patterns discussed.
- **Toyota Production System: Beyond Large-Scale Production** (Taiichi Ohno, 1988, Productivity Press): Details Toyota's manufacturing system emphasizing waste reduction and continuous improvement. Relevant for understanding lean principles applicable to optimizing IT operations.
- **The Phoenix Project: A Novel About IT, DevOps and Helping Your Business Win** (Gene Kim, Kevin Behr and George Spafford, 2013, IT Revolution Press): Introduces DevOps principles through a narrative about fixing a troubled IT project. Relevant for understanding the DevOps culture essential for Cloud Native.

- **Wiring the Winning Organization: Liberating Our Collective Greatness Through Slowification, Simplification, and Amplification** (Gene Kim and Steven J. Spear, 2023, IT Revolution Press): Explores creating high-performance organizations via principles like slowification, simplification and amplification. Relevant for structuring organizations for success and continuous improvement.
- **Product Lifecycle Management: Driving the Next Generation of Lean Thinking** (Michael Grieves, 2005, McGraw Hill): Describes managing a product's entire lifecycle for efficiency. Relevant to understanding the broader context of product evolution discussed.
- **The Innovator's Dilemma: When New Technologies Cause Great Firms to Fail** (Clayton M. Christensen, 1997, Harvard Business School Press): Explains why successful companies often fail to adapt to disruptive innovation. Foundational reading for understanding the core challenge addressed in this book.
- **Site Reliability Engineering: How Google Runs Production Systems** (edited by Betsy Beyer, Chris Jones, Jennifer Petoff and Niall Richard Murphy, 2016, O'Reilly Media): Shares Google's approach to building and maintaining reliable large-scale systems via SRE. Relevant for managing Cloud Native systems at scale.
- **The Site Reliability Workbook: Practical Ways to Implement SRE** (Betsy Beyer, Niall Richard Murphy, David K. Rensin, Kent Kawahara and Stephen Thorne, 2018, O'Reilly Media): Companion

book offering practical guidance for adopting SRE practices. Relevant for implementing reliable Cloud Native operations.

- **Kanban: Successful Evolutionary Change for Your Technology Business** (David J. Anderson, 2010, Blue Hole Press): Explains applying Kanban to improve workflow and enable continuous improvement. Relevant to Agile methodologies discussed as alternatives/complements.
- **Agile Estimating and Planning** (Mike Cohn, 2005, Prentice Hall): Details practical Agile techniques for estimation and planning in software projects. Relevant to the Agile methodologies preceding Cloud Native.
- **Three Horizons: A Framework for Managing Innovation** (Mehrdad Baghai, Stephen Coley and David White, 1999, Perseus Publishing/Basic Books): Model for balancing current operations with future innovation horizons. Directly relevant to the strategic frameworks discussed for managing innovation waves.
- **Cloud Native Transformation: Practical Patterns for Innovation** (Pini Reznik, Jamie Dobson and Michelle Gienow, 2019, O'Reilly Media): Outlines patterns and strategies for adopting Cloud Native technologies. Directly relevant as it addresses the book's central transformation theme.
- **Continuous Delivery: Reliable Software Releases through Build, Test, and Deployment Automation** (Jez Humble and David Farley, 2010, Addison-Wesley Professional): Definitive guide on automating the software release process for speed and reliability.

Essential reading for understanding CI/CD implementation.

- **Platform Strategy: Innovation Through Harmonization** (Gregor Hohpe, 2024, Self-published via Leanpub): Discusses creating and leveraging digital platforms. Relevant to the concept of IDPs and platform engineering discussed extensively.
- **The Software Architect Elevator: Redefining the Architect's Role in the Digital Enterprise** (Gregor Hohpe, 2020, O'Reilly Media): Guides architects in bridging technology and business strategy during transformations. Relevant for technical leadership roles in transformation.
- **How Buildings Learn: What Happens After They're Built** (Stewart Brand, 1994, Viking/Penguin Books): Explores how buildings adapt over time, using layers analogy. Relevant for the architectural layers and rates-of-change analogy applied to software.
- **A Pattern Language: Towns, Buildings, Construction** (Christopher Alexander et al., 1977, Oxford University Press): Presents design "patterns" for creating functional and living environments. Relevant to the concept of reusable patterns in architecture and potentially software.
- **The Timeless Way of Building** (Christopher Alexander, 1979, Oxford University Press): Philosophical treatise arguing for design rooted in natural order and human experience. Relevant for deeper thinking on sustainable and human-centric system design.
- **The Oregon Experiment** (Christopher Alexander, 1975, Oxford University Press): Describes a community planning approach shaped by users.

Relevant to user-centric design and potentially participatory platform development.

- **Skunk Works: A Personal Memoir of My Years at Lockheed** (Ben R. Rich and Leo Janos, 1994, Little, Brown and Company): Memoir detailing Lockheed's secretive, innovative Skunk Works projects. Relevant as a case study of successful Pioneering mode operations.
- **Team Topologies: Organizing Business and Technology Teams for Fast Flow** (Matthew Skelton and Manuel Pais, 2019, IT Revolution Press): Offers a model for structuring technology teams for speed and effectiveness. Directly relevant and a frequently referenced framework in this book.
- **Software Engineering at Google: Lessons Learned from Programming Over Time** (edited by Titus Winters, Tom Manshreck and Hyrum Wright, 2020, O'Reilly Media): Shares Google's practices for managing complex software systems sustainably over time. Relevant for large-scale software management principles.
- **Escape Velocity: Free Your Company's Future from the Pull of the Past** (Geoffrey A. Moore, 2011, Harper Business): Moore's roadmap for companies to break from legacy constraints and accelerate growth. Relevant to overcoming inertia during transformation.
- **Move Fast and Break Things: How Facebook, Google, and Amazon Cornered Culture and Undermined Democracy** (Jonathan Taplin, 2017, Little, Brown and Company/Macmillan): Critiques the impact of dominant tech platforms built on the "move fast" ethos. Relevant to discussions

on balancing speed, stability and broader consequences.

- **Reinventing Organizations: A Guide to Creating Organizations Inspired by the Next Stage of Human Consciousness** (Frederic Laloux, 2014, Nelson Parker): Explores new organizational paradigms like self-management and evolutionary purpose. Relevant to considering future organizational structures beyond traditional hierarchy.
- **Project to Product: How to Survive and Thrive in the Age of Digital Disruption with the Flow Framework** (Mik Kersten, 2018, IT Revolution Press): Advocates a product-centric approach over project-based thinking for digital transformation. Relevant to managing initiatives and value streams effectively.
- **Building Evolutionary Architectures: Support Constant Change** (Neal Ford, Rebecca Parsons and Patrick Kua, 2017, O'Reilly Media): Focuses on designing adaptable software systems that can evolve over time. Relevant to creating resilient and future-proof architectures.
- **The Art of Innovation: Lessons in Creativity from IDEO, America's Leading Design Firm** (Tom Kelley, 2001, Currency/Doubleday): Reveals IDEO's design thinking process for driving product innovation. Relevant for fostering creativity and user-centric design.
- **The HERO Transformation Playbook: A Step-By-Step Guide to Planning and Delivering your Transformation Programme Successfully** (Gary Transformation, 2020, Kindle Direct

Publishing): Uses the hero's journey metaphor for transformation. Relevant as an alternative framing for personal/organizational change.

- **The Digital Transformation Game Plan: 34 Contributions to Adopt Technology, Manage Change, and Engage Employees** (Edited by Gary O'Brien, Guo Xiao and Mike G. Williams, 2019, Palgrave Macmillan): A strategic guide for navigating digital transformation with multiple contributors. Relevant to the broader context of organizational change driven by technology.
- **Fundamentals of Software Architecture: An Engineering Approach** (Mark Richards and Neal Ford, 2020, O'Reilly Media): Introduces core software architecture concepts and design approaches. Relevant background for technical discussions on architecture choices.
- **Patterns of Enterprise Application Architecture** (Martin Fowler, 2002, Addison-Wesley Professional): Classic reference categorizing common design patterns in enterprise applications. Relevant for understanding established solutions to architectural challenges.
- **On the Origin of Species** (Charles Darwin, 1859): Darwin's seminal work on evolution by natural selection. Relevant metaphorically to the evolution and adaptation of technologies and organizations.
- **An Introduction to General Systems Thinking** (Gerald M. Weinberg, 1975/2001, Dorset House Publishing): Explains how to analyze complex, interrelated systems. Relevant for understanding the interconnectedness within organizations and technical ecosystems.

- **The Innovation Stack: Building an Unbeatable Business One Crazy Idea at a Time** (Jim McKelvey, 2020, Portfolio/Penguin): Shares how layering unique innovations can create competitive advantage. Relevant to strategies for differentiation through technology.
- **How Innovation Works: And Why It Flourishes in Freedom** (Matt Ridley, 2020, HarperCollins): Explores the process of innovation, emphasizing freedom and open exchange. Relevant to discussions on fostering an innovative culture.
- **Innovation and Entrepreneurship** (Peter F. Drucker, 1985, Harper Business): Drucker's classic work redefining innovation and entrepreneurship as purposeful disciplines. Relevant foundational reading on driving economic and organizational renewal.
- **What You Do Is Who You Are: How to Create Your Business Culture** (Ben Horowitz, 2019, Harper Business): Examines how leadership actions shape company culture. Directly relevant to this book's emphasis on culture's role in transformation.
- **Tribal Leadership: Leveraging Natural Groups to Build a Thriving Organization** (Dave Logan, John King and Halee Fischer-Wright, 2008, Harper Business): Discusses naturally forming "tribes" within organizations and how to leverage them. Relevant to understanding informal social structures during change.
- **The Infinite Game** (Simon Sinek, 2019, Portfolio/Penguin): Advocates prioritizing long-term vision and resilience over short-term wins. Relevant to

adopting a sustainable, strategic perspective on business and transformation.

- **Range: Why Generalists Triumph in a Specialized World** (David Epstein, 2019, Riverhead Books): Argues for the value of broad experience in complex problem-solving. Relevant to the evolving skill sets needed in tech, potentially favoring adaptability.
- **In the Plex: How Google Thinks, Works, and Shapes Our Lives** (Steven Levy, 2011, Simon & Schuster): Insider's view of Google's culture and operational approach. Relevant as a case study of a highly influential tech organization.
- **Teaming: How Organizations Learn, Innovate, and Compete in the Knowledge Economy** (Amy C. Edmondson, 2012, Jossey-Bass): Explains how teams collaborate and learn in dynamic environments. Relevant for building effective, adaptive teams.
- **Creativity, Inc.: Overcoming the Unseen Forces That Stand in the Way of True Inspiration** (Ed Catmull with Amy Wallace, 2014, Random House): Shares lessons from Pixar on nurturing creativity and innovation. Relevant for fostering an environment conducive to new ideas.
- **Loonshots: How to Nurture the Crazy Ideas That Win Wars, Cure Diseases, and Transform Industries** (Safi Bahcall, 2019, St. Martin's Press): Shows how nurturing radical ideas ("loonshots") can lead to breakthroughs. Relevant to the importance of the Pioneering zone.
- **Humble Consulting: How to Provide Real Help Faster** (Edgar H. Schein, 2009, Berrett-Koehler Publishers): Advises consultants/leaders on

providing effective help through engagement and humility. Relevant for internal change agents and leaders.

- **Thinking in Bets: Making Smarter Decisions When You Don't Have All the Facts** (Annie Duke, 2018, Portfolio/Penguin): Teaches decision-making under uncertainty using probabilistic thinking. Relevant for navigating the inherent uncertainties in transformation.
- **The Book of Why: The New Science of Cause and Effect** (Judea Pearl and Dana Mackenzie, 2018, Basic Books): Introduces a framework for understanding causality. Potentially relevant for deeper analysis of system behaviors and outcomes.
- **The Signal and the Noise: Why So Many Predictions Fail—but Some Don't** (Nate Silver, 2012, Penguin Press): Explores methods for improving predictions by distinguishing signal from noise. Relevant for forecasting technological trends and market shifts.
- **Shoe Dog: A Memoir by the Creator of Nike** (Phil Knight, 2016, Scribner): Nike co-founder's memoir on building a global brand through persistence. Relevant as an inspirational example of entrepreneurship.
- **Innovating: A Doer's Manifesto for Starting from a Hunch, Prototyping Problems, Scaling Up, and Learning to Be Productively Wrong** (Luis Perez-Breva, 2017, The MIT Press): Encourages experimentation and learning from failure through rapid prototyping. Relevant to the iterative processes in Pioneering mode.

- **The Captain Class: The Hidden Force That Creates the World's Greatest Teams** (Sam Walker, 2017, Random House): Explores how specific leadership traits drive sustained team excellence. Relevant to identifying effective transformational leadership characteristics.
- **Change by Design: How Design Thinking Transforms Organizations and Inspires Innovation** (Tim Brown, 2009, Harper Business): Shows how human-centered design thinking can drive innovation and organizational transformation. Relevant for user-centric platform/product development.
- **Radical Candor: Be a Kick-Ass Boss Without Losing Your Humanity** (Kim Scott, 2017, St. Martin's Press): Advocates for direct feedback combined with genuine care in management. Relevant for building trust and effective communication during change.
- **Extreme Ownership: How US Navy SEALs Lead and Win** (Jocko Willink and Leif Babin, 2015, St. Martin's Press): Teaches leadership principles centered on accountability and discipline. Relevant for fostering ownership and decisive action in teams.
- **The Alchemy of Growth: Practical Insights for Building the Enduring Enterprise** (Mehrdad Baghai, Stephen Coley and David White, 1999, Perseus Publishing/Basic Books): Offers insights for fostering sustainable, long-term growth through continuous innovation. Relevant to the overall goal of building adaptable organizations.

- **Vision, Leadership, and the Creation of Management Consulting** (Elizabeth Haas Edersheim, 2004, Wiley): Chronicles the evolution of management consulting and visionary leadership. Relevant historical context for strategic thinking and leadership.
- **Accelerate: The Science of Lean Software and DevOps: Building and Scaling High Performing Technology Organizations** (Nicole Forsgren, Jez Humble and Gene Kim, 2018, IT Revolution Press): Presents research identifying practices distinguishing high-performing tech organizations using lean/DevOps. Directly relevant evidence supporting DevOps benefits discussed.
- **Battle for Life and Beauty of the Earth: A Struggle between Two World-Systems** (Christopher Alexander, 2012, Oxford University Press): Examines conflicts between industrial development and nature, advocating for harmonious design. Relevant for deeper thinking on sustainability.
- **Cloud Native Development Patterns and Best Practices** (John Gilbert, 2018, Packt Publishing): Covers techniques for building scalable, resilient Cloud Native systems. Directly relevant to technical implementation details.
- **Thinking in Systems:** A Primer (Donella H. Meadows, edited by Diana Wright, 2008, Chelsea Green Publishing/Earthscan): Introduction to systems thinking for analyzing complex, interrelated systems. Relevant for understanding organizational and technological ecosystems.
- **The Box: How the Shipping Container Made the World Smaller and the World Economy Bigger**

(Marc Levinson, 2006, Princeton University Press): Story of how the shipping container revolutionized global trade. Relevant analogy for how seemingly simple technical standards (like containers) can have massive impact.

- **Ninety Percent of Everything: Inside Shipping, the Invisible Industry That Puts Clothes on Your Back, Gas in Your Car, and Food on Your Plate** (Rose George, 2013, Metropolitan Books): Exposes the critical but often invisible global shipping industry. Potentially relevant metaphorically to foundational infrastructure.
- **The Five Dysfunctions of a Team: A Leadership Fable** (Patrick Lencioni, 2002, Jossey-Bass): Identifies common pitfalls hindering team effectiveness using a fable format. Relevant for diagnosing and improving team dynamics.
- **How Bad Are Bananas?: The Carbon Footprint of Everything** (Mike Berners-Lee, 2010, Profile Books Ltd/Greystone Books): Quantifies the carbon footprint of everyday items. Relevant background for discussions on sustainability and environmental impact metrics.
- **Management Challenges for the 21st Century** (Peter F. Drucker, 1999, Harper Business): Drucker's examination of future challenges for organizations. Relevant for strategic foresight and long-term planning.
- **Patterns of Strategy** (Patrick Hoverstadt and Lucy Loh, 2017, Routledge): Explores common strategic patterns in business. Relevant for developing robust competitive strategies.

- **Fearless Change: Patterns for Introducing New Ideas** (Linda Rising and Mary Lynn Manns, 2004, Addison-Wesley Professional): Presents patterns for overcoming resistance when introducing new ideas. Relevant for managing the human side of change during transformation.

www.ingramcontent.com/pod-product-compliance
Lightning Source LLC
Chambersburg PA
CBHW070720200926
51611CB00006B/27
9781807785239